A WORLD HISTORY

A WORLD HISTORY

PAUL KELLOWAY

To Joan
With happy memories
of our time in London
and many thanks for
your continuing interest
in my book
Paul K

ASP

© Paul Kelloway 2005

First published 2005
Australian Scholarly Publishing Pty Ltd
Suite 102, 282 Collins Street, Melbourne, Victoria 3000
Tel: 03 9654 0250 *Fax*: 03 9663 0161
Email: aspic@ozemail.com.au
Web: www.scholarly.info

A Cataloguing-in-Publication entry for this title is
available from the National Library of Australia.

ISBN 1 74097 069 1

All rights reserved

Page design and typesetting by Shawn Low
Printing and binding by Mercury Printeam
Cover Design by Shaw Cunningham www.neithercorp.com

Contents

Introduction — vii

1	The First Civilisations	1
2	Civilisation and Empire in the Mediterranean	21
3	Civilisation in Indian and China	52
4	Christendom and the Origins of Europe	65
5	The Rivals of Christendom – Byzantium, the Slavs and Islam	104
6	China and India – from Early Middle Ages to Modern Times	127
7	South East Asia and Japan	143
8	Beyond the Frontiers	161
9	The Rise of the West	179
10	The Age of Revolution	205
11	The Nineteenth Century	226
12	The End of European Hegemony	263
13	One World 1945–2004	280
14	The Europeans in Australia	318

INTRODUCTION

This book is a history of the world in 100,000 words, the size of a short novel. It arises from the author's conviction that:

- the background of history goes far to explain the circumstances in which we live,
- this history can be presented in a way which will hold the interest of the average reader,
- BUT, given the many demands on our time, brevity is vital if that reader is to get to the end of the story, that is (for the moment) the present time.

Basically, history begins with the written record, i.e. more than 5000 years ago in Western Asia, some centuries later in Egypt, almost two millennia later in China, later still in most other countries. So, although it is possible and useful to penetrate further back with the aid of archaeology, history proper really begins about 3000 BC.

To condense the history of five millennia into 100,000 words requires not only concise expression but also careful selection of what to include and what to omit, what to recount at some length and what to squeeze into the shortest possible compass. Obviously the author's perspectives and prejudices tend to influence his choices and also his interpretations of events but the consensus of scholarship is a powerful check on individual bias. Hopefully, there is little in this book which departs too far from mainstream opinion.

The history of the human race is a story of courage and initiative, of ruthless war and rare peace, of long periods of stagnation and occasional initiatives which set the stream of history flowing in a new direction. Above all, it is our story, the explanation of how we come to be what we are.

It is clear that no part of the human record should be excluded from our story. Indeed it is the great achievement of our European ancestors to have broken down the isolation of one part of the world from another so that in our generation the notion of one world has become a reality, with consequences both enthralling and menacing. To live in this world we need to know at least an outline of how its parts originated and how they came together.

Properly told, this history is bound to arouse interest. Misused, it turns into propaganda, feeds prejudice and misunderstanding and arouses hatred. By the end of the twentieth century such perversion of history was perhaps less common than it had been at the beginning. It was by no means eliminated, with the tragic consequences to be seen, for example, in former Yugoslavia. Balanced and unbiased history can help to eliminate such prejudice and misunderstanding. I hope that this book will make a small contribution to this objective.

It is over fifty years since I graduated from the University of Sydney with honours in history. My studies left me with a deep interest in the subject which has remained my favourite reading matter over the intervening years. Over this time I worked for the the Australian public service, the Tasmanian public service, the United Nations World Food Programme and CAB International, an international organization specialising in agriculture and information. Much of this experience contributed to my understanding of the historical process. Retirement has given me the opportunity to think more about that process and to put some of my thoughts on paper.

Writing a book for the first time has been a pleasant but demanding experience. My perseverance to the end has been due, above all, to the understanding and unfailing encouragement of my wife, Pam.

Paul Kelloway
November 2004

Chapter One

The First Civilisations

The Origins of Agriculture

About 10,000 years ago, humanity took the crucial first steps from virtually total dependence on the environment towards modification and management of it. For countless millennia, men and women had lived as hunters and food gatherers, dependent for survival on the animals they could kill and the seeds and fruits they could gather. The constraints of this life style limited the total population of the world to perhaps four million.

These constraints were broken when some food gatherers gradually came to realize that it was possible to improve food supplies and make them more certain by sowing grain and looking after it. Probably the innovators were women who were traditionally responsible for seed gathering. Agriculture meant that human beings were no longer totally dependent on what nature provided; they could influence their chances of survival by deliberate, rational intervention.

This crucial step seems to have been first taken in Western Asia. This area, however, has been subject to more intense archaeological investigation than any other in the world and its arid climate is ideal for preserving the detritus of human occupation. In any case, it seems probable that the West Asian invention of agriculture was not unique. It was soon replicated in Egypt. Millennia later it would be replicated in other parts of the world – in China about 5000 BC, in South East Asia perhaps even earlier, by 5000 BC in Sub-Saharan Africa and by 2700 BC in America.

History before writing is critically dependent on archaeology. This discipline has become, in many ways, a very precise science although that does not prevent heated arguments about the interpretation of the data. But obviously the knowledge derived from archaeology is dependent on the sites investigated and that, in turn, on their identification as promising subjects.

The intensive investigation of Western Asia has yielded a rich return which largely determines our view of the development of agriculture and of the first civilisations. Could there be other sites, in other areas, not yet identified, where agriculture or civilisation is even older? The easy answer is that if such early development took place, some traces of it should have come to light by now.

One aspect of historical geography, however, should make one cautious. Climatic conditions in West Asia and North Africa ten thousand years ago were warmer than they are today and much of the Sahara and the Arabian desert were moist grasslands. What beginnings of agriculture or of civilisations may be buried under the deserts we really do not know.

One consequence of agriculture was an increase in the population capacity of a given area. Early farmers used slash and burn methods; they slashed the undergrowth and burnt it to get a clearing to sow their crop. In a few years the fertility of the soil would be exhausted and a new area would be cleared by the same methods. Only after this process had been repeated several times would the original area have recovered sufficiently to bear a useful crop. So each family, or group of families, needed a relatively large area to survive. Compared to hunting and gathering, however, the survival area was much smaller – perhaps initially one square kilometre per person compared to ten. Before 3000 BC world population had passed the ten million mark

Once launched on the process of manipulating the environment, early farming communities learned to adapt other crops. Grain was supplemented by fruit and vegetables – a large number of our fruits seem to have originated in West Asia.

If plants could be controlled and manipulated, why not animals? Sheep and goats were domesticated in West Asia by 8000 BC. Whether the first steps to domestication were taken by farmers or by hunters, who had domesticated the dog as early as 11,000 BC, is not clear but soon the typical farming community was engaged in mixed farming – crop growing and animal husbandry. Meat and milk thus became available; clothing resources improved as men and women learnt to shear, spin and weave.

Domestication of animals also made possible the development of an alternative way of life, in areas which would not support agriculture. By 6500 BC pastoralists were established on many of the fringes of settled agriculture. Conflict between pastoralist and agriculturalist is one of the recurrent themes of history but originally pastoralists may have lived in a sort of symbiosis with farmers, exchanging beasts for grain.

When domestication extended from sheep and goats to cattle and donkeys, human muscle was no longer the only source of power. The donkey was probably the first beast of burden. It, and even more the ox, made it possible to replace the hoe with the plough. This innovation changed the nature of West Asian agriculture – and eventually determined the pattern of those farming systems, from Western Europe to India, which grew out of it. With the plough a farmer could cultivate a much larger area than with the hoe. Hence a patch of land could be worked longer because its fertility did not have to be as high as with slash and burn to return a crop which would ensure survival. When farmers learnt to leave fields fallow and to plough in weeds, they had the means to maintain fertility and really permanent settlement became possible.

The plough also changed significantly the productive roles of men and women. In most primitive societies men hunt and women gather edible seeds, roots, berries etc. Hoe based farming was probably largely carried on by women, as it still is in Africa, but ploughing seems to have been men's work from the beginning –

certainly the earliest illustrations show men at the plough. This was perhaps one small step away from the exploitation of women, although there was still heavy work to be done to grind the grain as well as spinning and weaving. It also, however, reinforced the economic dominance of men who now assumed control of the major source of food.

Villages and Towns

Even with slash and burn methods, farming communities could be relatively stable compared to hunters and gatherers. Settlement could become more permanent and more possessions could be accumulated. Hoes and sickles could be supplemented by other tools. Pottery first appears about 7000 BC and the potter's wheel was in use by 3500 BC. The precarious dwellings of the hunters gave way to more permanent structures – mud brick houses in Western Asia.

Agricultural villages could be largely, but not entirely, self sufficient. They needed, for example, salt which is essential in a largely grain diet and obsidian or some other suitable stone to provide cutting teeth for the sickle. So rudimentary trade patterns developed and gradually specialised groups of miners and traders. These developments were given a substantial boost around about 4500 BC when copper began to be worked and copper ores smelted. Copper is a soft metal and its utility for tool making is limited but its use pioneered metallurgy. Bronze, an alloy of tin and copper, easier to cast and harder than pure copper, was developed by 3000 BC.

The settled way of life expanded. By 6000 BC agriculture had reached Eastern Europe; by 3500 BC it had spread as far as the Orkney Islands, to the north of Scotland. By 2200 BC the plough had come into use across Europe, making it possible to increase population to perhaps five million.

Just how this expansion took place is unknown. Maybe the original farming populations expanded and moved into new lands, generation after generation, pushing out or absorbing the quarter million or so hunters they found there. It is also quite feasible that many of these hunters took up agriculture or stock raising and so contributed to the expanding population of farmers and pastoralists.

The potential of population increase can be illustrated by comparison with a more recent case, well documented by censuses since 1664. The French speaking population of Canada in 1760, when the British took over and immigration from France came to an end, was 70,000. This population was derived from 10,000 immigrants, mostly in the seventeenth century. A century later, this population had grown to one million.

While the great majority of the population lived in villages, a few towns developed very early in West Asia. Jericho covered eight or ten acres by 6000 BC. It was walled and had a massive tower and a population of perhaps 3000 people. About the same date Catal Huyuk in Anatolia had a population of 6000.

These towns may have been based on trade and the possession of some strategic raw material – salt from the Dead Sea in the case of Jericho, obsidian at Catal Huyuk – although both communities also had their own agricultural base. Indeed, Jericho seems to have developed irrigation from the spring on which the settlement was originally based.

Towns, however, were exceptions to the general pattern of rural settlement in small villages. In Western Europe these villagers created the remarkable architecture of the megaliths – tombs, circles and avenues constructed of massive stones. One of the best known of these monuments, Stonehenge in England, includes several stones weighing fifty tons each and eighty odd pieces weighing five tons each which seem to have been transported 150 miles from the Welsh mountains. Megaliths are to be found along the coasts of Western Europe from Malta to Scandinavia. It used to be surmised that the culture of the megalith builders had spread from the East, perhaps from Crete or Mycenae. Radio-carbon dating, however, has shown that, while Stonehenge in its present form dates from about 2000 BC, many of these monuments are older than anything similar in the Eastern Mediterranean, some by as much as a thousand years. Their origin and inspiration therefore remain a mystery.

Impressive as the megaliths are, it was not their builders who were to take the vital steps to civilisation. The first civilized society built, not in stone, but in mud brick.

Origins of Civilisation in Western Asia

Between 4000 and 3000 B.C. the first civilisations were established in Western Asia. While not all later civilisations were derived from West Asia, no civilisation between Europe and India was untouched by its influence.

Change began when some farmers, perhaps stimulated by increasing aridity, began to practice irrigation. This began in small sites such as Jericho in Palestine and Choga Mami in northern Iraq where traces of limited redirection of streams have been dated before 5000 BC. Soon after agricultualists began to expand southwards into the alluvial plain of the Euphrates and the Tigris. This, the land which the Greeks and Romans called Mesopotamia – the land between the rivers – was the stage for the gradual development of the first civilisation known to us. This was the work of the Sumerians who inhabited the southern part of the plain.

In the great valleys of the Nile, the Tigris and the Euphrates and the Indus, the fertility of fields is renewed by the annual deposit of rich mud and silt by the flooding rivers. This annual renewal of the soil made permanent settlement extraordinarily productive. As population expanded, however, the scale and complexity of the irrigation works required grew. This called for a degree of organisation undreamed of in dryland farming. Social structures had to make it possible to mobilize and direct the labour of increasing numbers; this meant a differentiation between the mass of farmers and those who planned the works and organised the labour.

In this irrigated agriculture a farm family could generate far more food than it could eat. The surplus made it possible for more people to specialise in non-farm work and produce non-food goods such as pottery and tools. Skilled crafts emerged to provide luxury goods – jewellery and fine clothes, for example – for the directing and controlling group. Trade developed to mobilize the raw materials the river valleys lacked.

There was, however, a heavy price to be paid for this development: to make it possible the controlling groups rewarded themselves with the lion's share of production. This division of resources and benefits had important implications for the way in which civilisation developed. Obviously, the labour which the controlling groups appropriated was not available to meet the needs of others. The concentration of artisanship enabled the production of fine artifacts and the beginnings of a higher culture. But it also meant that most of the benefits of civilisation were focused on a small minority. The best artisan skills went to meet their demands rather than to improving the instruments of production.

Probably the very fertility of the irrigated river valleys militated against continuing technological developments. Existing equipment and methods would produce all the surplus required to support the directing groups and the artisans they needed. Sufficient labour resources were available for all the work needed to maintain and expand the irrigation systems. Population was low – perhaps two to three hundred thousand in Sumer in 3000 BC – and growing slowly; irrigated areas in a hot climate probably had a high incidence of water borne diseases. Thus, there was little impetus to continued innovation in agriculture which, along with the associated irrigation works and other public works, such as the construction of temples and palaces, continued to absorb the majority of the population.

Moreover, since that majority was left with little of the surplus it generated, nothing like a mass market, in which demand might stimulate innovation, could emerge.

So the social and economic structure which made the first civilisations possible also meant that, after the first massive changes had established the base, further change and development in them would be slow.

Writing

The river valley civilisations developed the key instrument for their own management and for our knowledge of them – writing. The earliest writing began somewhere in Western Asia in the fourth millenium BC as an effort to record goods and their movement. Pictographic signs could easily be devised to represent goods and other physical objects. Abstract ideas were more difficult until the rebus principle – the use of puns – was introduced. This approach requires a massive number of signs; Sumerian at this stage had over 2000. By 2300 BC signs were used to represent syllables and the number was reduced to 600.

The Sumerian signs, made with a reed stylus on a clay tablet, soon lost their pictographic quality and became simply an arrangement of wedge shaped indentations. The Egyptians, who wrote with a brush on papyrus made from reeds, preserved the picture character of their hieroglyphic script although they also developed a simplified form (hieratic) for every day use.

All these scripts required years of training and established the scribe as a subordinate but privileged member of the ruling group. Not until the alphabet was developed around about the end of the second millennium was it possible to learn to write without years of training. Even so, writing for long remained the privilege of a small minority.

Sumer

In Sumer by 3000 BC a group of cities had emerged to constitute a civilisation based on irrigated agriculture, a differentiated and stratified social structure, a common set of religious beliefs and long distance trade.

The Sumerians were almost certainly the descendants of the first farmers who had moved into the area soon after 5000 BC. Although their script can be read, scholars have not been able to classify their language. Probably the Sumerians were Caucasians, related to the Elamites and other early inhabitants of Western Asia long since submerged, to the Georgians and a few other small groups which still maintain their identity in the Caucasus, and perhaps to the Basques and other early inhabitants of Europe.

Archaeological evidence suggests that the cities of Sumer developed slowly between 5000 BC and 3000 BC. At Eridu a sequence of temples, growing steadily larger over two thousand years both epitomizes the development and emphasizes the central role of religion as the settlement grew from a village to a town to a city.

By 3000 BC the largest of these dozen or so cities supported a population of perhaps 10,000 or more and controlled a rural hinterland sufficient to feed them. Each city was seen as the domain of a god and its governance and management were vested in his priests. Later in the third millennium, perhaps as warfare between the cities emphasised the need for military leadership, ultimate power was vested in a single individual – and passed on to his sons – whose title we can translate as king. The king, however, was still regarded as the servant of the god and seems to have worked in close co-operation with the priesthood.

The Sumerians had thus devised the earliest form of the state – an entity which claims supreme power over the inhabitants of a defined territory, takes ultimate responsibility for controlling it and acknowledges no superior on earth. For, like the Greeks two thousand years later, the Sumerian city states jealously maintained their independence of one another. They were loosely associated in what the Greeks would later call an amphictyony, a religious grouping of states of a common culture with a central shrine. Nippur, the city where that shrine was located, and its god Enlil, enjoyed a primacy of honour but nothing more. The Sumerian city states were often at war with one another in disputes over boundaries or futile efforts by one city to establish domination over others.

Within each city, king, priesthood and a wealthy class exercised power and controlled the basic resource of irrigated land which in theory belonged to the god or gods. The land was parceled out to tenants and both priests and the wealthy held large and profitable areas which were worked by either sub-tenants or servants.

The surplus accumulated from the actual workers of the land and the luxury goods made by the artisans it fed provided the basis for a far ranging trading system. By 3000 BC well developed networks, many already hundreds of years old, linked the Sumerian cities with hundreds of trading points. Merchant caravans, with goods carried on pack asses, wound their way to Syria, Lebanon and Egypt, through the mountains to eastern Anatolia, across the Iranian plateau to Afghanistan, Baluchistan and the Indus Valley and probably into Turkmenistan. Water transport, being easier than land, played a key role wherever possible. The Persian Gulf and the Euphrates became a major axis of trade and Dilmun (Bahrein) a major focal point. In the west the system eventually expanded to include Cyprus, Crete, the Aegean and mainland Greece.

The Growth of Civilisation

It would be a mistake to think of civilisation being 'invented' in Sumer and simply diffused throughout Western Asia. Rather other centres developed at their own pace and in response to their own circumstances. Undoubtedly, however, they were stimulated by trading contacts and borrowed techniques and ideas from them. In this sense, Sumer was the centre of a system which transformed Western Asia from a collection of simple rural societies to an interrelated complex of cities and states.

The most striking developments were at both ends of the network – in the valleys of the Nile and the Indus.

The Nile valley was occupied by a Hamitic speaking people, related to the Berbers of North Africa and, less closely, to the Semites of Arabia. Irrigation developed at roughly the same time as Sumer. Geography, however, meant that irrigation was simpler until population became much more dense. Moreover, outside contacts were limited by the desert which surrounded the Nile, although some archaeological evidence suggests early contact with Sumer.

Egypt, unlike Sumer, achieved and maintained early unification. A substantial period of hostility between Upper (Valley) Egypt and Lower (Delta) Egypt ended about 3100 BC when the leader of the former established his supremacy over 'the Two Lands' and established a unified administration on a new site at Memphis, near their border. Egyptian tradition named this first pharaoh Menes. (Archaeologists are inclined to identify him with Narmer who has left some traces of conquest in their findings.) Menes thus established the first nation state. It was to last, with many vicissitudes and under foreign rule after 525 BC, for 3000 years, the cultural tradition it enshrined even longer.

Unification was soon marked by massive building works. The great pyramids, constructed to provide appropriate burial places for the pharaohs of the third and fourth dynasties are the largest and most enduring works of the ancient world. The largest of them, the pyramid of Khufu (Cheops), covers thirteen acres and contains over two million stone blocks weighing on average over two tons each. It rose to a height of 481 feet. The construction of the great pyramids must have required a massive mobilization of labour, probably by conscription during the slack agricultural season. The effort was too great to be sustained; after 2500 BC the pyramids become much smaller and their construction inferior; today they are only piles of rubble while the great pyramids stand almost as they were erected.

At the other end of the network civilisation developed in the Indus Valley in the second half of the third millennium BC. It seems likely that the Indus civilisation, while locally generated and showing distinctive indigenous elements, was heavily influenced by Sumer.

Empires and Invaders

Developments closer to home were of more immediate concern to the Sumerians. The attractions of civilisation were becoming clear to the neighbouring peoples. The tribes of the Zagros mountains cast envious eyes on the rich cities of the valleys. Semitic nomads from the steppe fringe of Arabia drifted into Sumer in increasing numbers.

We are so used to the military superiority of civilized powers that we tend to regard it as inherent in the stage of development. In fact, however, it has only become established in modern times as advanced technology has put increasingly greater firepower in the hands of armies with access to industrial production. The states of antiquity did not have this advantage and could easily find themselves confronted by barbarian tribes with equal or superior military technology. Since the tribes commonly had hardier, more ferocious, manpower, civilized states were always at risk of being overwhelmed by the less civilized people around them.

Further north in the river valleys other Semites developed their own city states, at first in cultural and perhaps political dependence on the Sumerian cities. Then in 2350 BC Sargon, a Semitic official in the service of the Sumerian city of Kish, usurped the royal power. Sargon proceeded, in a series of military campaigns, to establish not just a state but an empire including all of Sumeria as well as much more.

Sargon's empire met continuous resistance and lasted barely two hundred years. Nevertheless, Sargon had pioneered a new and dynamic political concept. The history of Western Asia after him becomes largely the story of successive attempts by one power or another to dominate the whole area. Independent city states might survive precariously on the fringes, in Syria and on the Mediterranean coast. But the heartland in Sumeria and further north would increasingly be seen as a single entity to be fought for and won or lost by conflicting powers.

Some of these powers were city states – the first was actually the Sumerian city of Ur. Others, however, were tribes from the arid semi-desert, the steppes or the mountains. Once installed in power, such tribes were usually rapidly assimilated to and simply replaced or incorporated the ruling elite they had overcome. Conquest was therefore often a setback rather than a disaster.

In this process the Sumerians disappeared as a separate people. Submerged by the unending flow of infiltrators from the arid fringes of Arabia, the inhabitants of Sumer became Semitic speaking. The collapse of Sumer may also have been partly due to the salination of the soil which seems to have reduced the productivity of their irrigation about the end of the third millennium.

Although the Semitic peoples had absorbed and replaced the Sumerians they showed a respect for them which can be compared with the traditional European respect for the heritage of Greece and Rome. Sumerian was retained, as Latin was for centuries in Roman Catholic worship, as a sacred language.

Babylonian and Assyrian kings showed a strong interest in the preservation of Mesopotamian history. They built libraries and employed scribes to copy the records of earlier times. To train these scribes, dictionaries were composed showing, for example, the contemporary equivalents of Sumerian words.

The work of the Mesopotamian librarians and scribes was, of course, recorded on clay tablets which are practically indestructible. Fire in the end destroyed the great libraries as their royal owners went down before new conquerors; the tablets were often broken as the buildings collapsed but the fire simply hardened and preserved them. Consequently the library collections remained in the ruins, to be rediscovered by modern archaeologists who found the dictionaries particularly useful in working their way back through the long forgotten languages of Mesopotamia.

In the second millennium leadership passed to the Semitic city of Babylon. Hammurapi (1792–1750 BC) established an empire which extended from the Persian Gulf to the important trading city of Mari on the Upper Euphrates. It collapsed on his death but not before he had inscribed on a massive basalt stele a remarkable code of 282 laws dealing with most aspects of Babylonian life. Compared with Sumerian law, the code included some major backward steps; it sanctioned the use of torture and discriminated against women.

It was presumably Hammurapi who arranged for the spread of an amended version of the traditional mythology in which Marduk, the god of Babylon, was vested with 'executive power' over all people by the supreme gods of the Sumerian pantheon. The supremacy of Marduk and the prestige of Babylon survived the collapse of Hammurapi's empire and the whole area of middle and southern Iraq passed into history as Babylonia.

Soon after Hammurapi's death, a new character appears on the West Asian scene – the horse. Pastoral tribes in the steppes of South Russia were the first to domesticate the horse; by 1700 BC it had been harnessed to a light, two wheeled chariot. Manned by a driver and an archer, the chariot had an impact on the battlefield comparable to the tank in the twentieth century. The first charioteers were barbarian tribesmen who overwhelmed the backward infantry armies of the civilized states as well as other, less mobile peoples.

Probably it was this new military technology which enabled the Kassites, a people from the Zagros mountains, to take control of Babylonia and the Hurrians further to the north to establish the new state of Mitanni. In Anatolia, the Hittites used it to create an empire by dominating the peoples around them.

The Hittites, and perhaps the dominant aristocracies among the Kassites and the Hurrians, spoke Indo-European languages, part of a vast language family which includes most European languages, Iranian and most of the languages of North India. The origins of the Indo-European peoples are unclear, and still controversial after generations of scholarship. The steppes of South Russia are preferred by most scholars but powerful arguments have also been put forward for Anatolia. What is not in doubt is that in the first half of the second millennium, hordes of Indo-European peoples invaded and established dominion over much of Western Asia and Northern India. Chariot warfare was the instrument of this explosion.

Even Egypt, so long secure within its desert fringes, fell victim to intruders – in this case Semitic not Indo-European – with the new military technology. The Hyksos, profiting by disunity and strife within Egypt, established a presence in the eastern delta and by 1650 BC had been recognized as pharaohs. Their supremacy lasted less than a century. The Egyptian pharaohs of the New Kingdom resolved to preempt future Semitic incursions and brought most of Syria and Palestine under their control.

Inevitably this expansion brought Egypt into contact and conflict with the other powers of Western Asia. The conflicts were eventually resolved and the region settled down, for some centuries, into a system of international relations and balance of power which, with its treaties, ambassadors and royal marriages inevitably brings to mind Europe in the eighteenth and nineteenth centuries.

This period of relative calm, probably accompanied by expanding trade and prosperity, came to an untimely end before the close of the second millennium. Egypt suffered from waves of invaders, largely Indo-European, known as the Sea Peoples although not all of them came by sea. They were repulsed but the fabric of the Egyptian state, already undermined by internal dissension, was weakened and its power never recovered. The Hittite state, weakened by similar incursions on land and attacked by the expanding power of Assyria, collapsed; the Hittites disappeared from history.

Part of the invaders' advantage was the use of iron weapons. Iron smelting had been developed a few hundred years before, probably by the Hittites. Iron ore was relatively plentiful and accessible. The weapons of war were therefore more widely available – a situation which suited barbarian tribes in which every man was a potential warrior. A little later Iranian tribes in central Asia mastered the difficult art of fighting on horseback. The new technique, more flexible and more widely available than the expensive chariot, spread rapidly across the steppes.

Within Mesopotamia, the Assyrians mastered the new techniques and expanded from their homeland on the upper Tigris; by the seventh century their empire included Egypt as well as Babylonia and much of the former Hittite state. The Assyrian military machine was the most efficient yet seen; it was also the most ruthless. Its policy of terror and destruction ensured that its rule would never be willingly accepted or supported by the subject peoples. Babylonia, now dominated by a fresh wave of Semitic migrants, the Chaldeans, asserted its independence and in 614 BC formed an alliance with the Medes, an Indo-European people in north western Iran. The alliance overthrew Assyria, destroyed its cities and virtually wiped out the Assyrian people.

The Great King's Peace

Babylonia fell heir to most of the Assyrian empire. But the future lay with the new power of Media or rather with the related Persian dynasty of Cyrus the Great which replaced it in a coup d'etat. Cyrus overthrew the Lydian kingdom in western Anatolia and extended his power from the Aegean to central Asia. In 539 BC, aided by discontent within, he occupied Babylon. His son, Cambyses, conquered Egypt in 525 BC and his son-in-law, Darius carried the boundaries of the empire to the Indus.

With remarkable enlightenment, Cyrus established a regime which rested, if not on the consent, at least on the acquiescence of the governed. Local gods and priesthoods were respected and local governing classes left undisturbed. A satrap or governor exercised overall power in each province, his powers carefully checked by the separate appointment of a tax collector and a garrison commander. Communications were fostered by road construction, notably the famous Royal Road which ran 2700 kilometres (1700 miles) from Susa in south western Iran to Sardis in western Anatolia. Improved communications and stable government over an immense area favoured trade. So too did the introduction of coined money, which the Persians took over from the Lydians.

The Persian Empire was not perfect. Dynastic disputes could lead to assassination or even civil war. By the fourth century it had to contend with nearly continuous rebellion in Egypt. But Egypt was almost alone in this refusal to accept the Persian peace. Western Asia, exhausted by centuries of warfare, seems to have welcomed it and presumably flourished accordingly.

The Beginnings of the Jewish People

When Cyrus conquered Babylon in 539 he found among its inhabitants a number of Jews, deported from Judah by the Babylonian King Nebuchadnezzar half a century before. Cyrus yielded to their entreaties to permit their return to their ancestral lands.

The Jews traced their origins back to Abraham whom their traditions described as 'a wandering Aramean'. Abraham migrated from the region of Ur to Haran in northern Mesopotamia and later took his family group southward to Palestine or Canaan as it was then known. This was most likely about the beginning of the second millennium. Abraham was one of the large number of Semitic nomads – known at this time as Amorites rather than Arameans – who lived a wandering life on the outskirts of settlement. But Abraham was different; he was convinced that his god had manifested himself to him and covenanted to make a great people of his descendants – and he passed that conviction on to them.

Consequently, when some of those descendants, having migrated to Egypt – possibly in the time of the Asiatic Pharaohs or Hyksos – found themselves enslaved by the next, Egyptian dynasty, they were very ready to follow a charismatic leader in a dash for freedom. Moses led the escapees into the desert of Sinai where they wandered for a generation or more. Under his leadership they became the nucleus of a people, convinced that God had spoken to Moses, revealed his law and covenanted with them to give them the land of Canaan. Then, probably having coalesced with kindred tribes, they moved into Canaan in the thirteenth century and, like other Semitic tribes before and after them in Mesopotamia and Syria, settled down to become cultivators and stock farmers.

The Israelite amphictyony – a loose union of tribes of common origin and worship – maintained its belief in its one God. In the eleventh century it came under pressure from the Philistines, a remnant of the Sea Peoples settled on the coast of Palestine, and elected Saul as king to organise defence. His successor, David, extended Israelite power from Damascus to the gulf of Aqaba and became the archetype of kingship for succeeding generations. David's son Solomon reigned in great magnificence but the burden of taxation and labour services, a novelty to his people, caused great discontent. On his death in 926 BC the kingdom split; Judah in the south remained loyal to his dynasty but Israel in the north seceded. The two kingdoms continued in uneasy and sometimes hostile relations until 722 BC when the Assyrians destroyed Israel and transported many of its inhabitants. Judah met the same fate at the hands of the Babylonians in 587 BC.

The period of the monarchy was marked by increasing social stratification and oppression. Royal marriages with Phoenician princesses led to the introduction of the cults of their gods which seemed more attractive than the austere God of the covenant. These tendencies led to the rise of prophets who felt themselves called by that God to denounce both false gods and injustice. Although the prophets frequently fell foul of royal authority they could not be silenced. Their stark and vivid preaching, preserved by their followers and eventually put in writing, left an indelible mark on the religion of Judah, establishing both that their God was the only God, lord of the universe, and that he demanded justice and compassion as well as worship.

Even the exile to Babylonia could not destroy this faith. The exile was seen as God's punishment for infidelity; if the people forsook their evil ways and returned to him, he would restore the kingdom. Cyrus' permission to return to Jerusalem was seen as the first step in this restoration. Not all the exiles returned; the beginnings of the Jewish diaspora are traced to this period. But Jerusalem and the temple were rebuilt; Judah became a separate province under a native governor, virtually a theocracy under the high priest. The Jewish community established there drew in on itself, rejecting association with the remaining population of Israel, the Samaritans. The traditional law attributed to Moses began to take definitive and detailed form; although the works of the prophets were also collected, along with histories, emphasis was placed on a strict observance of the law.

Civilisation at the Halfway Mark

It is worth reflecting that half the span of civilized history had passed by the time of Cyrus; his generation was as distant from the first cities of Sumer as from us. In the 2500 years that had elapsed from the beginnings of city life in Sumer the people of Western Asia and Egypt had defined and devised the institutions and instruments which made civilisation possible. From them we have inherited such fundamentals as the state, writing, the wheel and international trade as well as not insignificant beginnings in chemistry, metallurgy and mathematics. Sumer contributed and its Semitic successor states preserved some of the basic notions which entered the Hebrew bible, notably but by no means only in the flood story. Egypt, for its part, inspired much of the Wisdom literature in which Egyptians and Hebrews wrestled with themes as diverse as how to succeed in one's career and the meaning of life.

These achievements are the more impressive when we note that the total population of the area in 500 BC was of the order of fifteen million people.

Chapter Two

Civilisation and Empire in the Mediterranean

The First Sea Power

By 2000 BC the ceaseless quest for metals had spread Mesopotamian trading contacts as far as Cyprus, if not further into the Mediterranean. About the same time, farming communities in Crete, the Greek mainland and the southern Aegean islands began to supplement grain crops with the vine and the olive. The development of a longship (up to 40 feet long!), strongly built and furnished with sail and oars, gave them the means of transport needed to develop trade in wine and oil, as well as metal artifacts and ornaments. In consequence, many villages grew into small towns.

The most spectacular development occurred on Crete where a palace centred civilisation developed. At Knossos, on the north coast, the largest and most impressive of these palaces was decorated with vivid and lively pictures depicting dances, religious ceremonies and acrobats leaping over charging bulls. Later Greeks were so impressed with the size of this palace that they recounted all sorts of legends about the labyrinth, the monster that inhabited it and Theseus, the Greek hero who slew it. The name of the Knossos ruler in the Greek legends, Minos, has been adopted by archaeologists to describe the civilisation of Crete.

Minoan civilisation revolved around the palace which was home to the king and his officials and a vast store for grain, wine, oil and the output of a varied collection of artisans who produced both luxuries for the palace and artifacts for export. Minoan products were traded as far as Syria and Egypt and King Minos (or perhaps the Minos – the word may have been a title) and his people lived well on the proceeds. Careful records were kept on clay tablets, at first in a pictographic script and then in a linear one (Linear A) which has so far defied decipherment.

Greek tradition regarded the Minoan state as the first sea power (thallasocracy). In fact, although there is some evidence for destructive warfare between the various states about 1700 BC, Minoan civilisation seems to have been mainly peaceful. Unfortunately for it, some of its neighbours were not. About 1500 BC, Knossos and numerous other sites were either destroyed or abandoned. Knossos was rebuilt and the frescos in the new palace, for the first time, show military scenes.

There is little doubt that the destroyers were mainland Greeks who shared much of Minoan culture but had developed an aristocratic, warrior ethos. Apparently they took over Knossos where records appear in a new style of writing (Linear B) in Greek. Massive, fortified palaces at many sites in Greece – notably at Mycenae, which has given its name to this civilisation – testify to their military orientation and their determination not to go the same way as the Minoans.

Mycenaean trading networks expanded to surpass the Minoan. Their distinctive pottery has been found not only in the Aegean, Syria and Egypt but as far west as Sicily and Sardinia.

The Mycenaean states were monarchies with a strong aristocratic element. Although independent, they were capable of acting in concert on occasion. Towards the end of the second millennium, they combined to sack Troy, a prosperous non-Greek town which commanded the Hellespont and the entrance to the Black sea. Later Greek legend, eventually enshrined in the Iliad, ascribed the conflict to a dispute over Queen Helen. Some modern historians are inclined to suspect a geo-political war for control of the Hellespont and the growing trade of the Black Sea.

The sack of Troy was only one incident in the time of troubles which marked the end of the second millennium. The Mycenaean states, despite their military orientation, were overthrown by invaders from the north and their palaces and towns largely destroyed. Mycenaean warriors, fleeing before the invaders, were probably one of the Sea Peoples who invaded Egypt about this time.

The Phoenicians and the Opening of the Western Mediterranean

When the time of troubles eventually gave place to a new stability, the Minoan/Mycenaean role in the sea trade of the Eastern Mediterranean was initially taken by the Phoenicians.

Important trading cities had emerged on the coast of Syria (mainly in the present Lebanon) in the second millennium. Byblos has given its name to the Greek word for book and through that to the Bible. Ugarit contributed more than its name. By 1500 BC Semitic peoples in Syria and Palestine were experimenting with the first alphabets. A hundred years later scribes at Ugarit were writing in a true alphabet. The Phoenician alphabet which succeeded this was the origin of the Greek and Roman alphabets, of our current script and, in the opinion of some scholars, of all the alphabets in the world.

It was probably the quest for metals which led the Phoenician traders into the Western Mediterranean. Before long a string of trading stations or colonies was established from Tripoli to Morocco, around the straits of Gibralter, along the south coast of Spain, in the Bealearic Islands and in western Sicily, Sardinia and Corsica.

In 814 BC (traditional date) or by 750 BC (archaeological dating) Tyre established the colony of Carthage, not far from modern Tunis, and strategically situated near the narrowest point (apart from the Straits of Messina between Italy and Sicily) between the eastern and western Mediterranean. Carthage soon became the undisputed centre of Phoenician penetration of the Western Mediterranean. The Carthaginians were interested in trade, not political domination. For some centuries they left the tribes of the interior largely undisturbed. Profiting by this, and their wealth of tin, copper and silver, some of the tribes on the south coast of Spain established the first large political unit in western Europe, the kingdom of Tartessus which is mentioned in the Bible as the fabled, wealthy land of Tarshish.

At this stage a contemporary observer might well have assumed that the Western Mediterranean was destined to become a Carthaginian lake from which a Semitic style of civilisation might gradually penetrate the hinterland. The assumption would have been reasonable but wrong. Fifty or sixty years after (the traditional date of) the foundation of Carthage, the first Greek colonists appeared in southern Italy and established a town at Cumae (north of Naples). For the next two hundred years, Greek colonists poured into southern Italy, Sicily, the south coast of France and a few settlements on the east coast of Spain. Unlike the Phoenicians they came for settlement, as well as trade. Inevitably, the scene was set for conflict.

Both the Greeks and the Carthaginians, to say nothing of the Etruscans, who had established a powerful confederation of city states in central Italy, would have been astonished if they had been told the final victor in the conflict ahead. The little group of Latin speaking farmers, clustered on the hills around the Tiber which were to become the city of Rome, were merely obscure dependents of the Etruscans.

The Greatness and Failure of the Greeks

The invaders who drove out the Mycenean ruling class around the end of the second millennium were themselves Greek speaking, although with a distinctive dialect later identified as Dorian. Their success may have been due to their use of mounted warriors with iron weapons against the chariots and bronze weapons of the Myceneans.

The invasions produced several centuries of confusion. The Mycenean palaces were destroyed and writing disappeared. Some of the Myceneans fled across the Aegean and strengthened the Greek presence on the coast of Anatolia. The Dorian dialect became dominant in much of the Peloponnese, in Crete and on the south western coast of Anatolia. It seems unlikely, however, that the Dorians exterminated or pushed out all the previous population; the Mycenean legends survived to become the common cultural property of all Greece. Athens and the nearby islands remained substantially untouched by the Dorians and preserved the Ionian dialect.

By 800 BC the Greeks, while conscious of these separate dialects and the mixed history that lay behind them, saw themselves as one people. The epic tales of the Myceneans, long preserved by oral tradition, began to be written in a new, alphabetic script derived from the Phoenician. Finally, some time between 750 BC and 650 BC, these traditions took definitive shape in the two epic poems ascribed to Homer – the Iliad and the Odyssey – and gave the Greeks the basic resource for the development of their literature, their pantheon and their sense of identity.

The Greeks and European History

Like all epic traditions stemming from the early years of a developing culture, Homer preserves a very mixed bag of fact and fiction. The Greeks in general were not aware of this and tended to accept the epics as history. The precursor of European historians, Herodotus, questioned the detail of the Iliad – he remarked that if Helen had indeed been in Troy, she would have been handed over to the Greeks – but even he accepted the basic truth of the narrative.

So did the Romans and the Western Europeans. It was left to the nineteenth century critical historians to question the historical value of Homer, at first too drastically – Grote's authoritative history described it as purely mythical; twenty years later Schliemann excavated Troy!

The Romans adopted Greek culture and made it the foundation of their education. A core of Greek literature and philosophy survived the barbarian invasions in Latin translation. In the fifteenth century this core was expanded by material brought by Greek refugees from Byzantium. With the Renaissance, this expanded core, along with a body of Latin literature, became the basis of education in Europe. The cultures of West Asia and Egypt and the early development of Europe were buried and forgotten; Greece came to be seen as the origin and foundation of European civilisation. It was only when archaeology developed into a science, beginning at the end of the nineteenth century, that scholars were in a position to realize that Greek society had antecedents and origins. The Greek contribution to European civilisation remains unique and enormous. It is not diminished by accepting that it, in turn, built on what had gone before it.

By the eighth century Greek society was developing a structure very different from the Mycenean with its predominance of kings and aristocrats; change was beginning to draw some of the commoners into the heart of the political process. Probably the use of iron weapons was the foundation of this development – any prosperous farmer could acquire such weapons and every Greek state, always in actual or potential conflict with its neighbours, needed their military service. Moreover, Greek farmers, unlike their downtrodden counterparts in the old empires, were sufficiently close to their tribal background to be useful warriors. Then the phalanx came into use and rapidly became dominant on the battlefield. The phalanx was an array of armoured spearmen, usually eight deep, trained to advance and fight in unison. Properly drilled and motivated, the phalanx could only be held, if at all, by another phalanx; lighter infantry and cavalry would simply be swept off the battlefield. So the security and perhaps the existence of a state no longer depended on its aristocratic horsemen but on the commoners in the phalanx.

Those commoners soon began to draw political conclusions from military realities. If the state depended on them for survival, they would have a voice in its control and decisions. Between the eighth and the sixth century kings either disappeared or were reduced to purely formal, often religious, functions in most Greek states. This change was accompanied by a confused period of struggles in which the old aristocracy and the newly emerging middle class of wealthy merchants and prosperous farmers strove to put in place arrangements which gave them, rather than the common people, control of the state. In many cases the immediate beneficiaries were men whom the Greeks called tyrants. In Greek terminology a tyrant was not necessarily an oppressor but what we would call a dictator – a man who seized control of the state with the support of one of the conflicting factions and governed it according to his own will rather than according to laws and traditions. Many tyrants were admitted to have done great things for their states but it was inherent in their position that they would never be regarded as legitimate by all the population.

These changes were accompanied by others of equal moment. Growing populations rapidly outstripped the productive capacity of the limited available land. The Greeks reacted by sending out colonies – to the north coast of the Aegean, to Southern Italy and Sicily, to the coastlands of the Black Sea and even to Cyrenaica in North Africa. Some two million people lived in Greece at this time and the overseas population eventually reached half a million. These are not large figures from our perspective but they were at the time; the entire population of Italy, which probably received the bulk of the Greek colonists, was less than three million.

Greek colonies were independent from the moment of their establishment; their ties with the mother state were never more than those of sentiment and filial piety. Originally they were mostly agricultural settlements but some rapidly developed into trading centres through which Greek products were channelled into the barbarian hinterland. Many of the most famous cities of the Mediterranean originated as Greek colonies – Marseilles, Nice, Naples, Syracuse and Istanbul (Byzantium) to name but a few.

By the middle of the sixth century colonisation came to an end. The most attractive sites had been occupied and growing trade meant that surplus population from the land could largely be absorbed in urban, trade based work. Strangely enough, neither of the two states which were to take the lead in Greek affairs had participated in the wave of colonisation.

Dorian Sparta, dominant in its immediate area (Laconia), solved its population problem by conquering neighbouring Messenia and reducing most of its population to serfdom. To ensure their continued predominance, the Spartans turned themselves into a standing army, invulnerable on the battlefield but unresponsive to cultural and intellectual developments.

Athens followed a different and more tumultuous path which, however, was to lead not just to economic prosperity but to the cultural and intellectual leadership of Greece and much more. Its citadel on the Acropolis survived the Dorian invasions and pottery remains suggest that something of Mycenean culture survived. Certainly, by the middle of the sixth century, beautiful Attic pottery was to be found everywhere in the Mediterranean and the Black Sea. Much of it had been exported as containers of wine and oil.

In the seventh century, the supremacy of the aristocratic landowners (eupatrids or well born) was challenged by the new rich supported by impoverished and indebted tenant farmers. Athens avoided revolution by adopting a new constitution which cancelled all debts and abolished debt slavery. Further dissension culminated in the tyranny of Peisistratus and his sons (546 to 510).

The tyranny inaugurated the pre-eminence of Athens. Peisistratus fostered trade and industry, undertook an extensive building programme, introduced new, cohesion-building festivals – the origin of Greek drama – and attracted artists and poets to his court. Athenian coinage circulated all over the Aegean. Perhaps it was the prestige that Athens was acquiring that induced the Spartans, jealous of their pre-eminence, to support the overthrow of the Peisistratid regime. If so, it did them little good. After a short period of confusion, Cleisthenes devised a new constitution which increased the power of the people and integrated city and countryside. Athens was now set on the road to democracy and a rival to Sparta for paramountcy in Greece.

Persian Wars and Athenian Democracy

In 500 BC the Ionian cities on the coast of Anatolia revolted against Persia. Athens, conscious of her growing pre-eminence among the Ionian states, and nearby Eritria came to their assistance. The revolt was suppressed and the Persians advanced into Thrace and Macedonia. Symbolic tribute – earth and water – was demanded from all Greek states. Athens and Sparta refused. A Persian fleet and army crossed the Aegean and destroyed Eretria, deporting its inhabitants. The Persian host then landed on the Attic coast at Marathon only to be swept away by the Athenian phalanx.

It was ten years before the Persians were in a position to renew the conflict. In the meantime the Athenians had located a new, rich vein of silver at Laurium and wisely used the proceeds to built a fleet of 200 triremes. When the Persian host – perhaps 100,000 to 200,000 men, not the million of later Greek legend – crossed the Hellespont and subdued Thessaly, the population of Athens was removed to the island of Salamis. The Persians, overcoming the heroic resistance of 300 Spartans at the pass of Thermopylae, burnt Athens and their fleet sailed down the Attic coast. At Salamis, crowded in narrow waters where its superior numbers could not be deployed, it was soundly beaten by the Greeks. Next year, at Plataea, the land army again proved no match for the phalanx and the fleet was again beaten at Mycale, near Miletus on the coast of Anatolia.

Victory over the great power of the Persian empire produced a great burst of self-confidence and of intellectual and artistic creativity, especially at Athens which had taken the lead in the struggle. It is to the fifth century that we owe the development of Greek drama at Athens and the sculpture and architecture of the Parthenon. Western historical writing begins with Herodotus and takes a step towards the pursuit of objectivity and careful methodology with Thucydides – although the latter was not a historian of times past but a recorder and analyst of current events. Western philosophy takes shape with Socrates, Plato and Aristotle. It is not too much to say that Greece, and particularly Athens, laid half the foundations on which the European mind-set has developed ever since. (The other half, of course, was being laid by the Jews, to be developed by Christianity).

At Athens, these developments were accompanied by a progressive growth of democracy which placed control of the state in the hands of the popular assembly of citizens or Ecclesia. One factor in this was probably the importance of naval, rather than military power, in Athens' defence. No expensive equipment was needed to pull an oar so all citizens were liable to service in the fleet. The democratized constitution reflected this reality.

Obviously, the assembly needed leadership. This was supplied by Pericles, who first became prominent in 462 in advocating the revision of the constitution to place more power in the hands of the people. Pericles' patronage, culture and ability drew into his circle such men as Herodotus, Sophocles the dramatist and Phidias the sculptor; his eloquence swayed the assembly and, as paraphrased by

Thucydides, immortalized the name of Athens and her claim to be the model of democracy.

The Athenian idea of democracy, however, was very different from ours. Representative institutions were confined to a great council (boule) of 500 whose business was to prepare matters for decision by the assembly. The Greek concept of democracy was essentially direct – all the people should participate in decision making. But the Athenian citizen body was some 40,000 and the Pnyx, the meeting place of the assembly, could seat little more than 6,000.

Payment for attendance at the assembly, the council and the vast juries, numbering hundreds or even thousands, made citizenship valuable. The thousands of resident aliens who contributed much to the economy and culture of Athens were excluded.

Women also were excluded from active participation. Indeed the Greeks assigned women to a distinctly subordinate role; they could not own property or engage in transactions worth more than a measure of barley. If a woman's husband died without an heir, she and the property were awarded to the closest male relative of the husband prepared to marry her; for this purpose the relative could divorce his wife. Within the house, separate and secluded quarters were assigned to the women who only left the house in company. In short, Greek women were in much the same position as women in traditional Islamic societies. There is no more chilling description of the subordination of women to men than the boast of an Athenian orator. 'For this is what having a woman as a wife means, to have children by her...Call-girls (hetairai) we have for the sake of pleasure, mistresses for the daily refreshment of our bodies, but wives to bear us legitimate children and to look after the house faithfully.' In short, women were a resource to be exploited, just as slaves were.

Naturally, Athenian democracy also excluded slaves. There were about 100,000 of them, engaged in domestic service, trade and industry and even finance. Most of them were not badly treated by the standards of many slave societies. But in the mines at Laurium, as in Victorian England or contemporary Colombia, children were employed to work in shafts too narrow for an adult.

No Greek thinker of the period criticised either slavery or the subordination of women. For that matter, we search Greek writing in vain for the passionate call for justice to the poor which we find in Amos and other Jewish prophets.

All told, the Athenian democracy enfranchised less than 20 per cent of the population and exploited a good part of the rest. Other Greeks never criticised Athens for this – the situation in their cities was the same. It was a different matter, however, when Athens developed an empire which reduced the independence of other Greek states. For the Greeks were passionately convinced that every city state had a right to independence and to the control of its own destiny. To surrender even a portion of this control was somehow unworthy of Greeks.

Athens had taken the lead in the continuing struggle with the Persians and in 477 organised the League of Delos to ensure defence. The war was carried on in a desultory fashion, interrupted by conflict between Athens and Sparta, until 448. The settlement of that year provided that the Greek cities of the Anatolian coast would remain within the Persian empire but retain local autonomy.

The Delian League, which now embraced virtually all the Aegean cities, was gradually transformed into an Athenian empire. The situation was inherently unstable and in 431 Sparta was drawn into war with Athens. The Peloponnesian War extended to embrace on one side or the other virtually every Greek state in the Aegean and many in Italy. Athens finally admitted defeat; the Delian league was dissolved and an oligarchic government was established in Athens. The Spartan hegemony that followed was even more oppressive and resented. By 403 Athens had re-established democratic government; the power of the people was celebrated in 399 by condemning the philosopher Socrates to death for corrupting youth and introducing new gods.

Athens was visibly on the road to recovery and beginning to re-assert its claims to leadership. Sparta allied with Persia and the Great King dictated terms of peace in 387; Persian gold and Greek divisions had accomplished what Persian arms could not. The Greek states continued their endemic warfare. Phillip, King of Macedonia, saw his opportunity. He united his backward kingdom, built up a strong national army and developed a new system of tactics, combining heavy cavalry with the phalanx. In 338 he overwhelmed a Greek alliance and next year formed the Greek cities into a league for a war of conquest against Persia. His murder in 336 brought to the throne his 20 year old son Alexander.

In a series of victorious campaigns Alexander overwhelmed the Persian empire and proclaimed himself its king. He led his armies to its furthest boundaries and would have pressed on into India if his troops had not mutinied. In 323, at the age of 33, he died at Babylon.

Alexander seems to have envisaged some sort of merging of Greeks and Persians but we shall never know for certain how this remarkable man saw the future of his enormous realm, nor indeed whether he had any vision except unbounded conquest. What is certain is that he had changed the future of both Greece and West Asia and laid the basis for a new cultural regime – to which we owe a good deal of the inheritance which we tend to ascribe to the Greece of Pericles and Socrates.

Alexander's death was followed by a confused half century in which his generals and their heirs fought and intrigued to maximise their power. By 280 BC the framework of the Hellenistic world was established. The Antigonids ruled in Macedonia and dominated the Greek cities. The Ptolemies were Pharaohs of Egypt. The Seleucids had most of the rest but already an Iranian people, the Parthians, were beginning to press on their northern borders.

The Rise of Rome

When colonisation came to an end about 550 BC, Greek city states were dominant in eastern and southern Sicily and scattered along the Italian coast as far north as Cumae and Naples. Inland were Italian speaking tribes and along the Adriatic coast, in which the Greeks showed little interest, Illyrian tribes. None of these posed any threat to the Greeks. Further north, however, the league of Etruscan city states saw the intruders as a menace to their trading interests and perhaps more. Their response was to ally with the Carthaginians to defeat a Greek fleet at Alalia in Corsica. The Carthaginians, already established in Western Sicily, became dominant in Corsica and Sardinia. The Etruscans continued their expansion from their homeland in Tuscany, north into the Po valley at Bologna and Mantua and south into Latium and Campania as far as Cumae. There, in 474 BC, their southward advance was halted by the fleet of Syracuse, the greatest Greek city in the West.

The Etruscans themselves claimed an Eastern origin and certainly their language, as revealed by the few surviving inscriptions, is neither Italic nor even Indo-European. Their culture, however, seems to be a development of the prehistoric Villanovan culture. It is not impossible that an eastern influence was super-imposed on this some time around the beginning of the first millennium but there is little or no evidence to support this hypothesis. The so-called Orientalizing style in later Etruscan art is adequately explained by the Greek contacts.

In the course of their expansion, the Etruscans became dominant in the small city of Rome. Later (unreliable) tradition spoke of three Etruscan kings, the last of whom was overthrown in 509 BC. Rome was henceforth independent but its debt to the Etruscans was large. It was most obvious in the alphabet (which the Etruscans had derived from the Greeks), the symbols of authority such as the fasces, the axe tied in a bundle of rods (which Mussolini revived as the symbol of Fascism), the gladiatorial games and the divination of the will of the gods by the study of intestines and of the flight of birds. It seems likely that the Etruscan influence ran deep. Indeed, although Rome used the Latin language and always considered herself a Latin city, it is not impossible that an important Etruscan strain was absorbed into the Roman population.

The Roman aristocracy or patricians, who had come to power in 509 BC, struggled hard to preserve its prerogatives but was prepared in the last resort to compromise with, and co-opt, the leaders of the people or plebeians. By the end of the fourth century, Rome had developed a complex constitution with annual elections of two consuls and other office holders by carefully structured assemblies. Plebeians were eligible for election and in this way a new, mixed nobility of office holders emerged. This nobility directed the state through the senate, subject to check by the assemblies.

By a mixture of warfare and concessions Rome established her domination of the Latin cities around her and built a base for further expansion. In the process, a distinctly Roman concept of a colony was developed. Unlike Greek colonies, those established by Rome were never independent or destined for independence. But the citizens of a Roman colony, unlike the citizens of a Hellenistic city, were citizens, not subjects, of Rome. They had all the rights of a Roman citizen – they could even vote if they happened to be in Rome at the right time – while their city institutions gave them complete control of their own local government. As expansion proceeded, similar status was accorded to some existing Italian communities – citizenship without the right to vote (*civitas sine suffragio*), which distance from Rome would have made impossible in any case. Citizens obviously did not pay tribute – this was no Asian empire. Equally obviously, citizens were liable to military service, so that the Roman military pool was constantly expanding. These arrangements were supported by contact and intermarriage between the Roman and the Italian ruling classes. Indeed, it has been argued not unreasonably that one of the attractions of Rome to the ruling class in the Italian cities was that it offered an assurance against social conflict within.

Rome developed an effective military machine on the basis of its own rural population, supplemented before long by the levies of the colonies and the other communities with citizenship and eventually also of allied states. The Romans developed a more flexible battle order than the Greek phalanx with legions divided into units arrayed in a chequerboard pattern. They replaced the massive thrusting spear of the phalanx with two lighter spears which were thrown before battle was joined with the short sword. These arrangements perhaps strengthened the spirit with which Roman armies fought – Roman armies were sometimes defeated but they did not expect to be. Defeat was, in any case, only a prelude to victory. Rome won its wars, thanks to its spirit, its tactical system and its ever growing Italian manpower.

So, by a combination of military strength and shrewd, innovative institutional arrangements Rome built up an Italian commonwealth, approaching a national state while retaining both local government and central direction. It was a remarkable achievement, predicated above all on openness – a willingness to expand Roman power by extending citizenship – an approach which the Athenians and other Greeks, jealously guarding their citizenship and engaged in their internecine wars, would have found difficult to comprehend. The Roman Republic was a unique form of state, neither empire nor federation of equals but perhaps the most effective mechanism yet devised for governing a population approaching five million people.

Rome had treaties with Carthage dating back several centuries but when the momentum of expansion drew it into Sicily conflict broke out in 264. The Romans built a fleet and equipped the ships with boarding bridges so that they could use their military superiority at sea. The war dragged on for over twenty years but in the end Carthage was forced to yield Sicily, and then Sardinia and Corsica, to Rome and to pay a large indemnity. The new acquisitions were not brought into the commonwealth system but were organised as provinces subject to a Roman governor.

Recognizing that the peace was only an interlude, Carthage built up a land based empire in Spain and profited from its mines. War broke out again in 219. Hannibal led a Carthaginian army from Spain, across the Alps, into Italy and defeated the Romans in a series of battles, culminating at Cannae where the Romans lost 50,000 men. Thereafter the Romans refused to engage Hannibal and waged a war of attrition in Italy, using their command of the sea to prevent re-inforcement and to carry the war abroad. By 205 they had conquered Carthaginian Spain and next year landed a force in Africa. Hannibal was recalled to defend the homeland, only to be beaten in the decisive battle of Zama in 202. Carthage was forced to accept a humiliating peace.

The long struggle, which only ended with a third war and the destruction of Carthage in 146, settled the destiny of the Mediterranean peoples. Rome was now clearly dominant in the West and would soon extend its power to every people around the sea. Internally the long period of war had changed the nature of Roman society and subsequent expansion would continue this trend.

The Hellenistic World

The Eastern Mediterranean/West Asian world on which Roman power now burst had been transformed in the century since the conquests of Alexander. Despite their conflicts with one another, and the rise of independent states in Anatolia, the successors of Alexander (the Diadochi) succeeded in achieving a substantial measure of Hellenization in Western Asia. Greek remained the language of administration and culture and Greek elites, re-inforced by the migration of the talented and ambitious from the Greek homeland, were dominant in all the successor states.

The Seleucids founded Greek cities all over their vast kingdom, from Syria to the borders of India. The institutions of these cities were modeled on traditional Greek constitutions. But they were subject to royal orders and paid tribute to the royal treasury. Even this very un-Greek situation did not shake the Greeks' conviction of their superiority over barbarians.

The Greek kingdom of Bactria, roughly corresponding to present day Afghanistan, broke away from the Seleucid empire in 239 BC Battered by nomad invaders, a Greek state survived for a time in north India to preside over a fascinating admixture of Greek and Indian art and to offer patronage and protection to Buddhism.

Greek culture, backed by the power and patronage of absolute rulers, proved attractive to at least some of the native elites. A new, cosmopolitan, Greek speaking culture became dominant in much of Western Asia.

Needless to say, this new culture did not penetrate to the mass of peasant farmers; they continued to be exploited and were now alienated from their masters by a difference of language. This alienation was to have large consequences in the seventh century AD when Islam arose to challenge the supremacy of the Greek speaking, Christian empire. In the meantime, it fatally weakened the Diadochi when they were confronted with the advance of Rome and the revival of Iranian power.

Nowhere was the division between the Greek speaking elite and the peasant mass more pronounced than in Egypt. The Ptolemies did not just rule Egypt – they owned and exploited it to maintain the power of the state and a magnificent, cultured capital at Alexandria.

Under these conditions Greek culture was bound to undergo significant changes. It makes no sense, however, to regard this Hellenistic culture as obviously inferior to that of classical Greece.

Philosophy and science both made significant advances in the Hellenistic period. Stoicism and Epicureanism, which between them provided the intellectual framework for the educated class until the triumph of Christianity, are both Hellenistic products. The foundations of geometry were established by Euclid and of mechanics by Archimedes. Archimedes designed artillery (not, of course, powered by gunpowder) to assist Syracuse to resist the Roman siege. Hero of Alexandria (first century AD) has left us the diagram of an incipient steam engine but it is simply a demonstration piece. The fatal divorce between high culture and the world of work prevented these scientists from realizing their potential to touch off an industrial revolution – the urge to improve the means of production and save labour was absent from a society accustomed to rely on the labour of slaves and exploited peasants.

Even in sculpture, in which the classical age had made a unique contribution, some Hellenistic artists introduced a realism which contrasts with the stylized idealism of earlier sculpture and culminated in the marvelous portrait heads of first century Rome. The Ptolemies endowed Alexandria with the largest public library in the ancient world and gathered around it scholars who, among other achievements, established the foundations of grammar and of textual criticism. It was no accident that the massive task of translating the Jewish scriptures into Greek was undertaken at Alexandria.

The Jews in the Hellenistic World

Alexander's conquest and the successor states did not at first disturb the tight-knit community that had been built up around Jerusalem after Cyrus had authorized the return of the Jewish exiles. Trouble started when Antiochus Epiphanes resolved on the Hellenization of all his subjects. Some Jews found this attractive but others resisted. Under the leadership of the Maccabean family, they revolted and, as Seleucid power weakened, established a virtually independent state by 142 BC. Profiting by the confused situation in Western Asia, the Maccabean or Hasmonean dynasty extended its power into Transjordan, conquered Samaria and Judaized Galilee to the north of it.

The Hasmoneans could therefore claim to have restored the kingdom of David but the achievement was doubly precarious. Externally, it depended on the continuation of a power vacuum which would soon be filled by Rome. Internally, the dynasty was often divided by bitter power struggles and penetrated by the attractions of Hellenism which aroused the opposition of the devout. The future of Judaism did not rest with the Hasmoneans or the priesthood but with the group of devout laymen who preached a strict observance of the law and, as rabbis or teachers, exercised a great influence on the general population. The role of these Pharisees, preserving the Jewish commitment and sense of identity, became even more important when Rome annexed the kingdom in 63 BC. Rome recognized the Jews as a special case and made no attempt to impede their religion but Hellenism became even more pervasive.

The kingdom was restored in 37 BC under the rule of Herod but he was too obviously a Roman client and was, in any case, only half Jewish – his mother had been a Hasmonean but his father was an Idumean or Edomite, one of a neighbouring people traditionally enemies of Israel. Devout and nationalist Jews did not accept Herod; increasingly they looked forward to divine intervention to restore the line of David. Confused expectations of a coming Messiah – the anointed one or king – became common, and worried both the Romans and the priesthood who correctly saw them as subversive of the established order.

A succession of high-handed and corrupt Roman governors provoked many Jews beyond endurance. In AD66 their resentment and Messianic expectations spilled over into revolt. Its bloody suppression took several legions, led by the future emperors

Vespasian and Titus, four years. Jerusalem was plundered and the temple destroyed. A second uprising in 132 AD resulted in Hadrian razing Jerusalem to build a Hellenic city – Aelia Capitolina – and prohibiting Jews from entering, not only the city, but even the district around it.

These events might have meant the end of any ordinary people and their absorption into the Hellenistic-Aramean world around them. The Jews, however, already had a large diaspora throughout the Roman world – perhaps as much as ten percent of the total population of the Empire – and beyond; the ruling family of Adiabene, a Parthian client state in what is now Kurdistan were converted to Judaism in the first century AD.

Although there was tension and a few uprisings early in the second century AD, on the whole the Jews of the diaspora were an accepted part of the Roman world and willing to live as part of it; the Bible had already been translated into Greek in Alexandria and Jewish scholars such as Philo were active in trying to explain Judaism in Greek terms. With few exceptions the Jews of the diaspora did not support the uprisings in Judea, which they probably realized were hopeless. Under the influence of pharisaic rabbis, these Jews maintained the tradition of a life governed by the law, the study of the Scriptures and weekly prayer in meeting houses or synagogues. These observances made the Jews a people set apart from the world around them and ensured their continuation as a people for two thousand years without a state or territory of their own.

Rome – from Republic to Empire

Rome paid heavily for its triumph over Carthage. The long war devastated much of Italy and took farmers away from the land; further wars followed – in Spain, where the Romans imposed their power with difficulty and brutality, and in the East, where the

Diadochi were never a match for Rome but military action was frequent and lucrative. The quarrels of the Hellenistic states made it inevitable that Rome would be drawn in step by step as ally and arbiter. Initial reluctance to expand gave way to an impatience with Greek quarrels and then to an imperialist urge. By the first century BC the Hellenistic world had been reshaped into Roman provinces and Roman client kingdoms.

The size of the Roman inheritance had already been reduced by an Iranian revival, spearheaded by the Parthians, Indo-European nomads who ejected the Seleucids from Iran and Mesopotamia in the second century BC. They established a strong state which, as heir to the Persian kings, shook itself free of Greek influence and presided over a revival of Iranian traditions. The Parthian Empire set bounds to Roman expansion in the East but the whole Mediterranean basin was united under Roman control.

Frequent warfare meant that manpower poured out of Italy in the legions; booty and slaves poured in. Rome and Italy were transformed and not for the better. In much of Italy small farms gave way to large estates worked by slave labour. Rome itself grew exponentially as it became an imperial capital and developed an urban proletariat. Differences in wealth grew rapidly and obviously as the governing class ruthlessly exploited the new provinces. The senate lost its old ability to avoid conflict by judicious compromise. The Gracchi, popular leaders advocating modest land reform and other palliative measures, were murdered.

By the beginning of the first century BC Rome, triumphant abroad, was bitterly divided at home. The senatorial party sought to maintain the power of the senate and ensure that the benefits of empire flowed mainly to its members. The popular party sought greater power for the popular assemblies and land distribution for veterans and proletarians. The dangers of the situation were increased by the Roman custom of awarding the control of armies to former consuls and other high officers of state; hostile politicians were in control of Rome's armed power and, sooner or later, would use it to settle their differences.

Meantime, the Italian allied states were increasingly dissatisfied with their inferior position. When a proposal to extend citizenship to them led to the murder of its proponent, Drusus, the allies revolted in 91 BC. At this point the senate recovered something of its old ability to compromise and the war was ended by the extension of citizenship.

Willingness to compromise, however, did not extend to the social sphere. The result was a half century of intermittent civil war. In 48 BC Caesar, a popular leader of aristocratic ancestry, who had built up his military power in a nine year conquest of Gaul, seemed victorious. The cowed senate appointed him dictator for life and he started to use the power to introduce some order into the Roman world, reforming city governments in Italy, making arrangements for the better government of the provinces, reforming the calendar and even introducing some Gauls into the Senate. All this, plus his liaison with Cleopatra, the Ptolemaic ruler of Egypt, was too much for some of the senators. On 15 March (the Ides of March) in 44BC they murdered Caesar and inevitably precipitated another period of civil war. Caesar's great-nephew and heir, Octavian, emerged as the clear victor in 32 BC. He proceeded to devise a form of government which gave the Senate some of the forms of power while leaving real power with him as princeps or first citizen. The Senate accepted the situation with relief and bestowed on him the title of Augustus.

The civil wars were over. Rome and the whole Mediterranean settled down to two centuries of peace and prosperity. The crass exploitation of the provinces was brought under some sort of control. Road building improved communications and the frontiers were stabilized and successfully defended against barbarian incursions. An attempt to extend Roman power into Germany, however, failed disastrously when three legions were annihilated in AD 9.

In the East local government was left in the hands of the cities. The same model was applied as rapidly as possible in the West; North Africa, Spain, Gaul and Britain (conquered in the first century AD) became a network of cities, all furnished with public buildings, baths, amphitheatres and aqueducts. Many may have been little more than administrative centres under the control of the landowners of the surrounding countryside but they were instruments of acculturation, extending at least a veneer of common civilisation over the whole vast area of the Pax Romana, the Roman Peace.

Within this area, government rested, in a sense, on the consent of the governed. Just as Rome had earlier co-opted the Italian elites, the provincial elites were co-opted by the principate in a network of patronage and influence, honours and favours. The ultimate honours were Roman citizenship, which was judiciously extended, and even membership of the Senate. Within each city, the elite maintained control by the same sort of mechanisms, subject to minimal interference from provincial governors and the distant authority of the Senate and the Princeps. The system worked for two centuries, providing peace and stability to some fifty million people. Neither the occasional border war nor the brief conflicts between the legions when the succession to the Principate was in dispute disturbed this peace for long or for many people.

Even more remarkable, the peoples subject to the Pax Romana gradually came to form a single entity in which diversity did not lead to conflict. The expansion of Roman citizenship reached its logical conclusion; it was extended to all free men. Admittedly, it thus became less valuable, especially to the great majority classified as 'humiliores' and subject to harsher and more inhuman penalties than the 'honestiores', the oligarchs. But the Empire had at least remained true, in principle, to the Roman spirit of inclusiveness.

Gibbon, the great pioneer historian of the Decline and Fall of the Roman Empire, thought that the Age of the Antonines (96–192) was an unsurpassed golden age. Gibbon was an eighteenth century gentleman and his judgment reflects this perspective; like his own time, the Pax Romana was a fine time to live – but only if you were a member of the ruling class. The city governments were oligarchies under the control of the rich; the poor majority was controlled by a mixture of private favours and public display, such as games and building projects, backed on occasion by the force of bully boys employed by the rich. Justice was in their hands and was manipulated in their favor.

At least the ordinary city dwellers had the occasional games and festivals to enjoy. The peasants missed even this consolation. Illiterate, and in many provinces not even speaking Greek or Latin, they were effectively cut off from the benefits of Roman rule – except the basic one, peace – and increasingly exploited by landowners and the local elites. Such a regime did not promote innovation. Nor did the cities, where artisan production served limited demand – limited by the small number of the rich and the inadequate income of the majority. Surplus income went into conspicuous consumption, prestige building or land purchase. The Roman economy was stagnant and Roman society seemed likely to settle down, like China, to centuries of stability and little change.

Instability and Civil War

Instability, however, was inherent at the top. Augustus had intended the Principate to be hereditary and it did, indeed, pass to members of his family, not without murder and intervention by the Praetorian Guard, until Nero's suicide in AD 69 left no obvious heir. Then the full weakness of the Augustan settlement became brutally clear. Precisely because of the separation between the reality and the forms of power, the regime lacked the legitimacy to cope with a succession crisis. The position of the Senate had been eroded beyond repair; the succession was determined not by it but by a brief but bloody civil war between the frontier armies. The victor, Vespasian, inaugurated another period of stability but the legions had learnt their power. Future Principes would have to be generals; the style of Princeps gave way to Imperator – a word which originally meant general but soon came to have the connotations of our word derived from it, Emperor. Competent and conscientious generals held the power of the legions in check for more than a century and provided effective, if increasingly authoritarian, government. Adoption of successors gave the Empire four outstanding rulers in the Age of the Antonines but thereafter the system broke down and after 235 the legions made and unmade emperors every few years.

Frontier defence suffered from the new pre-occupation of the legions. German tribes, notably the Goths, penetrated the empire repeatedly in the third century and cities began to build walls which had been unnecessary for two centuries. The trans-Danubian province of Dacia, conquered by Trajan in 105, was abandoned by Aurelian in 275, leaving behind, according to Romanian nationalists, sufficient Latin speakers to survive through many vicissitudes and establish the national state of Romania in the nineteenth century. Aurelian repulsed a German invasion of Italy but found it prudent to surround Rome itself with the wall which still bears his name. The Pax Romana had come to an end and with it the prosperity it had engendered. As defence and the predatory legions became more expensive, taxation became more burdensome and corruption endemic. City self-government increasingly gave way to imperial control and detailed regulation.

A half century of chaos was brought to an end when Diocletian became Emperor in 284. He secured the frontiers and carried out a comprehensive re-organisation of the administration, dividing the Empire into twelve dioceses and over a hundred provinces. The smaller units indicated the detailed regulation of the economy – peasants were bound to the soil and city dwellers obliged to follow in their father's craft – in the interest of stabilizing the tax base and so ensuring support for the army. Citizens were replaced by subjects and imperial protocol modeled on the Persian to emphasise the majesty of the Emperor.

Diocletian divided the imperial power, and the Empire, between a college of two Augusti and two Caesares who would succeed them. This attempt to ensure orderly succession hardly survived his abdication in 305. Another round of civil war made Constantine sole ruler in the West in 312 and over the whole Empire in 324. His acceptance of Christianity opened a new period in the history of the Empire.

The Beginnings of Christianity

Christianity had originated about three hundred years earlier when the Roman governor of Judea, yielding to pressure from the Jewish priesthood and a supporting mob, crucified a wandering preacher from Galilee. The memories of Jesus which were eventually enshrined in the four Gospels (good news) leave no doubt that he was an extraordinary human being. His preaching and personality attracted the common people and a close following of disciples. The priesthood and the devout Pharisees, however, were outraged by his association with religious outcasts and women, his unorthodox teachings and his calm assumption of the authority to set aside provisions of the religious law. Even worse, he spoke and acted as if he had a special relationship with God whom he called his father, using a word 'Abba' which some scholars think is best translated as 'Daddy'. Sections of the people were ready to acclaim him as the Messiah and see him as a leader against the Romans. This latter role he firmly rejected, to the disappointment of the populace, but its implications left the authorities uneasy and served to persuade a reluctant governor to condemn him.

Presumably both Pilate and the priests slept easier with Jesus dead; the people would now be convinced that an executed criminal could not have been the popular leader of Messianic hopes and his close followers had disappeared in fear. Within a short period, however, those followers surfaced and began to tell all who would listen that God had raised Jesus from the dead, that they had seen him, spoken to him and eaten with him.

At first the followers of Jesus regarded themselves as part of Judaism, with a mission to convince the Jewish people that their master was, indeed, the saviour sent by God. Only gradually did they come to see their message as a universal one. The leader in this recognition was Paul, a Pharisee from Tarsus in Cilicia. Originally a leader of hostility to the Christians, he was converted by an experience on the road to Damascus; Paul had no doubt that this was an encounter with the risen Jesus, of whom he now became the champion. His preaching journeys carried him through Anatolia to Greece and eventually to Rome. His letters to the nascent Christian communities, carefully preserved, reveal a passionate, vehement, argumentative man; intellectual and imaginative, he spared no effort to spread the good news of Jesus and to penetrate to the heart of the mystery of his death and resurrection.

Paul's life-work is better documented than that of his colleagues but he was not alone in his missionary zeal. In Asia Minor a different tradition, eventually identified with John, arose and there were almost certainly others which have left no history. In Jerusalem itself there was a strong group of Jewish believers who were only with difficulty persuaded that it was possible to be a Christian without being a Jew. The conflict was resolved with the mediation of Peter who was acknowledged as the leader of those who had followed Jesus in his lifetime.

The common pre-occupation of these groups of believers was not only to spread the good news but also to understand the full significance of these extraordinary events. As they grappled with this problem they became convinced that the life, death and resurrection of Jesus were only comprehensible if he was more than a mere man.

This belief, in itself, posed no problems for the Roman authorities; the empire was full of gods and one more could easily be accommodated. But the Christians also inherited the Jewish conviction that there was only one God and could not, therefore, accept the worship of the gods of a city or of Rome or, when this came to be required, of the Emperor. Rome had accommodated this idiosyncrasy on the part of the Jews but, for some reason unknown to us, would not make a similar allowance for the spreading Christian communities. At first persecution was spasmodic, driven by mob hysteria or individual spite; only in the third century did it become empire wide although intermittent and unsuccessful.

By the third century, in fact, Christianity was a well established facet of life in the Roman empire and beyond. Many, perhaps most, cities in the empire had a Christian community and Christianity, preached in local languages, was already penetrating the countryside in Egypt, North Africa and parts of Asia Minor and of Gaul.

In each city the Christian community, which met for weekly worship, was presided over by a bishop elected by the members and accepted by neighbouring bishops. The bishops kept in touch with one another – provincial councils became common in the second half of the second century. Special respect was given to the views of the bishop of Rome, where Peter had been put to death and his tomb was already venerated. The bishops maintained, not without discussion and dissension, a common set of beliefs in which new converts (catechumens) were systematically trained. From the middle of the second century, Christian apologists had been writing explanations of their faith and debating with pagan counterparts; one of these, Celsus, writing about AD 150, already refers to 'the great Church'.

The Christian Social Conscience

From its beginnings Christian belief and practice included a concern for the poor and afflicted which, while building on its Jewish heritage, went beyond anything in the world around it. The Christian convert was taught that his salvation or damnation depended not only on belief in Jesus but also on his treatment of the poor.

Christianity thus integrated social concern with religious belief in a way which was quite novel to the Roman world. This vision, while not always fully acknowledged in practice, was never forgotten and became an integral part of the Christian tradition on which a new style of civilisation was built.

The spread of the Church and its penetration into the educated and official strata of society was no doubt facilitated by the vigorous efforts of the apologists but it may have owed more to the careful catechumenate and the systematic organisation of the bishops. Certainly people were impressed by the strong communal spirit of the Christians and their care for one another. Above all, the Christians spoke with assurance in an uncertain world; they knew that there was a life after death and offered believers in Jesus a part in it.

The spread of this strange religion alarmed emperors who were struggling to impart some cohesion to the state by requiring acceptance of an official religion. Beginning with Decius in AD 249 a series of horrific persecutions was launched. Although many Christians succumbed to fear, the Church survived. In 311 Galerius, the successor of Diocletian in the East of the Empire and an enthusiastic persecutor, admitted defeat. In an extraordinarily frank edict he recognized that Christianity could not be exterminated and therefore must be tolerated. In the West Constantine fought his way to power in the conflicts which followed the retirement of Diocletian. Constantine's mother was a Christian; although not yet one himself, he respected the power of the Christian God and put a Christian monogram on his standards. He showed his gratitude for victory by turning the Lateran Palace over to the Bishop of Rome and building the great churches of St.Peter and St.John Lateran. By 324 he was sole Emperor; next year he presided over a council of Christian bishops at Nicaea.

In 330 Constantine inaugurated his new capital at Byzantium, now renamed Constantinople; the dedication services were conducted by Christian bishops. The new capital was a choice of strategic genius, destined to survive as a Christian and imperial capital for eleven hundred years. Yet this was not the greatest of Constantine's achievements. His totally unexpected integration of Christian church and Empire determined the parameters of European history for much longer; in many ways we still live in its shadow.

CHAPTER THREE

CIVILISATION IN INDIA AND CHINA

The beginnings of civilisation in India and China were a good deal later than in West Asia and Egypt – around about the middle of the third millennium in India and up to a thousand years later in China. The Indian civilisation had significant trading links with Sumeria and, while maintaining its own culture, derived much from these contacts. Chinese is usually thought to have its own unique origins but some external stimuli cannot be ruled out.

The First Civilisation in India

Civilisation developed in the Indus valley in the third millennium BC, and came to an unexplained end in the second. All memory of this was lost; our knowledge depends almost entirely on archaeology.

Since Mohenjo-daro and Harappa, the first sites to be investigated, were excavated in the 1920's, many more have come to light, revealing a civilisation which embraced (in modern terms) all of Pakistan and spilled over into Afghanistan and into the adjacent provinces of India.

It seems likely that the Indus valley was first settled in the fourth millennium from neighbouring Baluchistan. Here agriculture had developed as early as the sixth millennium and substantial villages became centres of production of beads made of hard stones and of pottery. Trade in these items brought the people of Baluchistan into contact with Sumeria and the peoples in between; undoubtedly this contributed to their development. But neither their culture, nor that of the Indus cities, was simply derived from Sumer.

The people who created the Indus civilisation were very likely Dravidians like the Tamils and other peoples of modern south India. This hypothesis is re-inforced by the survival of a Dravidian language, Brahui, in modern Baluchistan. But the population of India also included Austro-Asiatic peoples related to the Khmers and Mons of South East Asia and Proto-Australoids, a grouping which also embraces the Australian aborigines and the Veddahs of Sri Lanka. It is not impossible that either or both of these formed at least part of the Indus people.

One of the striking elements of the Indus culture was a strong, even rigid, element of town planning. A raised acropolis dominated the city which was laid out in a grid pattern with streets of prescribed widths according to their function. Comprehensive water supply, sewerage and drainage systems were superior to anything constructed again in the Indian sub-continent until modern times. The dominant acropolis has suggested to some scholars a pronounced class structure with the ruling group fortified against any uprising of the subjects. It may equally well have been intended as a last defence against external enemies; there is some limited archaeological evidence of warfare between the cities and perhaps the gradual extension of the power of Mohenjo-daro and Harappa over their neighbours. What the relationship between the two great cities was and whether anything like a single empire ever came into existence remains unknown. Nor do we know what form authority took – whether it was monarchic, aristocratic or oligarchic. The men who ruled in the Indus cities have left us no great inscriptions, no statues, no libraries of baked tablets. They remain an enigma. Our knowledge of the Indus might be extended if its writing could be deciphered. But since the texts available are largely limited to brief inscriptions on seals, even this seems doubtful.

This civilisation disappeared before the middle of the second millennium. By 1700 BC the cities were abandoned, never to be re-occupied. It used to be thought that this was the work of Indo-

European invaders, the Arya, who appeared in the Indus valley in the second millennium and gradually expanded to become the dominant people in North India. This now seems unlikely; the Arya penetration of India seems to have been a couple of centuries later than the disintegration of the Indus civilisation.

Several alternative explanations have been suggested. One emphasises ecological factors: the immense cities and spreading villages, all constructed of baked brick, required enormous quantities of fuel, leading to deforestation and consequent uncontrollable flooding. Population moved out of the valley; decentralized dry farming in a wider area replaced irrigation. If correct, this explanation would make the Indus civilisation the first identified victim of its own ecological vandalism. Other explanations put forward include climatic change and natural catastrophes. The latter could include the blocking of the lower Indus by tectonic upheavals and the consequent flooding of much of the lower Indus valley. Certainly the Aryas do not seem to have spread south of the Punjab.

The Spread of the Aryas

The collapse of the Indus civilisation left India in a situation very different from that of Mesopotamia or Egypt. There, barbarian invaders could take over an established civilisation. After an initial wave of destruction they would then often absorb its culture and even become its champions and preservers. This possibility was denied to the Arya by the disappearance of the Indus civilisation before their arrival in India – the sub-continent was occupied by tribal societies little more advanced than themselves. Indian civilisation would have to be created by slow development

By 900 BC the Aryas had spread from the Punjab into the upper reaches of the Ganges valley. Helped by the spreading knowledge of iron working, they could now tackle the harder soils of the valley and gradually moved down it. In the process the cattle herders and cereal growers of the Punjab became farmers of irrigated rice. It rather looks as if the Aryas, as they spread down the Ganges, began to absorb the previous inhabitants.

Settlement became denser and some villages grew into cities; Delhi, Benares and Ayodhya all date from this period. The recent riots and bloodshed as Hindu militants fought to replace a mosque at Ayodhya with a Hindu temple are a reminder of the continuity of Indian culture and the memories it has preserved. Ayodhya is the centre of one of the great epics, the Ramayana, which, together with the Mahabharata, enshrine folk memories of the period of Aryan expansion. These epics, along with a body of hymns and other religious texts, were handed down by word of mouth until after many centuries they were committed to writing. They play a role in Hinduism which has been compared with that of the Bible in Christianity.

Aryan society had already devised a rudimentary caste system which divided people into brahmins or priests, warriors, commoners – farmers and artisans – and a fourth caste of servants or slaves. The fourth caste may have originated with pre-Aryan inhabitants enslaved or reduced to serfdom by the expanding Aryans. In the course of time this simple structure grew into a complex of several thousand sub-castes, each with their own rules and practices. Caste is very much an Indian institution, with no precise parallel elsewhere; one can only wonder whether pre-Aryan beliefs and practices were grafted onto the original simple distinction. Very likely this may also be the case with the idea of re-incarnation under which the soul is re-born in a higher or lower state according to a person's good or bad conduct. Perhaps this belief made lower caste life more bearable and so helped the system to be accepted and perpetuated.

Buddha and Asoka

Around the end of the sixth century BC, Siddhartha, a prince of a minor kingdom in the north-east, rejected caste and the rituals of contemporary religious practice. He taught his followers to regard the world as an illusion and to seek enlightenment which would lead, after successive re-incarnations, to absorption in the absolute and extinction of the individual personality (Nirvana). His followers, convinced that he had already achieved enlightenment, referred to him as Buddha (the enlightened one) and perpetuated his teachings through communities of monks and nuns following his 'Middle Way'. In the next few centuries Buddhism spread widely throughout India – without ever replacing the original beliefs in the gods and the associated practices – and eventually over most of East and South East Asia.

The Persian empire established by Cyrus and Darius extended as far as the Indus and perhaps stimulated the ambition of the Arya leaders. At all events the tribes in the Ganges valley coalesced into a number of kingdoms. By the mid fourth century these had been united into a single state ruled first by the Nanda dynasty and after 321 BC by the Maurya dynasty. Chandragupta, the first king of this dynasty, resisted the attack of Seleucus Nikator, one of the successors of Alexander. Seleucus made peace, ceding Baluchistan and all the territory east of Kabul in return for 500 war elephants.

Maurya power was extended over most of India in the next fifty years, bringing perhaps thirty million people into one state, but Asoka (272–231) became so revolted with the carnage involved that he desisted from further conquest and began to patronize Buddhism. Asoka's empire therefore never included the far south of India; it also did not include numerous tribal areas and held others in only nominal subjection.

The societies which the Maurya conquerors encountered in their drive into south India were organized largely on a tribal basis. The more advanced of them shared a common group of languages, known as Dravidian, and probably a common culture which may earlier have been influenced to some extent by the Indus Valley . Out of the encounter between the Aryan conquerors and the Dravidians, Hinduism gradually emerged as a synthesis of religious beliefs and practices, amorphous and undefined but with extraordinary resilience and absorptive capacity.

Asoka, however, was committed to Buddhism and endeavoured to promote it both inside and outside his empire. Envoys were sent to the Hellenistic kingdoms and to the emerging south Indian states and Sri Lanka to spread the message of Buddhism. This missionary drive, without parallel in ancient history, had mixed results. The impact on the Hellenistic culture seems to have been insignificant whereas the Sinhalese were converted and remain to this day committed to Buddhism. Even more significant was the impact on the emerging states of south India. Within the next few centuries they would become the bearers of Indian civilisation in its penetration of South East Asia. Their influence brought Buddhism to the region; it remains dominant in Burma, Thailand, Laos, Cambodia and Vietnam.

India Divided and Invaded

Asoka's empire began to disintegrate soon after his death and eventually collapsed. This left no power in India strong enough to defend the easily penetrated north east frontier against the waves of invaders who now began to push in from central Asia.

The first of these invaders was the Greek kingdom of Bactria, established in the wake of Alexander's conquests and the weakening of the Seleucid empire. From 170 BC the Greeks established small kingdoms in the northern Punjab, which acted as a conduit for Buddhism to central Asia and developed a fascinating synthesis of Indian and Greek art. For a short period their power seems to have penetrated to the mouth of the Indus and some distance down the Ganges. But they were cut off from Greece and the Hellenistic world by the Parthians who forced the Seleucids out of Iran and Mesopotamia. This deprived the Greco-Bactrians of easy access to Greek speaking recruits and left them isolated. Before long they were overthrown by Shaka nomads from Central Asia.

About the same time, an Indo-European group to the north of China, known to the Chinese as Yue-Chi, were defeated by the Huns and moved westwards. By the end of the first century AD, now known as the Kushans, they had established suzerainty over central Asia and north western India. The best known ruler of this empire, Kanishka, was a patron of Buddhism and no doubt facilitated its spread into China. The empire declined after his death and by the middle of the second century AD had been reduced to dependency by the Sassanid rulers of Persia. Only in the fourth century did a native dynasty, the Guptas, establish a brief supremacy over northern India.

Meantime, independent states in South India developed trading links across the Indian Ocean with the Mediterranean and around the islands and coasts of South East Asia. Trade between the Mediterranean and India grew after the first century AD when a Greek mariner, Hippalus, realized that the monsoon could be used to sail direct from the Red Sea to south India, instead of creeping around the coast. An astonishing number of Roman coins and other objects have been found in India and a smaller number in South East Asia. By the second century AD, if not earlier, India was the centre of a network of sea routes which linked the Roman Empire, India and China. The trade was of limited importance in the economies of the states concerned, being confined largely to luxury goods. But it provided a linkage between those states and broadened the intellectual horizons of those who participated in it or got to hear about the countries involved.

India never established a tradition of a unified state or, for that matter, a common language. Its political history was to be, like Europe, largely the story of competing states. Unlike Europe it did not find the mechanisms and structures which could resist successive waves of outside conquest. It did, however, find in Hinduism the basis for a diverse but integrated culture which preserved a sense of Indian identity for two thousand years, much of it under Moslem supremacy, and exercised a formative influence on the diverse peoples of South East Asia.

Origins of Chinese Civilisation

Several thousand years after agriculture appeared in West Asia, cultivation began in China. By 5000 BC dry farming was widespread in the valley of the Yellow river, growing millet, sorghum and other crops on the fertile loess soil. Presumably this was an indigenous development; although the warmer climate of the period suggests a possibility of some interaction across Central Asia, there is no positive evidence. By 3000 BC a village culture had spread through much of northern China based on large and often earthen-walled settlements. Irrigation and rice cultivation were common, possibly derived from the South, where they may have originated even earlier than 5000 BC.

Some time after 3000 BC the archaeological record uncovers evidence of a stratified society with sharp distinction between nobles and commoners and the development of expert crafts. Bronze appears before 2000 BC, using distinctive and presumably indigenous techniques.

The First Empires

Traditional Chinese history tells us that a measure of unity was introduced in the Yellow River valley soon after 2000 BC by the Xia dynasty, which was replaced by the Shang before 1500 BC. Archaeological evidence is lacking for the former but verifies the latter. The power of the Shang kingdom rested on a military aristocracy and they may never have exercised effective control over more than part of the North. That area had a population of perhaps five million people and the agricultural surplus which the Shang could command was sufficient to support luxury crafts and magnificent interments, accompanied by slaves and human sacrifices, for the monarchs.

The chariot, as well as wheat and goats, reached China about the same time as the Shang achieved supremacy; one cannot but speculate as to whether the Shang leadership were outside invaders; if so, they were soon absorbed into a culture which was already developing the distinctive patterns which were to become Chinese. Shang scribes developed the essentially pictographic script in which Chinese is still written. About 5000 characters have been identified in Shang sources and the language was identifiably Chinese, dependent on word order not inflection. Also identifiable is the domination of peasants by landlords and an emphasis on ancestor worship – both traits which were to continue into modern times.

The Shang monarchy was replaced by that of the Zhou, whose power base was in the North West, about 1100 BC. Perhaps it was to justify this replacement that the very Chinese concept of 'the mandate of heaven' was developed. As eventually formulated by scholars, this concept held that the quintessential function of the ruler was religious. He was the 'Son of Heaven'; by prescribed ritual and good government he kept the favor of heavenly powers and so preserved both the welfare of the state and the continuity of his dynasty. If, through inadequate ritual or bad government, he lost the mandate of heaven, he would be overthrown and power would pass to the founder of a new dynasty. Of course, just who had the new mandate could only be determined by uprisings and civil war. If the Roman Empire was absolutism tempered by military revolt, Chinese absolutism was to be tempered by revolution.

In point of fact, the Zhou power gradually disintegrated as local rulers asserted their independence. This led to an 'Epoch of the Warring States' (403 to 221 BC) which was only brought to an end when a border state, using cavalry and iron weapons, subdued the rest and restored a single monarchy. Chinese scholars have always regarded this time of troubles as a disgraceful aberration from China's natural condition as a unified state. In fact, China has been a unified state for only 60% of the time since 403 BC and for one-quarter of that under foreign dynasties.

Despite the waste and suffering involved in endemic warfare, the 'Epoch of the Warring States' was a most productive period in Chinese history. The Chinese began to spread into the valley of the Yang-Tse, ousting or absorbing the less advanced Yue peoples, and the population grew to 25 million. Part of the base of this advance may have been the introduction of iron tools. Iron working probably came from the west but the Chinese, being used to very high temperatures in their pottery making, produced cast iron two thousand years before its development in Europe.

The Formulation of a Chinese View of Life

Even more important, the Chinese view of life was given definitive formulation in this period. This formulation is associated firstly with the name of Confucius (K'ung-fu-tzu). Reacting against the 'Legalist' school of thought which advised rulers that might was right and there was no higher morality than reasons of state, Confucius articulated the traditional Chinese ideas into a system of ethics. This system, which came to dominate the thinking of educated Chinese, stressed respect for elders and superiors and called for adherence to traditional virtues such as benevolence and trustworthiness. Confucius and his followers – who put his teaching into writing – hoped to see both families and the state guided by these principles. Within the family, Confucian teaching, being based on traditional values, emphasised the authority of the father and the subordination of women.

Traditional Chinese nature worship was developed into a body of thought and practice known as the Tao or Way. This system, traditionally associated with the name of Lao-Tze, incorporated mystery and magic into an ill-defined but long-lived synthesis. Taoism answered, at least in part, the need for a supernatural dimension to life – a need which Confucian ethics did not contest but did not meet. Most educated Chinese seem to have incorporated elements of both into their approach to life.

This complex of beliefs accommodated Buddhism when it began to penetrate China in the early centuries of our era. While traditional Confucian scholars tended to frown on the new and foreign religion, many Chinese found in the Mahayana Buddhism transmitted to them, with its emphasis on Bodhisattvas or 'saints' who could help them to a better life after death, a consolation for the hard and uncertain reality of their lives. Buddhism was absorbed into the Chinese cultural complex; it did not replace Confucianism or Taoism, but supplemented them.

The Classical Stage of Chinese Civilisation

The Chin emperor who brought the 'Epoch of the Warring States' to an end in 221 BC was a man in a hurry. He imposed a uniform administration, standardized weights and measures, coins and script and expanded Chinese power to both north and south. He is also often credited with the construction of the Great Wall although he seems to have simply joined up a number of existing walls with earthen mounds. The massive conscription of labour necessary even for this effort may have been the last straw in provoking resistance to a ruthless and tyrannical regime; at all events, within fifteen years the Chin lost the mandate of heaven to the Han dynasty.

With the Han, who ruled, with a short intermission, from 206 BC to AD 220, Chinese entered its definitive, classical stage. The Han emperors created a bureaucracy which foreshadowed in many ways the celebrated scholar bureaucracy which the Tang dynasty (AD 618–907) would establish as the foundation of Chinese government.

The unity of China was reinforced by the preservation of the Chinese script. Alone among the great civilisations of the Old World, China never developed or adopted an alphabet. Writing therefore remained, of necessity, the preserve of a small elite. The Chinese script has, however, one great advantage. Because it is essentially pictographic – with many refinements such as the use of radicals to indicate the general subject to which a word refers – the meaning of each character is quite independent of the sound assigned to it. The languages spoken in north and south China are, in fact, mutually incomprehensible; they are not just dialects but are at least as far apart as, say, French and Spanish. But the same characters will be used to represent words of the same meaning; once they are committed to writing, the languages become mutually comprehensible.

This force for unity became very necessary as the Chinese of the Han period continued the expansion into the South begun under the Warring States. This massive expansion may well have involved absorbing substantial numbers of the Yue and other peoples, racially distinct from the Chinese and more closely akin to the Thais. Certainly, there are substantial cultural as well as language differences between North and South; the Chinese themselves are conscious of them, while continuing to regard themselves as one people. The mutual intelligibility of the written languages has obviously helped in this common identification.

Chinese expansion to the south was matched by the successful defence of the northern borders against the nomads. The Han broke the power of a people they called the Hsiung Nu who then began to move westward across the steppes; they may have been the people whom the Roman Empire knew as the Huns. The Han were also able to extend Chinese power through the oases of the Tarim basin and even across the Pamir mountains into the fertile valley of Ferghana. Trade in luxury items developed along this route which became known as the Silk Road and provided a tenuous link between Rome and China.

This successful, if transitory, assertion of empire no doubt reinforced the Chinese world view. In this view, the Son of Heaven was not merely ruler of China. Because of his unique relation with the heavenly powers, the whole world owed him allegiance; China, under his direct rule, was the 'Middle Kingdom' around which a ring of lesser, barbarian powers were tributary. The fact that this tribute was often little more than part of an exchange of gifts, which could even at times of Chinese weakness disguise 'protection payments' to threatening nomad tribes, disturbed the theoreticians of the 'Middle Kingdom' not a whit. Even the discovery, in Han times, that there were powerful empires – Rome and Persia – which knew nothing of China, did not modify the Chinese view of the 'Middle Kingdom' as the unique centre of a world otherwise composed of barbarians. This misconception was of little importance at the time but was to have serious consequences when China encountered the thrusting power of modern Europe.

The Chinese, not without reason, refer to themselves as 'Children of Han'. By the time the Han dynasty collapsed in AD 221, the mould of Chinese civilisation had been definitively set. Despite substantial periods of disunity and of foreign domination, China was to maintain its culture and its mind-set, virtually unchanged, and enter the twentieth century as a type of the archaic civilisations which had long since vanished in other parts of the world.

Chapter Four

CHRISTENDOM AND THE ORIGINS OF EUROPE

In the centuries after Constantine the post-classical synthesis of the Roman Empire was transformed into the genesis of three new and different societies:

- Western Europe developed an amalgam of Roman tradition and the raw culture of the German invaders out of which evolved medieval Christendom and eventually the Europe we know;
- Constantinople became the centre of a Greek (Byzantine), rather than Roman, Empire which eventually Christianized and civilized Russia and the Balkans;
- West Asia and North Africa were set on a different course by the Moslem Arab conquests of the seventh century.

The Barbarians and the Christian Empire

In 378 the Goths defeated and killed the Emperor Valens at Adrianople. The defeat of Valens was followed by a century of incursions and settlements by German tribal groups from beyond the Rhine Danube frontier. They were not large – probably less than a million in all compared to perhaps fifty million imperial subjects of whom twenty million were in the West. Clearly those subjects no longer thought the Empire worth fighting for; most people experienced the Empire as oppressive. What fighting there was they left to other Germans in the pay of the Empire. Before the end of the fifth century, Western Europe was controlled by a number of

German warlords who ruled their own peoples as kings and the local people as officials of a conveniently distant Emperor in Constantinople. In the sixth century, one of these emperors, Justinian, made an attempt to recover the West; successful in North Africa, his armies devastated Italy and made it easy prey for a new and more barbarous group of Germans, the Lombards.

In the East, the Empire had survived partly by diverting German invaders to the West. Now, weakened by Justinian's wars, it was overwhelmed by a new set of invaders, the Slavs. An amorphous mass of clans spread through most of the Balkans; only major cities remained under imperial control. But Constantinople prevented both the Slavs and more militarized invaders, the nomadic Avars, from spreading further. Anatolia, Syria and Egypt remained imperial and civilized. Increasingly, however, the latter two showed fissiparous tendencies which found an outlet in religious division.

Constantine's adoption of Christianity was designed to give the Empire new life by enlisting the support of the most dynamic element in society. In this he was largely successful; within a century the Empire was Christian. The divine Emperor became the Christian Emperor, God's vicegerent on earth and supreme alike in church and state.

Christians did not hesitate, therefore, to let the Emperor take the lead in resolving their differences. Early Christians, convinced that Jesus was more than human, had hailed him as the Christ, the anointed one of God and even as the Son of God. The educated Greek mind had to articulate an explanation of this which preserved the unity of God. The great Councils of the Church which wrestled with this question were dominated by the Emperors. When feelings on the question began to cause major riots and to become identified with the fissiparous tendencies in Egypt and Syria, the Emperors began to look for formulations which would preserve the peace and to try to impose them by force; heresy became a crime. These efforts failed; the Egyptians and Syrians formed heretical churches, separated nominally by refined points of doctrine but really by a growing consciousness of national identity. The most civilized and prosperous parts of the Empire were alienated from its ruling class which by the seventh century had become solidly Greek.

The Western Church was less interested in dogmatic disputes; it had inherited Roman legalism rather than Greek philosophy and it was pre-occupied with survival in a violent world. It was usually represented at Councils mainly by delegates of the bishop of Rome. The Pope was a loyal subject of the Emperor; Rome remained imperial territory after the Lombard invasions. But Constantinople was unable to provide for its continuing defence and administration; the Pope gradually found himself in the role of imperial governor. From time to time he also found himself at odds with an Emperor who, looking for compromise with the heretics, pushed doctrinal formulas beyond the bounds set by previous Councils. Rome, tracing its origins to St. Peter, regarded itself as the custodian of orthodoxy and claimed some pre-eminence over the whole Church, a claim acknowledged only grudgingly by Constantinople and, indeed, by leading bishoprics in the West.

The Rise of the Franks

Religion also separated the German kings in the West from their Roman subjects; they had been converted to Arianism – regarded by orthodox Christians as a heresy – before invading the Empire. The Frankish tribes, however, who occupied modern Belgium, were pagan. United by the aggressive and murderous Clovis, they rapidly extended their power over most of Gaul and became Catholic before the end of the fifth century. Common religion established a basis for the slow integration of Franks and Gallo-Romans. Clovis and his sons extended their power over most of Germany west of the Elbe. But repeated division of the kingdom between heirs, and recurrent warfare between them, weakened royal power, devastated the country and led to a continuing decline of cities. Real power fell into the hands of local strongmen. By the eighth century, few except clerics were educated or even literate.

The Role of the Monasteries

It was largely the monasteries which preserved such civilisation as there was. Monasticism started in Egypt and Syria, even before Constantine, as devout Christians sought to separate themselves from a sinful world. It spread to the West where Benedict of Nursia in the sixth century gave classic expression to its ideals and way of life. His Rule gradually became the common, although not universal, standard in the West. Monks copied and preserved the Bible, the Church Fathers and, with some misgivings, much of Latin literature. Even these isolated centres of education, however, were eventually threatened with barbarisation as the great families which had endowed them came to regard them as part of their patrimony.

Monastic and religious revival was stimulated from an unlikely source. In the fifth century, Britain, already abandoned by the Roman army, had been invaded by pagan German tribes from across the North Sea – Angles, Saxons and Jutes. In centuries of intermittent warfare, they pushed the Britons back towards Wales and the west and established a number of small, warring kingdoms. Their conversion was initiated by Pope Gregory the Great in 596. Monks from Ireland, converted in the fifth century and following a different style of Church organisation, were active in the north but the English were easily persuaded to follow the ways of St.Peter. Monasticism flourished, enriched by inputs from both Rome and Ireland. In the eighth century, English and Irish monks began to work in the German lands beyond the Rhine which were still largely pagan. The most prominent of these monks, Boniface, sought and received papal authority for the organisation of his mission and of the German church it created. Boniface also enjoyed great prestige in Gaul and induced the church there to acknowledge papal authority.

Spain and the Moslem Invasions

In Spain the Visigothic king and his people were converted to Catholicism in 589. The integration of church and state was manifested in the Councils of Toledo; summoned by the king and attended by nobles as well as bishops, the Councils legislated on both secular and religious matters. Isidore, bishop of Seville, developed a new political theory which rejected the authority of the Emperor and proclaimed that all Christian kings were equal. Isidore initiated the work of reforming and strengthening the Church which was carried on systematically throughout the seventh century, making Spain a beacon of learning and legislation in the West. Not even the Church, however, could prevent periodical violent struggles over the succession to the throne.

One of those succession struggles provided an opportunity for the Moslem conquest. The tide of militant Islam, which had burst out of Arabia in 636, had reached North Africa in 669. A hard struggle followed but North Africa was eventually conquered and converted, passing definitively out of the European culture sphere. In 711, profiting by a disputed succession, an Islamic army entered Spain and destroyed Visigothic power in a single battle. Resistance disintegrated and the Arabs rapidly conquered the whole country except the north west. Here, protected by almost impassible mountains, a Visigothic nobleman, Pelayo, mobilized local support and established the tiny Kingdom of Asturias.

The Arabs saw no particular reason why the tide of conquest should stop at the Pyrenees. A large Arab raiding party entered Gaul in 732, broke the local defences and penetrated as far north as Poitiers. There, it was defeated by the Franks under Charles Martel.

The battle was decisive. Charles profited by the opportunity to extend his control over Aquitaine and Provence.

The Carolingian Empire

Charles Martel was not king of the Franks but enjoyed the title of Mayor of the Palace, a position which might best be described as hereditary Shogun to the enfeebled Merovingian monarchs. In 751 Charles' son Pepin, with the consent of the leading men and the blessing of the Pope, deposed his nominal master and was acclaimed king.

The Pope was not long in asking for a reward. Rome was hard pressed by the advancing Lombard kingdom and deserted by Constantinople, which was involved in a bitter dispute with the papacy over the use of sacred images. Pope Stephen turned to the Franks. Pepin defeated the Lombards and handed over a large part of central Italy, from Rome to Ravenna, to the pope, thus originating the Papal States. When the Lombards renewed their attacks a generation later, Pepin's son Charlemagne deposed their monarch and proclaimed himself King of the Lombards.

Charlemagne was now without a rival in Western Europe. His dominion stretched from the Pyrenees to the Elbe and embraced most of Italy; on the map it bears an uncanny resemblance to the original six country EEC, established nearly twelve hundred years later. After a lifetime of bloody fighting he subdued the last independent Germans, the Saxons. Further south he shattered the nomad Avars, destroying their great camp on the Hungarian plain. Only his invasion of Muslim Spain was a failure – giving rise to the great medieval epic of Roland and Oliver – but he managed to establish frontier marches from which, together with Asturias, the Christian reconquest could later begin.

Charlemagne took the responsibilities of a Christian king seriously. He presided over councils of bishops to reform church discipline and assembled scholars from his own dominions, as well as Spain and England, to improve the education of clergy and multiply corrected texts, both sacred and secular. To these scholars we owe the small, clear script known as Carolingian minuscule; reintroduced in the fifteenth century, it became the basis of our printed alphabet.

The scope of Charlemagne's power was formally recognized in 800 when Pope Leo III crowned him as Emperor. Constantinople was less than pleased and so, apparently, was Charlemagne. He did not wish his power to be seen as coming from the Pope whom he regarded as his subject. But the idea of a Western Empire, and the Pope's role in the making of Emperors, now took hold in men's minds.

In fact, however, the Empire was fragile. Only a ruler of Charlemagne's prestige and energy could control so vast an area when the real source of power was the military force in the hands of local magnates. Disintegration, probably inevitable, was accelerated when the Empire was divided between his grandsons and came under new external attacks.

Vikings, Moslems and Magyars

Even before Charlemagne's death in 814 Viking raids had begun. An explosion of energy sent warriors from Norway and Denmark probing the coasts of the West in search of plunder. Finding resistance inadequate, they extended their raids inland up the river valleys until few parts of Europe or the Western Mediterranean were immune. The unpredictability of the annual raids meant that resistance could only be organized locally. This put a premium on the development of local power centres and spurred on the growth of feudalism. The Vikings in turn began to organize themselves in 'great armies', to winter in Gaul or Britain, and to think of conquest rather than raids.

This strategy had some success. The Danes destroyed most of the English kingdoms. Only Wessex survived, thanks to the leadership of Alfred, but he had to accept a division of the country with the Danes; his son and grandson reconquered the lost lands and established, for the first time, a unified Kingdom of England. The weaker Carolingian king in Gaul was obliged to recognize Danish settlement around the lower Seine in return for nominal allegiance; this developed into the quasi-independent Duchy of Normandy.

The ninth century also saw the development of Islamic sea power in the Mediterranean. Sicily was conquered and the coasts of Italy ravaged, Rome itself being attacked in 845. A permanent base was established at La Garde-Freinet in the Maritime Alps in 888 and maintained for almost a century, raiding widely and terrorising travellers between Gaul and Italy.

Islamic dominance of the western Mediterranean, however, was to be short-lived. In Italy many cities had somehow survived the devastation of centuries of warfare. In the south a string of coastal towns remained nominally part of the Byzantine Empire and profited by trade with it; when the Moslems established their predominance in the Western Mediterranean they did not hesitate to trade with them also, no doubt mixing in a little piracy when opportunity offered. Amalfi – today little more than a fishing village and tourist resort – developed the Tabula Amalfitana from which modern maritime commercial law is descended. By the tenth century the Italian ports were stronger than their Moslem rivals and ready to challenge their supremacy at sea.

At the end of the ninth century a new menace appeared in the East. The Magyars, a nomadic people of mixed Finnish and Turkish origin, settled in the Hungarian plain and began a series of devastating raids as far as Rome, Aquitaine and Paris which went on intermittently until 955.

From Carolingian to Holy Roman Empire

The descendents of Charlemagne proved powerless to cope with these attacks. The Empire was divided between his grandsons and then divided again. France and Germany became distinct kingdoms. The middle kingdom, originally assigned to Lothair, broke up into separate kingdoms of Italy, Provence, Burgundy and Lorraine (stretching from Alsace to the Netherlands).

Real power slipped into the hands of local warlords, mostly descendents of the counts appointed by Charlemagne. Whereas he had regarded such counts as local governors appointed and removed by his will, now they were hereditary magnates, furnished with armed force. After Poitiers, Charles Martel had created a force of cavalry. In the absence of an effective taxation system, he met the cost of horses and armour in the only way open to him; he endowed his mounted followers with lands. It was a foolish landholder who defied Charles Martel or Charlemagne. Now the situation was different; the office of count became hereditary and the most violent and unscrupulous imposed their power on the rest in a welter of conflict and strategic marriages. West of the Rhine, landholding, military power and jurisdiction were linked by a chain of oaths of homage to create the system of government we call feudal; lesser men found it advisable to 'commend' themselves to greater. In Germany both nobles and peasants retained freehold land but power coalesced into the four great duchies of Saxony, Franconia, Swabia and Bavaria.

The local warlords at least met the attacks of marauders and somehow prevented the complete dissolution of a society threatened by constant raids and devastation. They provided their vassals with some security against the depredations of others. While they had no intention of giving up the reality of power, they recognized the need for some sort of overall leadership. In 911 the German magnates elected one of their number, Conrad of Franconia, as king. He struggled in vain to exert his authority over the dukes; on his deathbed in 918 he directed his brother to transfer the royal regalia to Henry of Saxony.

Not without occasional battles with the dukes, the Saxon dynasty exerted real power in Germany and absorbed the former Middle Kingdom. In 961 Otto I made good his claim to be king of Italy; the next year the pope, looking for protection against the Roman nobility, crowned him as Emperor. Thus was initiated the 'Holy Roman Empire of the German Nation', which survived in increasingly vestigial form until 1806. Neither Otto nor his successors made any claim on the remainder of the Empire of Charlemagne, the kingdom of France. They did, however, attempt to impose suzerainty on the Slav states which were beginning to form to the east of Germany. Bohemia was forced inside the Empire, but kept its own king and remained substantially independent. The new kingdom of Poland – and also Hungary – escaped a similar fate, partly by using the support of popes already anxious that the Emperor was becoming not the protector but the master of the Church.

Capetians and Normans

In 987 the magnates in France elected Hugh Capet as king. The Capetians recognized their limits. They were by no means the strongest power in France and for a century they concentrated on building up their authority in their own domain around Paris. The rest of France fell under the control of dukes and counts who ruled virtually without interference by the king.

In 1066 one of these dukes, William of Normandy, seized the throne of England. William's claim was tendentious but he made it good by force and proceeded to ensure that none of his supporters could build up local power sufficient to challenge his authority. He rewarded his major followers, as expected, with large gifts of English lands but gifts composed, not of solid blocks of territory, but of estates scattered around the country. And he insisted that every oath of homage must include a qualifying clause giving priority to loyalty to the king. William thus made his conquest a strong kingdom in which feudalism was a mechanism for royal control. His successors developed the legal techniques to enforce that control; even so the anarchy of Stephen's reign showed how much power still depended on the personal quality of the king.

Technological Innovations

Beneath the surface of Western Europe other important changes had taken place. The introduction of the heavy, iron shod plough made it possible to cultivate the heavy soils of valleys; the light plough of Roman times, suitable for West Asia and the Mediterranean, had confined cultivation in Northern Europe to the less fertile uplands. The introduction of the horse collar made the horse an efficient plough and draft animal; the Roman neck band had meant that the harder the animal pulled, the closer it came to choking itself. Three field rotation probably improved yields, still wretchedly low by modern standards.

Even these innovations pale in comparison with the spread of the water-mill. The Romans had known the water mill but made little use of it; grain was largely ground by animal power or by hand. The water mill was the first major application of technology to save labour. Its spread across Europe – there were nearly six thousand in England, a country of three thousand villages and towns, when William the Conqueror made his great Doomsday survey in 1086 – marks the beginning of a new type of civilisation, geared not to the perpetuation of traditional ways but to their improvement. To build and maintain the mills required a new skilled trade; some of these millwrights would eventually pioneer improvements and new applications of the mill.

No less important was the innovation which accompanied Charles Martel's creation of a cavalry force. The stirrup, possibly derived from China via Persia, enabled the horseman to charge with the lance and strike with the sword, tactics which, without it, would only result in a humiliating and probably fatal fall. The mounted and armoured warrior, the knight, would dominate European battlefields until the thirteenth century.

Change in Social Structure

Underlying all these developments was a change in social structure. It is true that the peasants were the exploited base of medieval society but they were significantly better off than their ancient predecessors; even as serfs they had acknowledged and usually respected rights. As economy and society expanded, they also had avenues of escape; 'town air makes free' and so did the frontier. Marcher lords trying to settle frontier areas in East Germany or Spain, or even lords wanting to expand their cultivation into wasteland, asked no questions of new workers – when a ninth century count of Barcelona needed settlers, he simply offered freedom to all slaves, adulterers and criminals. The middle ages saw the beginnings of social mobility.

The collapse of central power was not an unmitigated disaster. Most people had experienced the late Roman state as oppressive. The removal of this burden evoked the rekindling of the local, family and individual initiative required to survive in a disorganised and violent environment. The new spirit reached its apex in the men who built up the dukedoms and counties which were the framework of tenth century Europe. The same spirit became apparent in the towns and in the pioneering peasants who spread German settlement to the Oder and beyond. Western Europe had given birth to a new type of civilisation and a new type of man.

Church and State

Over this civilisation presided the Church, itself greatly changed since Roman days. The conversion of the Empire had resulted in Christianity changing from conviction to habit. The conversion of the Germans entailed an even greater, unconscious change: the understanding of Christianity took on the hue of the German mind. Christ became the champion of humanity in a never ending war with the spirits of evil. The Church was no longer the assembly of believers but a sacred institution, intermediary between God and men. It performed the services of worship and prayer, on behalf of the people, the laity who were increasingly seen as subjects of the hierarchy.

The collapse of the Empire left bishops as natural leaders of their towns, just as the conversion of the aristocracy made available men used to authority. Some bishops led the defence of their towns against marauders. The choice of a new bishop traditionally rested with clergy and people, endorsed by the other bishops of the province. But their role in the emerging states and the wealth which accrued from gifts of land made bishoprics a natural target for great landholders, counts and kings. By the time of Charlemagne, education was confined to clergy and monks, making bishops the counselors of rulers and bishoprics a reward for service; rulers either ignored rights of election or saw to it that their candidate was elected. A great ruler might appoint great bishops; a great feudal family would use the local bishopric or abbey, which it may well have endowed, to provide for younger sons.

This situation, although not the abuse of it, was acceptable to churchmen because of the integration of church and state. The king, anointed at his coronation, was responsible to God for both and, if he needed the services of churchmen to rule effectively, they needed him to lead and defend. It was the mark of a good king to reform the church as well as the state. The papacy itself was rescued by the

Emperors from the domination of the violent and licentious Roman nobility. Henry III appointed a series of German popes with the approval of those striving for reform; the leadership of the Emperor seemed the best hope of attaining their objectives. Already in the papal chancery, however, some men were developing a different conception in which the Pope would be supreme over both Emperor and bishops.

Christendom Poised for Take-Off

The potential conflict between Pope and Emperor, however, had not yet come to a head. In the meantime, Western Europe had in Christianity a system of belief and practice which gave meaning to life and death, offered some control on the worst excesses of violence and cruelty and united it into a defined and vigorous civilisation. Not without reason did it describe itself as Christendom. The weaknesses of this society, its divisions and unresolved conflicts, were obvious. But the future would show that it was, in fact, the most dynamic society in the world. The foundations of the world we know had been established.

By the eleventh century Christendom was poised for take-off. No longer the hapless victim of external raiders, it was expanding vigorously on all frontiers. Military conquest, settlement, trade, religious conversion and acculturation were all instruments of this expansion, used in combinations appropriate to different circumstances. At the foundation of this drive stood an expanding population, an improving agriculture, a common religion and a state system slowly replacing chaos with some sort of order. This was an expanding economy and society and its growing population included a fair number of a new sort of man – self-confident, aggressive and oriented, not to the preservation of traditional ways, but to change and innovation.

In this new synthesis religion was largely a dynamic rather than a conservative force. Cathedral and monastery schools gave place to universities in which religious teaching addressed new intellectual problems and developed a new and dynamic synthesis. Great cathedrals articulated those teachings for the faithful and gave rise to a new and venturesome architecture. Conversion justified the spread of German settlement and the use of force on the Slav frontiers. Conversion brought Slavs, Magyars and Scandinavians into the orbit of Christendom and facilitated the state building of new monarchies. The Church blessed the reconquest of Spain from Islam and sponsored the Crusades.

The Normans in Southern Italy and Sicily

The archetype of the new self-confident European man was the Norman knight. Even before William's conquest of England, Norman adventurers were seeking their fortunes in the endemic warfare between Lombard and Byzantine in Southern Italy. The seven sons of William de Hautville, led by Robert Guiscard, arrived in the peninsula virtually penniless; they started as horse thieves and ended as kings. By 1059 Robert was acknowledged by the Pope as Duke of Apulia and Calabria. His brother Roger expelled the Arabs from Sicily and after Guiscard's death enforced his authority on the mainland. Roger's son Roger II persuaded the Pope to accept him as king (1129) and ruled the richest and best organised kingdom in Europe from Palermo. The Norman kingdom drew on Greek, Moslem and Italian skills to create a sophisticated administration and to patronize a synthesis of art forms which found marvelous expression in such works as the Capella Palatina with its mosaic walls and Islamic ceiling.

The Expansion of Christendom

Knightly adventurers strengthened the Spanish kingdoms in their constant wars with the petty states into which Moslem Spain had dissolved. In 1085 they captured Toledo, so alarming the Moslems that they called in the Almoravid rulers of Morocco. These proceeded to absorb the petty states and halted the Christian advance for a century. In any case the Christian kingdoms had enough to do to absorb their conquests. To encourage settlement, they granted extensive rights to new towns whose representatives sat with nobles and bishops in the Cortes or parliament. The Cortes of Leon, established in 1188, antedates by a century the English Parliament. The growing strength of the nobility is epitomized in the oath sworn by the Aragonese lords to the king on his coronation; they promised obedience but only if he respected their liberties.

Throughout northern Europe, more humble men accomplished an equally significant expansion, both internally and externally. The introduction of the three field rotation, coupled with the heavy plough, an improved scythe and the water mill, enabled an increasing population to open up vast areas of forest and wasteland for settlement. In times of expansion the worker prospers; the peasant would only come to the new villages in return for enhanced rights. If they were not on offer he could always go further East where German marcher lords were keen to settle the lands they conquered from the Slavs.

Between 1100 and 1300 the German frontier moved from the Elbe to the Oder and beyond. Even further East the emerging kingdoms of Poland and Hungary sought to develop their land and their revenue base by enticing German settlers with land and special privileges, both to rural areas and to new cities; Ottakar (1253–1278), the last great native king of Bohemia, established more than sixty German towns in his kingdom. Thus was initiated the German diaspora which lived peacefully from Bohemia to the

Volga until Hitler sought to use it for his aggression and Stalin in turn destroyed it.

The Growth of the Cities

In Italy the early development of the cities of the south, based largely on their trade with Byzantium, was challenged by their compatriots further north. Genoa and Pisa began to take advantage of a more prosperous hinterland and soon surpassed the cities of the south. In 1050 and 1071 respectively, in a rare show of co-operation rather than rivalry, they ejected the Moslems from Sardinia and Corsica. At the head of the Adriatic, refugees fleeing the violence of the mainland – tradition has it from Attila the Hun – had built Venice on the islands and mudflats of the lagoons. Venice had tenaciously maintained its theoretical allegiance to distant Byzantium and consequent independence of the Western Empire. In the eleventh century, virtually independent, it destroyed the pirates' nests of the Dalmatian coast and began to profit from the increasing prosperity of its hinterland and its connection with Byzantium. Already it was using sophisticated financial instruments to finance its merchant voyages.

If the Spanish towns claimed a role in the government of the kingdom, the cities of Northern Italy were intent on de facto independence. By the tenth century they had wrested virtual self-government from the bishops who, rather than secular counts, had previously controlled them, and set out on a successful campaign to absorb the countryside around them. Noble lords found themselves, willy-nilly, leading members of city communes and began to appreciate the advantages of trade. When the Emperor Frederick Barbarossa endeavoured to re-assert imperial control, the cities formed the Lombard League, inflicted a humiliating defeat on him at Legnano (1176) and forced him to agree that their allegiance to the Empire was purely nominal.

North of the Alps cities were less advanced. Some were new and others had to be virtually rebuilt – although the Roman town plan survived in a surprising number, suggesting that habitation had never entirely ceased. By Charlemagne's time, if not earlier, a new economic concentration was developing around the Rhine and the Meuse; well used trade routes linked this area, the English Channel and the Baltic. Canute, king of Denmark and Norway was accepted as king of England in 1016. His attempt to erect an empire around the North Sea failed with his death but the trade area survived and prospered. It would become the second pole of European development, rivaling and eventually surpassing Italy and the Mediterranean. As German settlement expanded in the East, the trading cities of north Germany formed the Hanseatic League to assert their trading rights and dominate the Baltic. All over Europe towns developed mechanisms of self government and looked for immunity from feudal controls. Except in Italy and Germany, however, where the central state was progressively eroded, they found the freedom of action they sought as self governing units in the emerging national states.

The Beginning of the National State

The model of the national state was initiated by William the Conqueror in England after 1066. England was small enough, and William's adaptation of the feudal system strong enough, for the country to be effectively controlled as a unit. Royal power was strengthened by the daemonic determination of Henry II (1154–1189) even though he spent more time on the continent than in England; his marriage to Eleanor of Aquitaine had made him feudal lord of most of France and an overmighty subject from the point of view of the French king. Phillip Augustus of France learnt from the English model; after 1202 he too required that all oaths of homage should reserve prior loyalty to the king.

It was Phillip who took the decisive step for the creation of both the French and the English nation states when he expelled King John, Henry II's son, from Normandy, Anjou and Touraine in 1202–1206. By annexing these vast regions to the royal domain, he made the king incomparably the strongest lord in France. Although the English king remained lord of the southern part of Aquitaine, the Duchy of Guyenne, this much smaller territory was clearly subordinate to his English interests. Disgruntled by the loss of their French lands, and fearful of John's arbitrary power in England, the barons united to force him to issue the Great Charter (Magna Carta) in 1215. The rights guaranteed in the Charter were largely for the barons but in the seventeenth century Parliament, careless of constitutional niceties, choose to regard them as the common rights of Englishmen – or at least those of landed and financial substance – and the banner of revolt.

Germany at first seemed to be following a path similar to France and England, especially when the Emperor was able to exert personal power over two of the great duchies. To strengthen his power the Emperor relied first on the bishops whom he appointed and whose lands provided the bulk of his armed force. While the use of bishoprics for this purpose had a long history, it was offensive to a new generation of church reformers who felt that it detracted from a bishop's first responsibility, the religious welfare of his diocese.

The Rise of the Papacy

The most influential source of reform thinking was the great abbey of Cluny, founded in the tenth century and soon the centre of a network of hundreds of daughter abbeys. Paradoxically, the ascendancy of the reform movement in Rome began with German popes appointed by the Emperor Henry III to rescue the papacy from the control of the Roman nobility. The reform movement worked with the Emperor and relied on his support but this changed in 1073 when Hildebrand became pope as Gregory VII. The new pope espoused and extended the most radical ideas of the reformers, denying the right of the monarch to appoint bishops and proclaiming the supremacy of the pope over kings and emperors.

Inevitably, these policies were resisted by the Emperor who relied on his bishops to exercise royal power in Germany. The conflict degenerated from argument to warfare – Gregory relying uneasily on Robert Guiscard and the Normans, who burnt part of Rome in their effort to enforce his authority there, and on his claims to depose Henry IV and mobilize the turbulent German nobility in support of a rival Emperor. The conflict was eventually settled in the concordat of Worms in 1122; the Emperor renounced his claim to invest a bishop with ring and crozier, the symbols of spiritual authority, and the Pope recognized his right to bestow the symbols of temporal authority. The emperor also acknowledged that canonical elections should be free; in fact few cathedral chapters would resist his will.

The papacy seemed to have won little out of the conflict. It was not the extreme claims of Gregory VII which were the basis of the steady extension of papal control over the Western Church in the twelfth century. That was the result of the administrative re-organisation of Urban II (1088–1099) – by no means the beginning of the papal bureaucracy which is very much the oldest in the world, as those who deal with the Vatican forget at their peril. The steady extension of papal jurisdiction was also inspired partly by the compilation of the decrees of earlier popes and councils. By 1140 Gratian had produced his great compilation, the Decretum, which became the basis for the systematic development of canon law. Innocent III (1198-1216), a great canon lawyer, carefully extended and defined papal claims to jurisdiction case by case; if he had in the back of his mind an overall theory of papal supremacy over earthly rulers, he was too cautious to do more than hint at it. Some of his successors were to be less cautious and that brought them into conflict with kings more secure in their power than the German Emperor.

For the Empire the conflict was disastrous. When Henry III rescued the papacy from the Roman nobility he was undoubtedly the greatest king in Europe, the master of an effective if somewhat fragile state, in which feudal institutions and feudal power were merely incipient. The conflict with the papacy gave rein to the fissiparous elements in Germany and fatally weakened imperial power. Frederick Barbarossa's heroic attempt to reconstruct imperial power by borrowing the feudal forms of France and England failed in its turn, broken by the alliance of a fearful papacy with the Lombard towns. His remarkable grandson, Frederick II, was not for nothing known as Stupor Mundi, the Wonder of the World. But he was first and foremost King of Sicily, inherited from his mother. He abandoned the attempt to govern a Germany again made fractious by papal intervention. Thereafter Germany was not to be an effective state until Bismarck put it together in 1870. Until then it would be little more than a loose collection of autonomous princes, each pursuing his own interest.

The Crusades

It is an indication of the growing power of the papacy, and the rude vigour of the new Europe, that in 1095, in the very middle of his struggle with the Emperor, Urban II was able to launch the First Crusade. Urban's action was in response to the request of the Byzantine Emperor, Alexius I Comnenus, for assistance after the disastrous defeat of Manzikert. Alexius had hoped for mercenaries and was less than pleased when he found himself giving transit to four tumultuous armies, led by distinguished lords intent on carving out principalities for themselves in the East; one of them was Bohemond, son of Robert Guiscard, last seen by the Byzantines besieging Durazzo in an attempt to extend Norman dominions at the expense of the Eastern Empire.

The Kingdom of Jerusalem and the subordinate principalities established by the Crusaders along the coast from Antioch to Gaza, and inland to Edessa and the Euphrates, could only survive while the Moslems remained weak and divided. Jerusalem fell in 1187 and Acre, the last bastion, in 1291. Although Islam retains unhappy memories of Christian aggression, the major impact of the Crusading ethos was on the West itself. Islam was defined as the enemy and the religion which had converted the Germans and the Slavs could only – with rare exceptions such as St.Francis – think of Islam in terms of war and subjugation.

The concept of the holy war was soon extended far beyond the conflict with Islam. In 1204 Venice diverted the Fourth Crusade to the conquest of Constantinople; the ephemeral Latin Empire thus created was cordially hated by the Greeks and its memory survives to this day. German crusading orders found themselves a doubtful mission in the Baltic where they Christianised and colonized the Prussians and the Latvians, creating for themselves a prosperous, powerful state. In 1209 Pope Innocent III proclaimed a crusade against the Albigensian heretics in the south of France and the Count of Toulouse who protected them. Soon the mechanism was being used against any prince who offended the Pope, undermining both the Crusading idea and the moral status of the papacy.

The Medieval Synthesis

Before the destructive effects of this undermining became apparent, however, Christendom achieved a remarkable intellectual synthesis. Thanks largely to translations from Arabic made mainly in Spain, the Western Church found itself confronted with the philosophical system of Aristotle. The logic of this system was persuasive – perhaps more than it should have been, a modern philosopher might say –

but much of it seemed to be inconsistent with Christian belief as then understood. A long generation of scholars and teachers wrestled with these apparent problems and in the end produced a system of thought which harmonized the new wisdom and the traditional religion with unsurpassed rigour and total logic. Their venturesome work occasionally worried the more conservative of the church authorities; Edward Tempier, Archbishop of Paris, has achieved a dubious immortality as the man who condemned some propositions of Thomas Aquinas, the greatest of medieval theologians. These, however, were isolated incidents; the medieval church on the whole accepted the pioneering work of its theologians and was rewarded with a compelling synthesis of faith and reason.

This highly intellectual synthesis had little impact on the ordinary faithful. Dualist heresies derived from the East spread and so did a more homespun piety which challenged the clerical monopoly of preaching and condemned the wealth and the sins of clergy. Repression, typified by the Albigensian crusade, could keep these movements in check but had little effect on hearts and minds. A more effective answer was found in the new orders of preaching friars.

Francis of Assisi, son of a wealthy merchant of that city and happy leader of its gilded youth, became convinced that God was calling him to rebuild his Church. After a false start in which he understood Church to mean a local building fallen into decay, he realized that his vocation was to bring the institution of the Church back to the ideals of the Gospel. The combination of this basic message and Francis' charismatic personality attracted followers by the thousand. No doubt to the dismay of some in the curia, Francis received papal approval. The new order lived in poverty and preached to the people. Soon, along with the Dominicans, they became a dominant influence in the new universities. The Dominicans were founded by the Spanish priest, Dominic Guzman, to preach against heresy but they shared the Franciscan ideal of poverty.

The concept of the university as an independent community of scholars was one of the greatest achievements of the middle ages, full of significance for the future of European civilisation. Not only philosophy and theology but also law became objects of academic study. This latter furnished the Church with canon lawyers and reinforced the inherited tendency in the West to conceive of religion in legal terms. To the kings and princes the universities contributed a renewed knowledge of Roman law which, with its basic assumption that the will of the ruler was the supreme law, they found both congenial and useful.

Even Louis IX, the saintly king of France, who earnestly strove to rule his kingdom with justice and recognized the rights of his feudal lords, found such men useful. His grandson Philip the Fair inherited Louis' staff of Roman lawyers. Both kings regarded themselves as responsible to God for the church as well as for everything else in their kingdom; Louis IX said as much to the pope himself at the Council of Lyons in 1247. Consequently, when Philip found himself confronted in Boniface VIII with a pope who claimed supreme power in intemperate terms, he did not hesitate. He sent William Nogaret with a force of mercenaries to seize the Pope and bring him to France for trial. Nogaret seized Boniface at his residence in Anagni, outside Rome. The citizens came to the Pope's rescue but Boniface died a month later. In 1305 the cardinals elected a Frenchman who was persuaded to take up residence in Avignon, just outside the French border. His successors remained there for more than half a century. Not all of them wished to be creatures of the king of France but inevitably they were regarded as such by other states unfriendly to what was now, clearly, the greatest state in Europe. This provided yet another reason for other kings to imitate Philip and assert with renewed vigour their control over the church in their states.

Christendom, A Plural Society

In fact Christendom by 1300 was already a plural society; equilibrium could only be maintained by a precarious balance, not only between church and state, but also between kings, nobles and cities (and within cities between classes), lawyers and universities, bishops, monks and friars. Aquinas, Dominican friar and saint, did not hesitate to enunciate the autonomy of the state as well as of the church in their own spheres: 'in those things that pertain to civil good, the secular power is to be obeyed rather than the spiritual' . Even with the ambiguous reference to papal power which follows, this cannot have made welcome reading in the Rome of Innocent IV, canon lawyer and inveterate opponent of Frederick II; but it was not contested.

This thrusting society, expanding in the Baltic and the Mediterranean, and developing new technologies like the windmill and the ocean going cogs of the northern traders, was ready to take advantage of the opportunities opened up by the Mongol conquest of Asia. It seems to have hardly noticed the Mongol incursions of 1241-42, the brunt of which fell on Poland and Hungary, demonstrating the instinctive wisdom of Christendom in building buffer states rather than, like Trajan in Dacia, wantonly destroying them. The Mongols withdrew on the death of the Great Khan and contented themselves with holding Russia in tribute. What Europe noticed was the opportunity opened up by the Pax Mongolica. Italian and other merchants rapidly realized the potential of trade across this vast area; Marco Polo was simply the most articulate of them. Popes and even Louis IX sent missionaries in a vain – but by no means irrational – effort to convert the new power. Ironically, it was along this route which was opening up to Europe a new vision of the world, that the scourge of bubonic plague, the Black Death, arrived in 1347.

The Challenge to Authority

The disintegration of the High Medieval synthesis was, in fact, inherent in the society it supported. Typically, Aquinas, who had formulated that synthesis with incomparable logic, had said that the argument from authority was the weakest of all arguments. Many who had never read his works, or perhaps even knew his name, acted by instinct on this proposition.

Kings challenged the authority of the Church and found churchmen willing to support them; in some countries loyalty and a sense of identity began to be focused on the nation rather than Christendom and the local lord. Nobles and towns challenged their kings and developed the doctrine, already implicit in the feudal state, that taxation depended on consent. Cities, in turn, found that the supremacy of a well born and wealthy patriciate was no longer taken for granted by exploited and tumultuous artisans. Pushed far enough by the devastations of warfare and the exactions of landowners, even peasants might revolt; 'when Adam delved and Eve span', they demanded, 'who was then the gentleman?' Such sudden and unorganised revolts were inevitably suppressed with worse atrocities than they had committed; they remained a sign that the old order could no longer be taken for granted.

The Black Death

The old order was undermined also by the Black Death. Bubonic plague was brought to Europe by a Mongol army besieging Caffa, in the Crimea, in 1346. Carried by fleas which infested black rats and then infected humans, it was soon transmitted to the Mediterranean ports; by 1350 it had spread all over Europe. European populations had no resistance to the new disease and no knowledge of how it was transmitted. In England, estimates suggest that it reduced the population by 20% to 45%; the overall impact in much of Europe was probably of the same order. For those who contracted the disease, it was commonly fatal; before antibiotics became available even modern hospital care could not reduce the mortality rate below 60%. Recurrent outbreaks persisted for over a hundred years before the population, having acquired some degree of immunity, returned to its pre-1346 level. Even after that, occasional outbreaks were to be expected. Only gradually did European authorities learn to contain their spread by effective quarantine, pioneered by Ragusa and Venice in the fourteenth century. The last great outbreak in northern Europe was in London in 1665; in the western Mediterranean around Marseilles in 1720–21.

It is difficult to imagine the profound social impact of such an experience. People were used to sudden and unexpected death but not on this scale. Many probably saw it as God's punishment of a wicked world; others looked for more immediate explanations – attacks on Jews, accused of poisoning wells, were particularly frequent in Germany and stimulated a migration to Poland and the growth of the Jewish population in Eastern Europe. Social tensions were exacerbated and the economic effects of such a decline in the work force, though differing from place to place, were large and disruptive.

The scarcity of labour increased the tendency already apparent for landlords to abandon demesne farming – keeping part of their land in their own hands, to be worked by the labour services due from serfs, or increasingly by hired labour – and rent out all their land. Serfdom disappeared in Western Europe, replaced by tenant farming and wage labour. In the East, and much of Germany, the landowners' reaction was different; they succeeded in increasing the burdens of serfdom and attaching them to most of the rural population.

City life seems to have been affected less by contraction than by changes in the balance of advantage. As the English developed a cloth making industry, for example, Flemish cities were hard hit by their competition as well as by that of workers in their own countryside. As patterns of trade changed, some cities declined while others grew – Antwerp replaced Bruges as the latter's access to the sea silted up. The loose league of north German cities, the Hanseatic League, dominated Baltic trade after 1370 and extended its tentacles from London to Novgorod. Barcelona, working closely with the crown of Aragon, achieved dominance in trade with Sicily and North Africa.

The changing world of the fourteenth century shattered the stability of the thirteenth century world view. Some people, like the characters in the Decameron, took refuge from the horrors of the Black Death in hedonism. Others turned to a more personal religion. Men like Gert Groot (1340–1382), who founded the Brethren of the Common Life in the Netherlands, were not heretics but they were building their Christian lives on personal devotion more than on the worship of the Church.

Rising Nation States and Declining Empire

It is a mark of the robustness of medieval society that it was able to survive this onslaught of disease without total disintegration. The core of incipient nation states continued their development unchecked. England, France, Portugal, the Scandinavian kingdoms, as well as Hungary and Poland, were established as powerful states in each of which a central government claimed and increasingly exercised a degree of control, carefully balanced with more local powers but very different from the feudal matrix of earlier centuries. The Spanish state we know had not yet come into existence, its future territory being divided between three Christian kingdoms – Castile, Aragon and Navarre – and the Islamic remnant of Granada. Despite their differences, the Christian states of the peninsula shared a common heritage and the eventual unification of Castile and Aragon has an air of inevitability which is deceptive. Portugal fought hard and successfully to preserve its separate identity; despite a good deal of turmoil from time to time all the Spanish kingdoms were well established, functioning states which might well have developed into three distinct nations.

Far different was the situation in Germany and Italy. The long struggle between Pope and Emperor had destroyed the effective power of the latter, not least because it had resulted in the Empire becoming definitively elective and the Electors took care not to elect anyone who could challenge their power. In 1356 the Golden Bull settled the composition of the electoral college at seven – three archbishops, the King of Bohemia and three secular princes – and made them virtually independent. They exercised control of their own legal systems without appeal and had the right to issue coinage. The seven preserved their electoral monopoly, with its lucrative potential for bribes, for centuries but the other privileges were soon extended to other princes while the rising towns took every opportunity to increase their independence of both Emperor and princes. In effect, Germany had ceased to exist as a state and the Imperial title was little more than an honour and, occasionally, an opportunity to increase the holdings of the Emperor's family; Rudolf of Hapsburg, elected Emperor in 1273 as a minor lord in Alsace and Switzerland, started the family's rise to European power by securing Austria and Styria for his sons.

Rudolf's success seemed a threat to a group of peasant cantons around Lake Lucerne. In 1291 they came together in an 'Eternal Union' to defend their rights against his rising power; they were soon joined by other cantons and adjacent cities. The Swiss infantry defeated the Hapsburgs twice in the fourteenth century; in between times they supplemented their meagre resources by service as mercenaries, notching up an impressive string of victories. By 1500 the Swiss Confederation was recognized as virtually independent.

Imperial power was even more nominal in Italy. The north was divided between rival city states independent in all but name. Social strife within and frequent war with neighbouring states eventually resulted in three 'great powers' – Venice, Milan and Florence – absorbing many of the smaller states and menacing the rest. From 1278 the Papal States were formally recognized as outside the Empire; for a long time most of its territory was divided between independent cities and rising despots. Naples and Sicily were independent kingdoms, the first ruled by the Angevin offshoot of the French monarchy, the second by the expanding house of Aragon.

With the Empire reduced to a nonentity, the pre-eminence of France in the early fourteenth century was unmistakable, if not always unchallenged. The transfer of the papal seat to Avignon – where it had been established since 1305 – however offensive to Italians, seemed natural to the French. Gregory XI returned to Rome in 1377, persuaded by the urging of Catherine of Siena. When he died in 1378, the Cardinals split and Christendom found itself with two rival popes, one in Rome and one in Avignon. The schism was not healed until the Emperor Sigismund assembled a Council at Constance in 1414. In 1417, having disposed of the existing claimants, the Council elected Odo Colonna and ruled that Councils should be called at regular intervals.

Martin V, a member of one of the great Roman families, had no intention of ceding papal power to a succession of Councils. By negotiating concordats with individual states he succeeded in emasculating the conciliar movement. The price was high. Not only were kings put in effective control of the Church in their domains but the papacy forfeited its historic role of leading the reform which more thoughtful elements in the Church saw as overdue. Succeeding popes, pre-occupied with strengthening their position as secular rulers in the Papal States and in Italy, treated the Church elsewhere as little more than a source of revenue. As the kings of the time strengthened their control over their states, they also came to exercise effective control over the Church.

Rising Sense of Nationhood

Voting at Constance had been by nations, an indication of a new national spirit becoming increasingly dominant in the thinking of, at least, the articulate and powerful in European society. When dynastic inheritance fell foul of national identity, the latter increasingly prevailed. The Scots rejected the claims of the English king, Edward I, and made good their independence at Bannockburn (1314). The Portuguese, finding that the legitimate heiress was married to the King of Castile, turned to her uncle, deterred neither by his illegitimacy nor by his vows as head of the military Order of Avis. A switch of allegiance from Avignon to Rome secured a speedy release from his vows and English archers helped him to defeat the Castilian army at Aljubarrota in 1385. Scandinavia appeared ready to transcend nationalism when the Union of Kalmar, formalised in 1397, brought Denmark, Norway and Sweden together under the king of Denmark. But the Swedes never really accepted the Union; by 1448 they had elected their own, Swedish, king.

National identity co-existed uneasily with feudal loyalty and dynastic ambition. Edward III and Henry V of England did not hesitate to use dynastic pretensions to claim the throne of France. The intermittent 'Hundred Years War' which ensued became progressively more national in orientation. In the end, after the charismatic intervention of Joan of Arc and the development of an effective artillery, the French were able to drive the English out. The long conflict demonstrated and strengthened the power of national feeling and its potential as a focus of loyalty both to defend a realm and to support aggression.

Yet dynasticism was not dead. Kings and princes still dreamed and schemed to build up the power and prestige of their houses and sought, when necessary, to use national feeling in one domain as an instrument while restraining it in another.

Typically, the recovery of France was impeded by the ambitions of the Valois Dukes of Burgundy, an offshoot of the royal house who put together, largely by marriages, the considerable territory of French and Imperial Burgundy, most of the Netherlands and Luxembourg. Burgundy itself was a large and wealthy area, already building up a trade in the wine which has made it famous; the Netherlands, with their cloth manufactures and their trade, were the hub of commerce in northern Europe. Contemporaries were fascinated by the power and wealth of the 'Great Dukes of the West'; their alliance made possible the near triumph of the English in France and their return to French allegiance made eventual English defeat certain. For a short period it seemed that they might succeed in recreating the ninth century Middle Kingdom of Lothair, between France and Germany. While they never created a set of common institutions for their disparate collection of territories, they did succeed in doubling their revenue from them and becoming a force in Europe. Burgundy was destroyed, not by lack of national unity, but by the reckless aggression of the last duke, aptly known as Charles the Rash. Outmanoeuvred by the devious 'spider king', Louis XI of France, and defeated by the Swiss, Charles was killed in 1477 at the Battle of Nancy. He left as heiress the nineteen year old Mary whose marriage to Maximilian of Austria gave the Hapsburgs a new addition to their rising power.

The Nobility and the Middle Class

Whatever their dynastic ambitions, monarchs had to reckon with other foci of wealth and power. In England, France and the Iberian kingdoms it was clear that the time when feudatories could seek to establish quasi-independent territories had passed. The ambitions of the nobility therefore turned to the control of the kingdom and to securing for themselves the maximum share in its resources. Kings had to reckon with their power; those who failed to do so successfully might, like Edward II and Richard II in England, and Pedro the Cruel in Castile, pay for it with their lives, especially if a rival member of the dynasty seized the chance to supplant them.

Increasingly, kings found that they also had to accommodate their policies to the rising power of the emerging middle class. Government needed money, especially when it became involved in war, and money could only come from the merchants and entrepreneurs who dominated the towns and the landlords whose estates generated a marketable surplus.

No medieval king was strong enough even to think of imposing taxes on these people by his own fiat; he had to extort their consent and this meant summoning their representatives to meet and agree. Parliament in England, Cortes in Castile and Estates General in France all found that money could be bargained for privileges and promises, not always honoured, to redress grievances. Their members, however, not being possessed of the force necessary to confront king and nobles, had to tread warily. In France, the Estates General, in the patriotic spirit of the concluding years of the war with England, was induced in 1439 to vote the taille (head and property tax) which the Crown interpreted to be perpetual; thereafter the Estates seldom met. The Castilian Cortes was emasculated by the victory of the nobles over Pedro the Cruel in 1369; the towns were nevertheless capable of playing an assertive role in the confused power struggles of the country until they mounted an unsuccessful revolt against Charles V a century and a half later. In both France and Spain the nobility, as well as the clergy, were exempt from royal taxes. In effect, monarchy and nobility had made an alliance at the expense of the towns and the merchants. In England the nobility almost exterminated itself in the bloody conflict of the Wars of the Roses (1455–1485), a struggle for power between two rival branches of the monarchy. The Welsh gentleman who eventually emerged as Henry VII had no intention of sharing real power with anyone but he was careful to work in harmony with Parliament and especially with the town elite and landed gentry represented in the House of Commons.

Progress in Technology

The wealth of most towns was based largely on trade and traditional artisan production. Increasingly, however, improvements in technology played a part. Before the end of the thirteenth century, two innovations of enormous significance had appeared – spectacles and the weight driven clock. The progress of the clock across Europe was rapid – before long no self-respecting town could be without one. The town clock initiated a new attitude to time – it could now be measured and therefore valued – which rapidly became a distinguishing part of the European mind-set. Moreover, while the initial production of clocks was made possible by existing skills, its spread required an increase in the numbers of precision metal workers. This strengthened the base of European technology; many clockmakers played a key role in later mechanical innovations. Spring driven clocks appeared in the fourteenth century and this made possible the production of watches, calling for even more precise work.

The influence of spectacles was more subtle. They enabled an educated man to keep reading all his life, whereas previously many had worn out their eyes by the age of, say, forty. The demand for them was such that by the early fourteenth century Venice was producing them in a mode which can be called factory production. Perhaps the use of spectacles contributed to the increase in the demand for books, especially for use by laymen. Vernacular literatures grew apace in the fourteenth century, with the work of such writers as Chaucer in England and Dante in Italy. Merchants needed reading and writing ability for more practical reasons; Florence, with a population not much over a hundred thousand, was said to have ten thousand children in school. Literacy was no longer a monopoly of the clergy and the increased demand for books gave rise to a regular trade of copying and book production long before the invention of printing. Books were made cheaper by the use of paper, introduced from the Islamic world which in turn had borrowed it from China; significantly, Europe improved its production by the use of water power.

The widespread use of water power naturally stimulated an interest in hydraulic engineering. Canals and locks were widespread in the fourteenth century, helped by such devices as the drainage mill, a windmill that operated a drainage scoop.

The immediate effect of these, and other, innovations was to increase productivity and, for substantial numbers of people, the standard of living. By 1500 not only was technology in Europe more advanced than in antiquity and at least equal to anything else in the world but European technological advance was cumulative and accelerating.

Less obvious, but in the long run more profound in its consequences was the impact of all this on the European mind. For centuries European culture had manifested dynamic as well as conservative elements; by the fifteenth century large parts of it had acquired a problem-solving orientation. It no longer accepted that the boundaries to achievement were immutable; they constituted problems to be addressed and overcome.

The Impact of Printing

This cumulative effect yielded a remarkable dividend in 1453 when Johan Gutenberg launched the art of printing with moveable type. His invention required fine metallurgy to cast the type and the solution which Gutenberg found drew on inherited knowledge – his father had been goldsmith to the Archbishop of Mainz. The Chinese had invented moveable type in 1045 but the innovation never came into widespread use, probably because it was not adapted to a script with thousands of characters. By contrast, Gutenberg's invention had an impact which can be compared with the computer revolution of our generation – it was a quantum leap in the speed and accessibility of information and ideas. The significance of Gutenberg's invention was immediately appreciated – by 1480 nearly four hundred printing presses were releasing an unparalleled flood of books on Europe, by 1500 they had produced more books than the region had seen in the previous thousand years. And these books, while still expensive, were cheap by comparison with hand transcribed copies – certainly beyond the reach of peasant or labourer (who, in any case, could not read) but well within the reach of gentry and merchants. A much enlarged reading public was created within a generation – sixty editions of Erasmus' 'Colloquies' were published in eight years. Printing also made it possible to carry argument and propaganda beyond royal courts and universities to a wider public – in 1520 four thousand copies of Luther's appeal 'To the Christian Nobility of the German Nation' were sold in three weeks. Such widespread and rapid circulation of ideas would have been inconceivable before printing.

The first books to be printed were works of religion – Gutenberg himself accomplished the massive task of printing the Bible in 1456 – and the romances which were the favourite reading of the literate and leisured. Before long the publishers found a new market in the Greek and Latin classics and works based on them. Interest in the classics had been growing steadily since the fourteenth century, stimulated partly by greater contact with Byzantium – Manuel Chrysoloras, a celebrated Byzantine scholar, was persuaded to accept the first professorship of Greek in Western Europe at the University of Florence in 1397. A new, largely lay, intelligentsia came into existence which took its inspiration from the classics rather than the philosophy and theology of the universities.

The new movement was not anti-religious but it tended to look directly to the Bible and to the personal religion typical of the

Brethren of the Common Life, rather than to systematic theology and the doctrinal authority of the church. Indeed the humanists, as they are generally called, tended to despise the medieval theologians because their Latin, a living language used to grapple with profound intellectual problems, was inelegant by classical standards. Many of the humanists' own works strike us as sterile imitations of their classical mentors but in their own day they had great appeal.

Such men found ready employment in the courts of monarchs where their writing skills and flexibility in argument were very useful. One of them, Lorenzo Valla, used the developing science of textual criticism to demonstrate that the Donation of Constantine, on which much of the papal claim to temporal authority had been built for centuries, was a forgery. Being steeped in the works of pre-Christian authors, the humanists began to develop purely secular notions of the power and role of the state. While the humanists might write of the glories of the Roman republic, few of them hesitated to support the power of a king or even a city tyrant. Preoccupied with service to rulers, with the beauties of classical Latin and with the advancement of their own reputation, the humanists achieved intellectual domination of Europe. There was, however, no synthesis comparable to the thirteenth century masterpiece of Thomas Aquinas. For better or worse, Europe was set on a path of intellectual development in which various branches of study would increasingly assert their autonomy and go their own way.

Overseas Exploration

The humanists' adventures of the mind were more than matched by the real adventures of the sea-farers. Well before the end of the thirteenth century, Genoa had pioneered the sea route to England and Flanders; Venice soon followed. Mediterranean and Baltic ship-building were thus brought into stimulating contact. The result was the carrack, a three-masted vessel combining the advantages of square and lateen rigging and furnished with a sternpost rudder. First developed in the Basque region on the Bay of Biscay about 1400, its use spread rapidly both in the north and in the Mediterranean, improving sailing times and reliability and reducing the costs of transport. (The lateen rigged caravel remained important for smaller cargoes and was largely used in the voyages of exploration.) Navigation was improved by the introduction of the compass and the astrolabe, or its simpler and easier version, the quadrant.

With these advantages, European seafarers began to penetrate the Atlantic. Before the end of the thirteenth century Genoese merchants were active on the Atlantic coast of Morocco and even penetrated to Sjilimassa in the centre of the Sahara. Early in the next century they began the conquest of the Canary Islands, an effort in which they soon gave place to the Portuguese, the Norman French and eventually the Castilians. It was the Portuguese, however, who persisted in further exploration down the coast of Africa. Much of the inspiration came from the remarkable royal prince, Henry, whom a nineteenth century scholar named the Navigator. Henry presided over the discovery and settlement of Madeira and the Azores and the initially difficult and unrewarding exploration of the African coast. When he died in 1460 the rewards of exploration had become obvious and it was pursued under the control and purposeful direction of the Crown; John II established a commission of mathematical experts to resolve the problem of finding latitude by solar observation. In 1488 Diaz rounded the Cape of Good Hope and entered the Indian Ocean. It was another ten years, perhaps partly occupied with more exploratory voyages which have left no trace, before Vasco da Gama led the first Portuguese fleet to India and opened the way which would eventually lead to the European domination of Asia.

It had taken the Portuguese almost a century of persistent effort to reach their goal. Castile was set on a quicker path to empire when it was persuaded to sponsor a Genoese adventurer. By 1492 most educated Europeans believed the world was round and Colombus was by no means alone in thinking that it was possible to reach Asia by sailing west around the globe; but he had a single minded, almost paranoid, determination to do it. After a voyage of thirty-three days he sighted an island in the Bahamas, which he promptly and wrongly identified as an outer island of Japan. Only gradually did it become clear that the globe was much larger than Columbus had thought, that a whole continent separated Europe from Asia and that Spain had acquired, not an alternative route to Asia, but a vast New World empire.

CHAPTER FIVE

THE RIVALS OF CHRISTENDOM
Byzantium, the Slavs and Islam

The Roman Empire, destroyed in the West, survived for centuries in the East around the nucleus of Constantinople. Before its last remnants were destroyed by the Turks in 1453, it had put its mark on the people of the Balkans, the Caucasus and Russia. Under its influence, and later that of the Turks and Mongols, they developed a style of civilisation which differed in important respects from that of Western Europe. Since the seventeenth century, Western historians have termed this Empire 'Byzantine'. Even though the term was never used at the time, it is now too well established to be ignored.

Byzantium represented an alternative style of post-classical civilisation, closer perhaps to its Greek and Roman origins than Western Christendom was. In the seventh century Muhammed created the new and militant religion which rapidly became dominant in the Middle East and North Africa. Islam eventually reduced the Eastern Empire to a vestige of its former self and finally completed its conquest in 1453.

In the sixth century Justinian's attempt to reconquer the West overstrained the Empire's resources and left it exposed in a dangerous environment. Beyond the Danube the Avars, Mongolian nomads pushed West by the Turks, had taken the place of the Huns. For the next thousand years the southern plains of the modern Ukraine were to be dominated by succeeding combinations of Turkish or Mongol tribes; until the Magyars formed a stable kingdom there at the end of the tenth century, their range would extend across the Carpathians into the Hungarian plain. The instability of these combinations, often stimulated by pressure from new tribes moving West, was a potential threat to the Empire. From its outpost in the Crimea, Byzantium used its diplomatic skills to set one tribe against another – a risky game which sometimes had unexpected results.

In the sixth century the Avars dominated the Slav tribes between the Volga and the Elbe and occasionally raided the Empire. Urged on by the Avars, an amorphous wave of Slavs infiltrated the frontiers and gradually occupied virtually the whole of the Balkans. The Slavs lacked anything like the national or tribal structures of the Germans but they came to settle in substantial numbers. The language of Thrace disappeared; that of Illyricum survived only in the isolated mountains of Albania. Even Greece almost succumbed; only centuries later did it again become entirely Greek speaking.

Persians and Moslems

In the seventh century, the Empire's ability to react to this influx was constrained by two successive life and death struggles. In 607 the sporadic border warfare with the Persians became a more serious struggle; the Persians occupied Syria and Egypt. By 626 their army was besieging Constantinople in alliance with the Avars. The siege failed thanks to Byzantine control of the sea and the Emperor Heraclius occupied the Persian capital, Ctesiphon in Iraq. The Persian nobles murdered the Shah and agreed to withdraw from their conquests. Heraclius returned to Constantinople in triumph but both empires were exhausted by twenty years of warfare. Six years later, the hitherto inconsequential Arab tribes, newly converted to Islam, achieved their first victory over a Byzantine army. Within a decade they occupied Syria and Egypt and destroyed the Persian Empire.

The Byzantine Empire was obviously threatened with the same fate. Constantinople resisted a great siege by the combined forces of the Arabs and the Avars in 670–674, thanks to its defensive position and the timely invention of 'Greek Fire', a secret mixture which was discharged from tubes and ignited on impact. The secret was so well kept that the composition is unknown but Greek Fire enabled the Byzantines to destroy the new Arab fleet and retain control of the Aegean – a rare example, before modern times, of a decisive military technology in the hands of a civilized power.

The loss of Syria and Egypt deprived the Empire of the greater part of its tax base and the source of Constantinople's grain supply. Neither mercenary armies nor an idle aristocracy could be supported from the limited resources remaining. Byzantium responded to the crisis by creating a peasant army in Anatolia and remunerating the soldiers with land grants. The Empire was well aware that its future depended on these soldiers and the law was modified to protect their rights. At the same time, administrative changes begun by Heraclius were continued – supreme power in each province (theme) was vested in the military commander (strategos). Under the strategos, however, civil administration continued and Constantinople remained firmly in control – the Empire was not feudalized.

The Empire Becomes Greek

The loss of Syria and Egypt had one compensating advantage – the Empire was now overwhelmingly Greek in language and Orthodox in religion. This gave it a cohesion and a sense of identity to underpin the continuing resistance to Islam. Paradoxically, its subjects, equally conscious of their Greek speech and their imperial heritage, continued to refer to themselves as Romans and displayed bitter resentment later when Westerners referred to the Emperor of the Greeks.

In the Balkans a new challenge emerged when the Bulgars, probably descendents of the Huns, crossed the Danube and established their hegemony over the Slav tribes in the area of modern Bulgaria. A succession of warlike Khans posed a continuing threat to Constantinople but could never overcome its defences. What they could and did do was to mould a state and a people in uncomfortable proximity to the imperial capital. Linguistically, the Bulgars were absorbed by the Slavs but this did not prevent them from establishing a powerful empire which by the ninth century stretched from Thessaly to Moldavia and into Hungary.

The Conversion of the Slavs

Only in the ninth century did Byzantium find an effective response to the incursions of the Slavs by converting them to Christianity. The missionary brothers Cyril and Methodius began the work of translating the Bible into Slavonic. Pushed out of Bohemia by the pressure of the neighbouring German church, the Byzantine missionaries converted the Bulgarian Khan Boris about 865 and the Serbs soon afterwards. Further north, the Croats were converted by Western missionaries, so establishing a division which has persisted to the twentieth century, with the tragic consequences to be seen since the break-up of Yugoslavia.

The conversion of 865 brought the Bulgarians within the Byzantine cultural sphere but did not end the conflict between them. In 913 the Bulgarian Khan Symeon conceived the project of ending the conflict by marrying his daughter to the boy Emperor; in due course his grandson would succeed to both thrones. The history of the Balkans might have been different had Symeon's scheme come to fruition but other contenders for the Byzantine throne had a different and more exclusive vision. The young Emperor was overthrown and his successors devoted themselves to the destruction of the Bulgarian state. By 1018 they had succeeded but the Bulgarian sense of identity persisted, to be articulated in a second empire when Byzantine military power was weakened two centuries later.

The Byzantine cultural sphere was expanded by the conversion of Russia in 988. The Slavic and some of the Finnish tribes there had fallen under the control of invading Swedes in the ninth century. In the first flush of their voyaging the invaders tried an attack on Constantinople but its failure convinced them that more was to be gained by trade and alliance – a Russian army supported the Byzantines in their attack on Bulgaria and the so-called Varangian Guard formed the core of the imperial army for generations. By 988 the Swedes were already speaking the language of their Slav subjects and developing a rudimentary state in which power was divided between a number of, usually hostile, descendents of the original house of Rurik. Conversion brought the Russians within the ambit of civilisation; Orthodoxy, even more than distance, set them apart from Western Europe. Thus even before the Mongol conquest in the thirteenth century their development was beginning to follow a different pattern.

Even though the Russian principalities remained outside the Byzantine power sphere, that power was at an impressive height in the eleventh century. The great empire of the Abbasid Caliphs was no more, dissolved into a collection of hostile emirates. The Caliph survived only as a religious leader and even in this sphere his role was challenged by a Shia dynasty, the Fatimids, who ruled Egypt and Syria. Byzantium had recovered the great cities of Antioch and Edessa, as well as Crete and Cyprus, and was pressing the frontier forward into northern Mesopotamia.

Weaknesses in the Byzantine System

The empire's apparent strength, however, concealed a number of weaknesses. The peasant armies of previous centuries had been replaced by mercenaries and great landowners were extending their control over the peasantry, curtailing at once their freedom and the imperial tax base. The Empire remained essentially a backward rural economy with limited trade and urban development. The craft workshops of Constantinople produced luxury goods which were the envy of the West but they operated largely in a command economy dominated by the Imperial court. Constantinople preserved much of classical learning and developed a literature and above all an art of its own. But this high culture was the preserve of a privileged and parasitic minority which increasingly battened on a suppressed peasantry.

Patriarch and Emperor – church and state – were two parts of a divinely ordained system; a Patriarch might challenge a particular Imperial decree on religious grounds, especially if he had the support of the people, but he would never challenge the right of the Emperor to control the church. Unlike the West, therefore, Byzantium never experienced the Church as an alternative focus of power and loyalty. Rome and Byzantium, in fact, understood one another less as their paths diverged; in 1054 they excommunicated one another in a quarrel which both now seem to recognize as unnecessary. The schism reinforced the division between East and West and the mutual hostility of different societies, one thrusting and innovative, the other proud and conservative.

Supreme in church and state, the power of the Emperor was unrestrained by any constitutional check; but the prestige attached to the office, rather than the person of the occupant. A weak, incompetent or juvenile Emperor might be supplanted and probably killed by an ambitious relative or commander; Byzantium was ruled by several dynasties for a few generations but none of them ever acquired the legitimacy of Western monarchies. The Empire was heir to Rome in many ways and not least in being a despotism tempered by assassination. It might look magnificent and was certainly resilient. But it was essentially brittle.

Manzikert and its Consequences

Both brittleness and resilience were demonstrated after 1071 when the Seljuk Turks, already dominant in the former Arab Caliphate, defeated a Byzantine army at Manzikert and occupied Anatolia. The Empire, under attack from the Normans in the West and Patzinak Turks across the Danube, had now lost a large part of its Greek heartland. Emperor Alexius I Comnenus sought Venetian assistance against the Normans and agreed a high price – exemption from all levies on their trade with the Empire. With the peasant armies of earlier centuries emasculated, he also sought mercenaries from the West. Alexius was dismayed when the response took the tumultuous form of the First Crusade but he managed the crusading lords skilfully; the Empire, if little stronger, was no weaker for their transit and their conquests in Syria and Palestine. Inevitably, however, this and succeeding Crusades intensified the suspicion and hostility between East and West. The passage of unruly armies added to the resentment caused by the Venetian trade privileges. The Greeks saw little advantage in the creation of Crusading statelets in territory they regarded as rightfully theirs; the installation of a Latin patriarch in Jerusalem added insult to injury. The Crusaders envied Byzantine wealth and mistrusted its diplomatic wiles. The Venetians, having suffered a massacre in Constantinople in 1183, shared and nurtured their suspicions.

Consequently when the son of a deposed Emperor sought help from a Crusading army assembled at Venice he found a ready hearing. The Crusaders and the Venetians entered Constantinople in 1203 and restored Isaac II and his son. The parties promptly fell out and in 1204 the Westerners took Constantinople again; after thoroughly looting the city, they installed a Latin Emperor and Patriarch.

The Crusaders were too few to create a durable state. By 1261 a Greek emperor was back in Constantinople. Only Venice, which erected an empire of its own in the Greek islands, was a lasting beneficiary. Bulgaria and Serbia seized the opportunity to expand in the Balkans but neither was able to seize the great prize, Constantinople. The restored Empire, however, was too weak to resist the continuing expansion of the Turks, now under the effective leadership of the Ottoman dynasty. In 1354 they occupied the Gallipoli peninsula and began the expansion in the Balkans which, by 1529, had taken them to the gates of Vienna.

The Ottoman Conquest

Byzantine emperors and their officials soon realized that only Western support would enable them to resist the Ottoman expansion. Western monarchs, increasingly pre-occupied with their own ambitions and quarrels, showed little interest in coming to Byzantium's rescue. Only the Papacy was receptive and its price was clear – restoration of Church unity on Papal terms. Some Emperors were willing to contemplate this price but their people were not. Nor could the Popes in fact mobilize Western support. Consequently the Union concluded at the Council of Florence in 1439 and the last ditch effort of 1452 were abortive. Fifteenth century siege artillery and Ottoman military organization meant that Constantinople was no longer impregnable. The last Byzantine Emperor, Constantine XI Paleologus, died fighting the final Turkish assault of 1453.

The fall of Constantinople, however traumatic, did not spell the end of a Byzantine style of civilisation. The Ottomans had no interest in the mass conversion of their Christian, tax-paying subjects. On the contrary, they looked to the Christian bishops, and pre-eminently to the Patriarch of Constantinople, to serve as their agents in the government of their people. Paradoxically, the Patriarchate, with no Emperor to interest himself in religious matters and regarded by Turkish officials as the prime source of advice on all matters concerning Christians throughout the Empire, was probably stronger that it had ever been. Unfortunately Turkish custom expected substantial payments for high office so that the Orthodox Church soon fell under the control of venal careerists rather than men of genuine religion. But the religion of the people, already accustomed to expect little from any authority, continued undisturbed. The Byzantine mode of Christianity continued as an essential constituent of the national identity of Greeks and Bulgarians, Serbs and Romanians.

The Origins of Russia

The Swedish invaders who, beginning in the ninth century, established supremacy in Russia, were interested in trade and tribute – and opportunities for raiding and conquest further afield – not land, which was too poor, sparsely occupied and undeveloped to attract them.

Consequently they established not territorial states but a network of armed trading stations from which they fanned out to collect tribute from the surrounding areas and used it to trade with Byzantium and with the Islamic states of Central Asia. The great river systems of Russia provided the means of transport; easy portages connected them into one enormous network stretching from the Baltic to the Black Sea and the Caspian. With the Mediterranean trade routes interrupted by Moslem domination, and the development of trade in the Baltic, the Russian rivers became for a time a main artery of trade between northern Europe and the East. The trading posts profited accordingly and some of them developed into substantial cities.

Over most of the river network the invaders found themselves dealing with Slavic tribes who had settled in the mixed forest or wooded steppe and carved out scattered settlements, largely based on slash and burn agriculture, supplemented by hunting and fishing.

Further north, among the swamps and forests, were Finnish hunters and trappers whose furs were a valuable item for tribute and trade. Their word for Swedes – Ruotsi – may be the origin of the word Rus'.

Neither the Slavs nor the Finns were sufficiently organized or powerful to resist the Rus' who rapidly took control of the whole vast area from the Baltic to Kiev. South of Kiev, however, the woodland gives way to the open steppe where the black earth country is good for agriculture but also ideal for nomads. The traders therefore had to run the gauntlet of nomad raiders and settlement was impossible.

In the second half of the ninth century Rurik and his son Oleg succeeded in imposing their supremacy on all the settlements; Oleg fixed his capital at Kiev where the tribute could conveniently be centralized and yearly trading expeditions to Constantinople prepared for the dangerous run through the Dnieper rapids and the nomad dominated steppe. As successive Grand Princes of Kiev and princes of other cities, largely members of the Rurik family, began to exert control of the tribes around them the Rus' intermarried with the Slavs and co-opted their leaders. Before long the Rus' had lost their Swedish language; the nation which was slowly taking shape would keep the name Russian but would be Slavic in speech and culture. In the north the Slavs gradually absorbed the Finnish tribes; the Great Russians, as they are now known, probably include a substantial proportion of Finnish ancestry. Paradoxically, the inhabitants of the present Finland were protected from being submerged in the same way by their proximity to Sweden; their land became part of the Kingdom of Sweden and their Swedish lords maintained their national identity. So, consequently, did the Finnish inhabitants.

Russia's Distinctive Development

The nature of its origins marked out the nascent Russian state for a development quite different from that of the West. The power of the princes and their retainers was not rooted in the rural areas but in trading cities; the rural inhabitants were simply a source of tribute, exacted at first by methods which must often have been little different from plunder. Lacking traditions of state and government, the princes regarded their territories as their private property, their patrimony or *votchina*. The princes held their *votchiny* by right of descent and managed them with a servile staff. They quarreled and warred incessantly among themselves, so that the Grand Prince of Kiev never developed into an effective sovereign, but they maintained control of their patrimonies. Feudalism never developed in Russia and neither, consequently, did the notion that the ruler had obligations to his subjects. The right of the princes and nobles to unfettered control of the peasantry provided the foundation on which a harsh and exploitative system of serfdom would eventually be built and maintained until the nineteenth century.

Conversion to Christianity in the eleventh century brought the Russians within the Byzantine ambit and ensured that Russian religious development would be Orthodox, thus erecting a substantial divide between them and the West; Russia, like Byzantium, would never experience the Church as an alternative focus of loyalty and power. Byzantine cultural influence, however, while strong in religion, was limited by distance and by increasing nomad domination of the steppe. The river trade declined in importance because of this domination and the recovery of trade in the Mediterranean and the West.

The Mongols and the Rise of Moscow

In the thirteenth century Russia's separate development received a fatal re-inforcement from the Mongol empire. When the Mongol armies turned back from the West in 1242 they remained in control of most of Russia. The southern principalities had been destroyed and the more northerly thoroughly ravaged and subdued. The Khan of the Golden Horde, one of the major khanates into which the Mongol empire was divided, was the sovereign of Russia and the surviving princes were little more than his tribute collectors. The Khans appointed residents to see that the princes did their duty and used their armies ruthlessly to overthrow and replace insubordinate princes. They also controlled the succession to principalities and exacted both tribute and humiliating obeisance as its price. Russia, already distinct from the West in religion, culture and government, assumed much of the character of an oriental despotism.

Under this regime, success came to the princes who were most ruthless in exploiting their own people and most servile and unscrupulous in their dealings with the Khans. The princes of Moscow, hitherto a minor principality in the north, distinguished themselves as effective servants of their overlords. Ivan I helped the Khan in 1327 to put down a revolt in Tver and was rewarded by appointment as Grand Prince and Farmer General of the tribute throughout all Russia. Ivan and his successors used this position to control and then absorb the other principalities. In 1478 this process culminated in the subjection of the great trading city of Novgorod. The Grand Prince successfully asserted his independence of a declining Golden Horde and begun to use the title of Tsar, previously applied only to the Byzantine Emperor and the Khan.

The fall of Byzantium to the Ottoman Turks in 1453 reinforced these claims. In the last years of the Empire the Russian church had viewed Byzantium's raprochments with Rome with horror and considered them good ground for establishing its own patriarchate.

The Muscovite ruler was obviously called on by God to ensure the survival of the true religion and it was only appropriate that he should proclaim himself Tsar or Emperor. Devout Orthodox and Russian patriots alike regarded Moscow as the Third Rome, set apart from the rest of Europe with an imperial destiny sanctioned by God.

A very significant change was also introduced in the style used to describe the position of the monarch in relation to his subjects. The Russian language at this time used *'gospodin'* to describe a ruler in relation to his free subjects and *'gosudar'* in relation to his serfs and slaves. From early in the fifteenth century, the Grand Princes insisted on being addressed as *'gosudar'* by all their subjects. In 1533, when Ivan IV ascended the throne as a child, *gosudar* became part of the official title of the Tsar of Russia. In effect, the royal government was asserting that the Tsar was not only the ruler of Russia; he was its proprietor. Not only serfs and peasant tenants lacked rights to land; so too did nobles and great landowners. The whole land belonged to the Tsar; it was his patrimony and he might dispose of it as he pleased. When Ivan IV grew to manhood he set himself to bring this concept to its logical conclusion: if all Russia was the Tsar's patrimony, no one else could be more than a tenant. Ivan used this concept to undermine the position of the traditional nobility and build up the position of the Tsar's low grade servitors, many of them of slave origin. Some of these servitors were rewarded with estates but these were held on conditional tenure and could be reclaimed by the crown if the holder failed to render satisfactory service. The result was to create a new nobility totally dependent on the Tsar's favor.

No doubt two centuries of Mongol domination is some part of the explanation for the development of Russia into a complete autocracy. But the patrimonial (*votchiny*) concept was even more fundamental and traces back to the way in which the Russian state was first put together as a mechanism for the exploitation of a backward people by ruthless invaders.

Further West the Russians had been glad to accept the expanding power of Lithuania, rather than subservience to the Khan. The pagan Lithuanians, stimulated into unity by the aggression of the Teutonic knights, expanded their nascent state in the fourteenth century to embrace the west Russians to the Dnieper and beyond. Kiev became a city of the Lithuanian state – a state in which the Russians were more numerous and culturally more advanced than the Lithuanians. A second, different Russia might have developed on this basis. The Lithuanians, however, accepted Catholicism and in 1386 marriage established a dynastic union between Lithuania and Poland. The combined state, which included the present territory of Belarus and much of the Ukraine, inevitably fell under the leadership of the more advanced partner. Tension between Russian Orthodox and Polish-Lithuanian Catholic was the inevitable result. It provided, in Muscovite eyes, another ground for the ambition of the new Tsar to extend his patrimony to embrace all the Russians. Only in recent years has it become clear that Moscow's eventual success in this ambition has failed to erase feelings which have now been articulated as a separate national sense for the Ukrainians and for at least some of the Belarussians.

Muhammad and the Beginnings of Islam

In 634 a Byzantine army was defeated by Arab tribes at Ajnadayn outside Gaza. Within ten years the Arabs were masters of Syria and Egypt and the Empire was fighting for its life. The Persian Empire, defeated at Qadisiya in 637, was completely destroyed.

These conquests announced the arrival on the world scene of a new religion. Islam was established by the preaching and writing of Muhammad, a merchant of Mecca, who claimed to be THE Prophet, chosen by God to complete the revelations of Judaism and

Christianity. Muhammad's ability to convey his vision, his simple monotheism and uncomplicated code of conduct struck a chord with some of his Arab contemporaries; his shrewd dealings with conflicting interests, his ability to build coalitions and the military prowess of his followers enabled him to dominate the tribes of Eastern Arabia. His revelations began to take shape in the Quran, the sacred scripture of Islam – although the definitive version was not compiled until some years after his death – and Islam began to form a religious state in Eastern Arabia.

On Muhammad's death in 632, the incipient state almost disintegrated in a welter of tribal conflict. Abu Bakr, his Successor or Caliph, managed to hold the community together and to direct its energies to raiding the outside world. Very likely its overwhelming success was as surprising to the Arabs as it was to the Byzantines and the Persians.

Islamic Conquests

Muhammad had promised the rewards of Paradise to warriors who fell fighting for Islam but religious fanaticism seems to have had little to do with the original Arab conquests. They fought initially for booty and then, as the opportunities opened up before them, for dominion and its rewards. Their military elan overwhelmed the armies of Byzantium and Persia, exhausted by two decades of warfare which had ended only in 628. Even so, the Arab conquests would hardly have been possible if the Empires' subjects had felt them worth fighting for; obviously, like the Roman subjects faced with the Germans in the West two centuries before, they did not. The oppression of the tax gatherer was reinforced by differences of religion; the Syrians and the Egyptians were heretics to the Byzantine authorities (and vice versa) while much of the population of Iraq was Nestorian Christian, often persecuted by the Zoroastrian Persians. To Christians and Jews Islam offered religious toleration in return for a poll tax. Moreover, the Arabs were few in number and from the outset were willing to recognize the position of local elites as second class but necessary collaborators.

The successors of Muhammed therefore found that maintaining their power over their new subjects was not difficult. The tide of conquest could proceed, subduing North Africa and reaching Spain in 711, extending through Iran and into Central Asia by 713. Not since Alexander had so much been conquered by so few in such a short time. Like Alexander's empire, however, Islam found problems with the ambitions and interests of its own supporters.

Islam's Internal Problems

Those problems centred around the tribal rivalries of the Arab armies and the quasi-religious question of the succession to the Prophet. Both questions aroused strong feelings and inevitably they intersected and led to violent conflict. When Ali, the fourth Caliph and son-in-law of the Prophet, was murdered in 661, his followers split with main-stream (Sunni) Islam to found the Shia movement. To this day the Shia, divided into a number of different sects, maintain a complex of religious and political beliefs revolving around the martyred Ali and the anticipated eventual triumph of his cause.

The Umayyad Caliphs who succeeded Ali were committed to the continued expansion of the Islamic state and the maintenance of Arab supremacy; conversion of non-Moslems was not desirable because it would reduce the income from the poll tax and involve a dilution of the benefits reaped by the imperial people, the Arabs. The Ummayeds established their capital at Damascus and began the arduous process of turning a conquest empire into an organized imperial state. In this process they relied heavily on Christian Syrians for administration and on the Arab army in Syria for military force. It was this latter aspect that aroused the opposition of

Arab armies elsewhere. Other Arabs, notably those from Yemen, who had begun to settle in towns and villages, wanted peace rather than the continuous frontier wars to which the Umayyads were committed. To this opposition was added the discontent of the *'mawali'*, non-Arab clients attached to the various Arab tribes who received a lesser share of the rewards of the expanding conquests. By 749, a rival lineage descended from an uncle of the Prophet, the Abbasids, had put together a coalition of discontented Arabs, *'mawali'* and Shia dissidents and overthrew the Ummayeds.

The Flowering of the Abbasid Caliphate

Much to the annoyance of their Shia supporters, the Abbasids annexed the Caliphate themselves. They did not, however, disappoint the *'mawali'*. Under the Abbasids, the Islamic state ceased to be simply an instrument of Arab domination; the discrimination between Arab conquerors and other subjects was replaced by a new order in which only Islam mattered. The Abbasid state took on the colour of a traditional West Asian monarchy in which power depended, not on national or tribal origins but simply on the ruler's favor – the most famous family of Viziers (chief ministers), the Barmicides, are said to have been of Mongolian origin. From a new capital at Baghdad, the Caliph, surrounded by courtiers and ministers, reigned in great splendour over a mixed population of many nationalities and cultures. Inevitably, with the location of the capital at Baghdad, Persian notables became influential and the Persian style of government became a model for the Caliphate.

It was consistent with this model for the Caliphs to foster literature, art and scholarship. They patronized the translation of Greek and Persian texts into Arabic. They encouraged the study of philosophy and efforts to reconcile it with Islam. A community of

Islamic scholarship reached from Central Asia to Spain, where it was to provide invaluable inputs for medieval Europe.

Islam gradually extended to embrace the greater part of the population, first in the towns and then throughout the countryside. Moslem law and practice developed under the leadership of the *ulama*, groups of learned men who studied and interpreted the Quran and the *hadith* or sayings attributed to the Prophet. In this way, the *Sharia*, Islamic law, was developed to apply to both religious and secular life; Islam has never recognized a distinction between the two fields. Since learning required leisure and a financial base, the *ulama* institutionalized an alliance between the authority of the Caliphate and the urban elites; the Islamic state left the basic social structure undisturbed.

The conversion of the countryside was largely the work of the Sufis, holy men dedicated to the pursuit of perfection and mystical experience. Some *Sufis* founded schools of disciples which developed into religious brotherhoods with their own traditions and attracted large followings. *Sufi* tombs became objects of devotion and outstanding *Sufis* came to occupy a place in popular religion analogous to saints in Christianity. Even so, conversion was slow – not until the fourteenth century was it virtually complete in Egypt and Syria, although a substantial Christian minority has remained in both until the present day.

The Diffusion of Arabic

Parallel with, and very likely connected with, the spread of Islam was the spread of the Arabic language which eventually supplanted all the Semitic and most of the Hamitic languages in the state. Coptic in Egypt survived until the seventeenth century and like Syriac is still the language of worship in the Christian community. In the far west, the Maghreb, Berber maintained itself in rural areas, a source of differentiation between Berber and Arab and occasional conflict which perhaps has not yet played itself out. As it came to be spoken by various peoples over this huge area, Arabic developed regional variations which make mutual communication difficult. In the Abbasid court and administration, however, a classical Arabic was developed which became the basis of a written language, extending over the whole Empire and beyond, and fulfilling a function rather like Medieval Latin in the West. This classical language still provides a bond of unity between Arab states and cultures.

Significantly for the future, Arabic did not replace Persian. Strong as the influence of Islam was on the development of Persian identity and Persian culture, this would always remain distinct from Arabic. Persian culture was destined to have a large influence on Islamic societies in Central Asia, India and as far as Indonesia. Only in the sixteenth century, however, was the distinctive style of modern Iran developed when the Safavid Shahs used persecution to impose their own variety of Shia beliefs on a society which had up till then embraced all forms of Islam.

The Decline of the Abbasids

The splendour of the Abbasid Caliphate concealed the usual weaknesses of a West Asian monarchy. The Empire was far too extensive to be controlled effectively and was weakened by the endemic corruption of officials. Tax farmers exploited the peasants who, like those in the Roman Empire centuries before, found it necessary to 'commend' themselves to great landlords and hold their land as tenants. Shia revolts and peasant risings became widespread in Iraq and Syria, complicated by conflict between rival military factions. In northern Mesopotamia cultivation gave way to pastoralism. The maintenance of irrigation works was neglected and Southern Iraq, once the most productive part of the Empire, reverted to a watery wasteland.

As the initial elan of conquest was replaced by softer life styles, military power waned. The Byzantine Empire recovered and, although Arab armies besieged Constantinople, they could not take it; in fact they could not push the boundaries of the Caliphate beyond the Taurus ranges which form the natural frontier of Anatolia. The disintegration of Abbasid power was foreshadowed on their accession when a Umayyad survivor established an independent emirate in Spain. By the early ninth century independent emirates were established in North Africa and Central Asia; before its end they embraced Egypt and much of Iran. In 967–972 a line of Shia Caliphs established themselves in Egypt and extended their power to Syria.

Military weakness drove the Caliphs to make increasing use of Turkish tribes from Central Asia who soon began to exploit their opportunities. The Caliphs also developed an institution which was to become typical of Islamic states. They recruited and organised slaves to make up an important component of their armed power. The institution worked for a short time but slave regiments inevitably discovered their own power and began to dominate their employers and the state. Slave dynasties eventually came to power in Egypt and in Delhi. Before that could happen in Baghdad, however, a Persian family, the Buwayhids, had made themselves masters of the city and the Caliph(945). The Abbasid dynasty survived until 1258 but the Caliphs functioned only as nominal religious leaders.

The Buwayhids were no more capable of maintaining effective power than the Abbasids. West Asia dissolved into a congeries of ephemeral warring emirates incapable of organising a continuing state or of defending the central Asian frontiers against the nomad Turkish tribes. These soon became dominant in the area and, led by the Seljuks, defeated the Byzantine Empire decisively at Manzikert in 1071. For a short time a Seljuk sultan ruled from the Aegean to the oases of central Asia but this state, too, followed the usual cycle of disintegration. There was nothing at first to indicate that one of the successor states, the Ottoman Turks, would succeed in erecting a longer lived empire but in 1353 they seized Gallipoli and began the conquests that were to take them to the gates of Vienna.

In an uncanny anticipation of twentieth century terrorism the Shia sect of the Assassins established a headquarters at Alamut south of the Caspian in 1090 and developed the art of assassination and a network of secret cells to further their aims.

West Asia after the Abbasids

Thus when the Mongols turned their world conquering armies towards West Asia in the thirteenth century they at first met with little resistance. They wiped out the Assassins in 1256 and savagely destroyed the Abbasid Caliphate in 1258. Their advance was halted by the Mamluk slave army of Egypt in 1260 at the battle of Ayn Jalut (Goliath's Spring); their Persian khanate, despite their inevitable conversion to Islam and a short period of high culture, proved as ephemeral as its predecessors. Nor did the Turkish Timurlane's conquests at the end of the fourteenth century prove any more lasting. Not until the Ottomans and the Persian Safavids established their empires in the fifteenth and sixteenth centuries was West Asia to know another period of stability, although for the Arabs it was also a period of subjection and stagnation.

By the time the Mongols destroyed the Caliphate in 1258, West Asia, and also North Africa, had become securely Islamic. The style of civilization thus entrenched, however, owed as much to the traditions of West Asian society as to Islam. The Caliphs were the successors of the Prophet but they inherited the mantle and governmental system of Persian, Hellenistic and earlier monarchs.

The regime therefore perpetuated West Asian social structures. A cultured and educated class of officials, wealthy merchants and great landowners was supported by the exploitation of a subservient peasantry. Successive invaders, Arab or Turkish, slotted into this system with their leading men enjoying the perquisites of power and lesser mortals gradually being reduced to peasant status.

Unlike Christendom, this society proved unable to defend its border with the nomads, thus becoming subject to periodical and devastating invasions. The Central Asian borders were more open than the European but this alone hardly explains the difference. Islamic West Asia failed to develop the military structure – feudalism – which enabled Western Europe first to defend itself and then to pass over to the attack. Even more important the imperial power of the Caliphate in the early centuries, while insufficient to maintain an effective state indefinitely, prevented the emergence of local centres of power, either noble or urban. After that, the collapse of the Central Asian borders meant that any centre of power would eventually be submerged by a new wave of nomad invaders. This, together with the extension of the Ottoman Empire to embrace virtually all the Arab lands, meant that only Persia could develop the rudiments of an early modern state.

Unlike Western Europe, therefore, West Asia did not develop a new style of civilisation in the Middle Ages but perpetuated the old one, impregnated with a new religion but otherwise essentially unchanged. Inevitably, as Western Europe gathered strength, West Asia was surpassed and subordinated. The belated awakening of its people to this, beginning in the nineteenth century, linked with their growing consciousness of Islamic and Arab identity, constitutes one of the most significant parameters of our time.

The Further Spread of Islam

Long before the nineteenth century, however, Islam had spread beyond its heartland of West Asia and the southern shore of the Mediterranean. In Africa, the emerging states of the Sahel became Islamic without exception. On the East Coast, a number of small trading cities were established by Arab merchants; inevitably they were Islamic. Serious Moslem penetration of India began with Mahmud of Ghur in the eleventh century and later provided the base for Moslem penetration of Indonesia and Malaysia.

CHAPTER SIX

CHINA AND INDIA
From Early Middle Ages to Modern Times

The end of the Roman Empire in the West was roughly paralleled by the fall of the Han dynasty in China in the third century. It was succeeded by a number of kingdoms, some under nomad control; China was divided for several centuries, until unity was restored by the Sui dynasty in the sixth century. The Tang dynasty, who succeeded the Sui, ruled for three centuries; their work resulted in the preservation of the archaic state and society. It survived, with many vicissitudes, until the twentieth century.

In India, the Gupta empire lasted from the fourth to the beginning of the sixth century. Its collapse left the sub-continent without effective defence and a series of invaders poured through the north-eastern frontier. India's remarkable absorptive capacity seemed at first capable of coping with them all. All this changed, however, when Mahmud of Ghur initiated centuries of Islamic conquest. The resilience of Hindu religion and culture ensured their survival but not until 1949 were the Hindus masters of their own country.

China – The Preservation of an Archaic Civilisation

When the Han dynasty collapsed in 220 AD, China entered on a time of troubles somewhat similar to that which the Roman Empire was to experience a little later. Whereas the Roman world, at least in Western Europe, was eventually transformed into a new style of civilisation, the Chinese tradition proved more resilient. By the end of the sixth century the Chinese empire had been restored in essentially its archaic form and had begun to develop the key institution, the scholar bureaucracy, which would ensure its survival into the twentieth century.

China Divided and Re-united

For a short time the empire was divided into three kingdoms, in the north, the south and the south-west, perhaps reflecting cultural divisions now largely submerged. Re-unification was achieved in A.D. 280 but was short-lived. Northern China fell under the control of nomad invaders who, like the German invaders in the Roman Empire, entered into symbiotic relations with the great families, and gradually came under the influence of Chinese culture.

Many of the great families and their followers, however, fled south to the Yang-tse valley. There they built up a pattern of great estates with their own military power, not unlike early medieval Europe. It seems likely that much of the population of the south was still T'ai or Viet (Yue) and its effective Sinification only dates from this period. Although the northern elite despised these people, Chinese culture absorbed some important southern traits and the balance of population and production shifted from the Yellow River valley to the Yangtze and the south.

With real power in the hands of the great families, the south was ruled by a succession of short lived dynasties. Despite the size and wealth of the south, it was easily conquered by the Sui dynasty, which had already unified the north, in 589. Realizing that the productivity of the south was needed to support both his capital and his frontier armies, the second Sui emperor constructed the Grand Canal, linking the Yang-tse with the Yellow River. Probably the massive conscription of labour for this work touched off the peasant revolt which resulted in his overthrow. He was replaced by a family of mixed Chinese-Turkish descent who initiated the Tang dynasty.

The Tang thus found themselves at the head of an empire of 50 million people which had old traditions of unity but had not been governed as a single state for three centuries. Their major preoccupation was therefore to find a means of government which would ensure the continuation of the united state under their dynasty. They introduced land reforms designed to establish a taxpaying peasantry, subject to militia service and conscript labour, and outside the control of the great landowners. This reform, however, was perhaps more notional than real; the power of the landowners in the countryside was not to be broken so easily.

The Creation of the Scholar Gentry

Far more effective was the creation of a bureaucratic administration. Building on practices developed in the northern states, the Tang superimposed a bureaucratic elite, recruited by competitive examination, on the aristocratic structure of society. At first examination candidates vied for appointment with aristocratic nominees; only later, under the Sung dynasty, did examination success become, at least in principle, the sole method of appointment. In practice, moreover, preparation for these examinations required years of study which normally only the wealthy could afford. Birth and land ownership therefore remained important but no longer decisive on their own; an exceptional candidate might come from the growing merchant class or more rarely from a peasant family which, in effect, invested in his future by supporting him during long years of study.

The scholar bureaucracy remained the key element in Chinese government until modern times; even foreign conquerors recognized that the country could not be administered without them. It is noteworthy that the Mongols, who refused to rely entirely on the bureaucracy, maintained their control of China for a far shorter period than the Manchus who co-opted it into their regime from the start.

Drawn very largely from the land owning class, the bureaucracy was an instrument of stability. This conservatism was re-inforced when the initial, broad range of examination subjects gave way to an increasing concentration on Confucianism. The scholar bureaucracy thus played a key role in the massive continuity of Chinese culture. The price was a resistance to innovation which, at times, cost China dearly.

Nevertheless, the bureaucracy enabled the Tang and their successors to administer an immense country, the population of which stabilized at about fifty million. Administration was centralized down to county level and a corps of censors carried out regular audit and inspection. At the grass roots, however, it relied on local and informal controls. Here the gentry and landowners played a key role in social control and in preserving the traditional structure in which the labour of the peasants supported both the state and their own high culture. The empire, like all archaic states, institutionalised a system which delivered most of the benefits to a small elite.

The Tang and their successors were thus enabled to preside over an empire ruled by a bureaucracy based on a combination of traditional scholarship and wealth derived from land-ownership. The scholar gentry, as they are often described, gradually replaced the old aristocracy. China had no tradition of primogeniture and aristocratic wealth was soon dissipated by division between heirs made all the more numerous by the acceptance of concubinage. Office, on the other hand, inevitably accumulated wealth – remuneration was high, the censors could not always detect corruption and the primacy of family obligations in Confucian ethics provided a strong incentive to use every opportunity to add to family wealth.

Weaknesses of the Chinese System

The strength of this system is amply demonstrated by its longevity. Like all systems of government, however, it also had built-in weaknesses. The pyramid of authority culminated in the person of the Emperor and the efficacy of the administration depended, in the last resort, on him. A strong and committed emperor could dominate the system and make it work. Typically, the first emperors of each dynasty were such men but within a few generations they gave place to idle and dissolute rulers, dominated by their favourites, their concubines and the palace eunuchs, all interested in accumulating wealth rather than in effective government. A rapacious and luxurious court meant rising taxes, neglected and corrupt administration and popular discontent; most likely it would be accompanied by weak defence and rising tribute to hostile nomads, again requiring higher taxes. Eventually the dynasty would lose the mandate of heaven, to be replaced either by a rebel leader or an invading nomad. Such, at any rate, is the picture which the voluminous official histories give us. There is probably a substantial amount of truth in it but some caution is in order. The official histories were compiled by scholars serving the new dynasty; they had an interest in blackening the reputation both of the superseded dynasty and of power wielders such as the eunuchs outside the circle of the scholar bureaucracy. Moreover they developed a theory of the dynastic cycle under which this course of events had to occur. The temptation to select those facts which proved the theory and illustrated the dangers of ignoring bureaucratic advice may well have been overwhelming.

Undoubtedly, however, the dependence of the system on the personality of the emperor was one of its weaknesses. Another was its total lack of any institutional means of interaction with either local opinion or those levels of society below the scholar gentry. A chain of command ran down through provinces and prefectures to the county magistrate appointed from the capital. Below him only informal mechanisms existed; when the system was working well peasant households might be organized in groups of hundreds and thousands but this was only for the purpose of tax collection and responsibility for the good behaviour of their members; the Communist system of neighbourhood control of the individual has a long history. Neither in town or country were there institutional means of dealing with local matters – merchants, artisans and peasants should all carry out official orders, not come together to regulate themselves. Even the merchant guilds which developed under the Sung dynasty were confined to dealing with their own mercantile affairs and acting as government agents. Chinese cities never developed self-governing councils.

This style of government perhaps served the interests of the land-owning gentry who had privileged access to the district magistrate, a man of their own class. But it left the peasants defenceless and the merchants and artisans firmly subordinated to the interlinked network of land-owners and officials.

From this subordination the merchant could escape by buying land and having his sons compete for government appointment – in times of rampant corruption this could even be bought – or at least for the first degree which made a man a gentleman. The gentry class was never closed and this was part of the strength of the system; it co-opted those who might otherwise have questioned it. The process of converting the wealthiest and most ambitious merchants into rentiers, however, hardly promoted commercial development.

Sung China – Trade and Technology

The Sung dynasty ruled all China from 960 to 1127 and the south to 1279 when it was finally overthrown by the Mongols. Sung China was technologically and commercially innovative. Its industry and trade were well in advance of Europe. It had a large and prosperous merchant class which traded all over the Empire and beyond and had begun to develop financial instruments and proto-banking institutions. Yet this class never developed further in the way that the European merchant class did. The Mongol conquest opened up trade still further but it was foreigners, Arabs and Europeans, who took advantage of it. Even allowing for the trauma of the Mongol conquest, one cannot but think that the constant drain of capital and ambition into land-ownership was at least part of the explanation.

China Draws in on Itself

When the Mongols – succumbing to dynastic decline even more rapidly than a Chinese dynasty – were ousted in 1368 and replaced by the Chinese Ming dynasty, Chinese fleets, under the command of the eunuch admiral Cheng Ho, sailed as far as India, the Persian Gulf and East Africa. These were massive expeditions, showing the Chinese flag in force. How much commerce accompanied them is unclear but certainly by the fifteenth century Chinese sailors were prominent in East Asia and expanding further afield. This promising development was brought to a sudden end in 1433 by imperial decree; the expeditions were expensive and the money, in the view of the emperor and his advisers, was better spent on frontier defence and building works.

The lack of vision shown in this decision reflected the growth of thought control in the imperial bureaucracy. Already in the ninth century the Tang had launched a short but violent persecution of Buddhism which succeeded in reducing the power and prestige of the monasteries and undermining Buddhist scholarship. Buddhism, which had shown signs of becoming an alternative to Confucianism, was reduced to a popular religion, a consolation for the peasants but not of intellectual interest to scholars. When Matteo Ricci, the great Jesuit missionary of the sixteenth century, resolved to assimilate himself to Chinese culture he began by adopting the garb of a monk and studying the teachings of Buddhism; he soon realized that this approach in fact cut him off from educated Chinese and that he must turn himself into a Confucian scholar.

In the eleventh century an attempt by a radical minister, Wang An-shih to reform the examination system and introduce practical concerns of policy and administration was sabotaged and then reversed. The entrenchment of scholarly orthodoxy was completed in 1313 when the commentaries of the great scholar Chu Hsi were prescribed as the standard for the examinations. The Chinese bureaucracy, the most educated in the world, was also the most conservative and the least open to new ideas. Stability was bought at the cost of stagnation.

For many centuries the peasantry were buffered from the worst effects of this stagnation. A large and fertile country presented lots of opportunities for the expansion of cultivation; the south was not fully occupied until Sung times and then the Mongol conquest of Nan-Chao, and the consequent southern migration of its Thai population opened up a new province (Yunnan) to Chinese settlement. Moreover, under the Sung, new, quick growing rice varieties were introduced from Vietnam, making double cropping possible in much of the south. Then, as a result of the European contact with America, maize and sweet potato were introduced into China and permitted heavy food crops on land unsuitable for rice.

Consequently, China's population which had been stable under the Tang and Sung, and drastically reduced by the Mongol invasion, began to expand again under the Ming and reached 150 million by the time they were replaced by the invading Manchus in 1644.

China under the Manchu

After the initial turmoil of conquest, the Manchu emperors of the Ching dynasty gave China a long period of stable, effective government. Already largely Sinified, they immediately adopted the traditional system and patronized the scholar bureaucracy. Three long-lived and hard-working emperors made the system function at its best until the end of the eighteenth century. Mixing Manchu military traditions and Chinese numbers, they extended the empire to embrace Tibet, Sinkiang and Mongolia as well as Manchuria. Eighteenth century China could be seen as by far the largest and most systematically governed state in the world.

From the perspective of Beijing the Chinese vision of the middle kingdom appeared to be no less than the reality. The nomads had been subdued, the surrounding minor kingdoms in South-East Asia and Korea were respectful and the western barbarians were seeking to trade with the middle kingdom and obviously to learn from it. When Great Britain sent an envoy to Beijing to seek greater trade openings, the emperor responded by saying that China did not need imports and graciously exhorting the subordinate monarch of Britain to be even more respectful in future embassies.

Hubris (excessive pride), as European scholars, from their Greek classics, could have told their Confucian counterparts, leads inevitably to catastrophe. In the nineteenth century the gap between Chinese and European power would grow apace as the latter developed and the former stagnated; the succession of great emperors would give way to nonentities who could not save the system from corruption, let alone lead it in responding to new challenges; and the growth of Chinese population, now unmatched by agricultural development, would produce misery and revolt. None of this scenario was within the narrow purview of the Confucian scholar and his whole education inhibited him from opening his mind to it. The scholar bureaucracy had preserved an archaic civilisation beyond its time and the inevitable adjustment was to be delayed and painful.

India – Islamic Conquest and Hindu Survival

From their centre in the lower Ganges valley the Gupta dynasty extended their power over most of north India in the fourth century. Their empire was largely a collection of tributary states around a central core subject to direct rule, with the fissiparous tendencies inherent in such a structure. A disputed succession in 467 provided the opportunity for the subject states to assert their independence. A brief unity was again imposed on the Ganges valley and the Punjab by Harsha of Kanauj in the seventh century. His attempt to extend his power into southern India, however, was defeated. Harsha's murder in 647 was followed by centuries in which no single power could dominate the sub-continent. Instead, a plethora of dynasties formed and reformed states which fought one another in largely inconclusive wars.

The Islamic Conquests

Most of these states paid little attention to an Arab army which appeared at the mouth of the Indus in 712 and conquered Sind in the name of Islam. Surprisingly, their confidence was justified. For the time being, the Moslem expansion into India had reached its limit. The Arab rulers of Sind tolerated Hinduism, employed brahmin officials and became the channel through which the Indian numerical and decimal system reached the Arab world.

The next Islamic intruder was very different. Mahmud of Ghazni was a Turk, engaged in putting together an empire which eventually stretched from the Punjab to the Caspian Sea. When he found that Indian armies were too ponderous to contest the field with his nomad horse-archers, he seems to have regarded India as a resource to be plundered; its inhabitants were idolaters and in Mahmud's simple understanding of Islam it was meritorious to despoil and kill them. Between the year 1000 and his death in 1030 he launched seventeen invasions of India, destroying temples and palaces, looting their treasures, slaughtering thousands of people and carrying others off to slavery.

Mahmud made no attempt to occupy any territory beyond the Punjab. His successors left India in peace, perhaps convinced that it had been despoiled so thoroughly that further raids would bring little reward. The Indian states resumed their rivalry and internecine wars. Gradually the Hindu temples were rebuilt. Significantly, however, the Buddhist monasteries were not. Within India, Hinduism had virtually absorbed Buddhism, recognizing the Buddha as an incarnation of the god Vishnu.

The next Moslem invader came, not merely for plunder, but for empire. In 1151 the governor of Ghur overthrew the Ghaznavid dynasty. His successor, Muhammed, began the conquest of north India in 1175. When he died in 1206 his domains extended from the Hindu Kush to Bengal. The Indian portion immediately fell to his slave general Kutb-ud-din Aibak, initiating half a millennium in which northern India was to be ruled by a succession of Turkish and Afghan dynasties, culminating in the Mughal/Turkish house of Babur and Akbar.

The Sultanate of Delhi

The establishment of the Sultanate of Delhi, as the Moslem state is generally described, reduced the Indians in the north to subjects of an alien conqueror. After the first wave of conquest and rapine, the Sultans realized that a permanent state required some accommodation with their Hindu subjects. Persecution gave way to toleration and looting to tax collecting. Difference of religion, however, was a formidable obstacle to the merger of conquerors and conquered. Moreover, since non-believers were liable to a poll tax, the Sultans had a very practical reason to refrain from efforts to convert their subjects.

Some conversion, however, there was. Sufis, Moslem holy men, could hardly be restrained by an Islamic government and their lifestyle and personality could have a powerful impact on ordinary Hindus. Islam, which proclaimed that all men were equal before God, could make a strong appeal to lower caste Hindus. For centuries, as settlement expanded, primitive peoples on the margin of society had been absorbed into the lowest castes. Islam now offered such people a more acceptable alternative. The population of East Bengal, in particular, found this offer irresistible. Their decision for Islam is reflected to-day in the solidly Moslem population which ensured the incorporation of this area into Pakistan. Unfortunately the many differences between the people of East and West Pakistan eventually led to civil war and the independence of East Pakistan as Bangladesh.

The defection of primitive and lower caste people did not impair the solid Hindu majority. Hinduism had survived the challenge of Buddhism largely because it provided the ceremonies and rituals which related to the high and low points of daily life – birth and marriage, sickness and death. By comparison with its colour and activity and its ability to provide an appropriate god for every occasion, Islam seemed to most Indians austere and unattractive. Those who did convert sometimes developed a mixture of Hinduism and Islam which purists of the latter religion would certainly not approve. So Hinduism survived, and with it Indian culture and identity.

The gulf between Moslem and Hindu, of course, increased the gap between ruler and ruled. At first north India was simply an occupied country whose rulers maintained their position partly by calling on periodical reinforcements from their fellow nomads, largely Turks, from Central Asia. The Delhi Court was heavily influenced by Persian culture; Persian remained the official language, even under British rule, until 1835. By the thirteenth century the Tughluq Sultans were willing to incorporate Hindu nobles into their power structure, but always in a subordinate capacity. A blend of Persian and Indian culture began to develop, symbolized in some ways by the development of the Urdu language, basically Hindi but written in Arabic characters and incorporating Persian and Turkish words

The Delhi Sultanates were almost entirely confined to north India. Only one Sultan, Muhammad bin Tughluq (1325–51), made a serious attempt to conquer the south. Becoming convinced that his aim could not be achieved while his capital remained far away at Delhi, he shifted it and its population to Daulatabad in the Deccan. For a few years his power was acknowledged almost to the tip of the Indian peninsula. But it soon became apparent that north India could not be ruled from Daulatabad and the capital had to be returned to Delhi. Even before Muhammad died, one of his generals had established an independent state, the Bahmani Sultanate, in the Western Deccan. The rest of his ephemeral conquests largely fell to the new Hindu state of Vijayanagara which absorbed the other kingdoms of the south. It flourished until it was defeated by a coalition of small Muslim states, the successors of the Bahmani Sultanate, in 1565.

The Tughluq Sultanate survived Muhammad's unsuccessful adventure. The next challenge was more serious. In 1398 Timur launched an attack which culminated in the sack of Delhi and the enslavement of its skilled artisans, carried away to work on the beautification of Samarkand. Like all Timur's military campaigns, this one was little more than a plundering raid but it weakened the Tughluq hold on power and led to their replacement by two short lived dynasties. The second of these, the Afghan Lodi dynasty, found itself confronted by an invader who intended, not simply to raid, but to conquer and rule.

The Grand Mughals

Babur could claim both Genghiz Khan and Timur as his ancestors. Ejected from his hereditary valley of Ferghana by the Uzbeg Turks, he seized Samarkand at the age of fourteen but could not hold it. Eventually he managed to install himself in Kabul and in 1526 defeated Ibrahim Lodi at Panipat, outside Delhi. Having defeated a Rajput confederacy, he seemed to have secured the Delhi Sultanate but in 1530 he died, leaving his conquests unconsolidated. His heir Humayun was ejected from Delhi by another Afghan, Sher Shah, and spent many years as an exile at the Persian court. In 1555 he recovered Delhi only to die six months later.

Humayun's son Akbar brought to the task of governance the courage and humanity of Babur as well as a wide ranging intellectual curiosity and the ability to devise and impose new forms of administration. Above all he understood that his state could only be successful with the support of its Hindu subjects. He abolished the poll tax, reduced the royal demand on the peasant's harvest to one-third, employed Hindu ministers, generals and counsellors and included a Rajput princess among his wives. With a unified state to call on, he extended Mughal power in the west to Sind and Gujerat, in the east to Bengal and in the south into the Deccan.

To consolidate his empire Akbar even tried to launch a new religious synthesis, drawing on Islamic, Hindu and Christian elements. Like most such efforts its support was largely confined to those who sought the Emperor's favor. With his death in 1605, this experiment came to an end. Something of Akbar's tolerant approach to his Hindu subjects, however, continued under his successors, Jahangir and Shah Jahan. The structure which Akbar had created was strong enough to survive their weaknesses and the empire was even slightly extended.

Aurrangzeb and the End of Mughal Power

Shah Jahan was succeeded in 1658 by his son Aurangzeb. The new emperor was a devout and fanatical Sunni Moslem. He immediately set out to reverse the tolerant regime which Akbar had created and to extend Mughal power over the whole sub-continent. Both enterprises ended in disaster.

The re-imposition of the poll tax on non-Moslems brought the Rajput princes, loyal servants of the empire and an invaluable military resource, to revolt. The crass disregard of Hindu feelings, manifested in such actions as the erection of a mosque dominating the most sacred of Hindu cities, Banaras, destroyed all hope of developing the united state and people of Akbar's dreams.

Aurangzeb did indeed succeed in extending his empire to embrace almost all India. But his conquests were to prove ephemeral. The Marathas, who inhabited the Western Ghats (the hill country behind Bombay and Goa), broke out in rebellion. Their leader, Shivaji, proved himself a master of guerilla war and raided across the country as far south as Tanjore. His son and successor lacked his great qualities; the Marathas remained formidable but their state was little more than a predatory confederacy of local dynasties.

In his determination to conquer the south, Aurangzeb himself took charge of his armies there in 1683. He never returned to Delhi; until his death in 1707 he ruled the empire from his military headquarters, established a few miles from the ruined city of Daulatabad, from which Muhammad Tughluq had briefly attempted to conquer and rule all India in the fourteenth century. Muhammad had eventually acknowledged that it was impossible to rule north India from the Deccan or south India from Delhi.

Aurangzeb, more stubborn than Muhammad, persisted until his death. When the strains imposed by a generation of war and the hostility aroused by persecution, not only of Hindus but of non-

Sunni Moslems, are added to the traumas of war, it is not surprising that Aurangzeb's policies led to the end of the Mughal empire. The Rajputs, already in rebellion for thirty years, achieved de facto independence. In 1724 the governor of the Deccan became effectively independent, establishing the line of Nizams of Hyderabad which survived until 1949. Worse was to come. In 1739 the Turkish adventurer who ruled Persia as Nadir Shah sacked Delhi. In 1757 Delhi was sacked again, this time by the Afghans. The Emperor called in the Marathas who, however, went down to defeat on the historic field of Panipat. History might have repeated itself with an Afghan dynasty in Delhi but the victorious warriors insisted on withdrawing to their own country. So the way was open for the only effective power left in India, the British.

Chapter Seven

SOUTH EAST ASIA AND JAPAN

East of India and south of China lies the peninsula and island world of South East Asia. Subject to influence from both these major civilisations, the peoples of South East Asia absorbed much from them but nevertheless developed their own distinctive cultures.

So too did Japan which borrowed much from China but always absorbed it into its own unique culture. Eventually, two centuries of isolation and peace enabled that culture to mature and flourish and to develop the unique strength which enabled Japan to claim a place in the European dominated comity of nations while other Asian countries were still either colonies or second class dependencies of the European system.

The Peoples of South East Asia

During the Han period, when Chinese records begin to give us some information about South-East Asia, the region was dominated by peoples of two major language groups.

The coastal areas south of Vietnam to the gulf of Siam, as well as the Malayan peninsula and the islands of Indonesia and the Philippines, were dominated by Austronesian, or Malayo-Polynesian, speakers. Sea-farers for centuries, if not millennia, these people had already penetrated far into the Pacific; in the first century of our era others settled in Madagascar.

Behind the Austronesians on the coast, mainland South East Asia was dominated by agriculturalists speaking Austro-Asiatic languages, especially Mon in the west and Khmer in the east. Another major member of this language family is Munda, spoken by isolated and backward tribes in parts of India – which raises interesting, but unanswerable, questions about the original distribution of these peoples. Some linguists see Vietnamese also as a member of this group, despite its being, unlike them, a tonal language.

Scattered among the Austro-Asiatic and Austronesian speakers were many remnants of earlier populations, some akin to the Veddahs of Sri Lanka and the aboriginal peoples of Australia, others related to the dominant peoples. Mostly hunter-gatherers or slash and burn agriculturalists, they occupied the less accessible uplands and were destined to play a largely passive role in South East Asian history.

The southward flood of Chinese conquest under the Han dynasty reached Vietnam in 111 BC. At that time, the chief city, Co Loa, near Hanoi, covered a site of 600 hectares and was elaborately fortified with three sets of ramparts and moats. Irrigated rice fed the dense population required to support these massive works. It is quite likely that much of the population of South China, absorbed into the spreading Han state, was related to these people and the Han emperors no doubt expected to absorb the Vietnamese also. They were to be disappointed; the Vietnamese maintained their separate identity and re-asserted their independence a thousand years later.

Further south, civilized states were already beginning to emerge but under Indian, rather than Chinese influence. By the beginning of the Christian era, South Indian merchants and the occasional brahmin and warrior were bringing trade, Buddhism and Hinduism to the mainland. Paradoxically, much of the knowledge we have of them comes from Chinese records, supplemented by archaeology and linguistic analysis.

The Early Kingdoms of the Mainland

The first recorded Chinese visitor, in AD 250, found two powerful kingdoms controlling the coast south of Vietnam. Funan, centred on the Mekong delta, was based on irrigated rice cultivation but had extensive trading interests and claimed control along the coast as far as the Kra isthmus. Here east and west flowing rivers were close enough to make portage of cargo between the two easy. The route provided an entree for Indian trade, ideas and religion. By AD 250 Funan was already a Hindu style kingdom; Funan was actually a dynastic name meaning 'king of the mountain' and probably referring to Indian cosmological beliefs. Buddhism and Hinduism were already present and court records were kept in Sanskrit.

North of Funan, a smaller Austronesian state jealously maintained its independence. Hemmed in between the mountains and the sea, Champa was, even more than Funan, a maritime state. Its geographical position, however, limited its trading opportunities and the Chams soon acquired a bad reputation for piracy. Squeezed between the Vietnamese and Funan, and later the Khmer empire, the Chams managed to maintain their independence until 1471.

Even more remarkable is the Vietnamese achievement. Conquered by Han China, the Vietnamese remained, not without revolts, Chinese subjects for a thousand years. They absorbed a great deal of Chinese culture, including Confucianism and the tradition of the scholar gentry but still maintained their sense of Vietnamese identity. When the Tang dynasty collapsed, the Vietnamese asserted and maintained their independence – the only people subject to Chinese control for a millennium to have recovered their independence. In parenthesis, one cannot but think that if Washington policy makers had been conscious of this unique history, they might have been more reluctant to involve the United States in war with Vietnam.

Indian Influence

Apart from Vietnam, Chinese influence in South East Asia before modern times was much less significant than Indian. Many states in the region accepted tributary status from time to time but this was mostly a nominal acknowledgement of China's paramountcy in return for trading privileges. The Mongol attempts to assert real power by invading Vietnam and Java were miserable failures.

Most exposed to Indian influence were the Mons, who occupied (in modern terms) southern Burma and eastern Thailand. Much of India's impact on South East Asia was mediated by these people who took control of the portages across the Kra isthmus when Funan's power collapsed towards the close of the sixth century.

Trade between India and China provided the vehicle which brought Indian influence; who sailed the ships is less clear. Certainly it is unlikely that the Austronesians would have been content for long to leave it all to the Indians; Austronesians had already sailed to Madagascar and settled the Pacific from Fiji to Tahiti, an area which would expand to embrace Hawaii and New Zealand. Probably we should think in terms of a polyglot sea-faring community with initiatives coming from both Indians and Austronesians and stretching eventually from Egypt and Persia to China and the outer islands of Indonesia.

Equally, it would be a mistake to think of the Indianisation of South East Asia. The peoples of the region appropriated only what they wanted – caste, for example, was ignored and the position of women was less repressed than in India – and integrated it into their own cultures. Despite many differences those cultures maintained a basic unity which entitles South East Asia to be regarded as a distinct cultural zone. One reason for the survival of these basic attitudes and values was that Indian culture and religions were imported by the monarchs and their courts and only slowly and imperfectly percolated among the mass of peasants, who assimilated Hinduism and Buddhism to their own basic beliefs.

The supremacy of Funan was brought to an end by the Khmer kingdom of Chenla further up the Mekong. The historical framework of the mainland for the next millennium was to be largely determined by successive invasions from the north. The kingdom which the Khmers eventually established on the ruins, and the model, of Funan came to dominate the valleys of the Menam (most of modern Thailand) and the Mekong, reducing the Mon states in the former to vassalage. It established an extensive road network and an impressive system of irrigation. In the twelfth century it created the magnificent temple complex of Angkor Wat, one of the architectural wonders of the world. The price of this, and many other architectural achievements, however, was the constant forced labour of hundreds of thousands of peasants. When the Thai incursions from the north became a real threat to the Khmer empire in the thirteenth century, the exhausted state lacked the power to contain them.

Invaders from the North

The Thai peoples had their homeland in the mountain spine of southern China centred around Yunnan. Here they had maintained a prickly independence in the kingdom of Nan Chao for centuries, resisting Chinese attacks and, in the ninth century, raiding as far as northern Burma and Hanoi.

Like the Germans on the borders of the Roman empire, some of the Thais served as mercenaries in Khmer armies; again like the Germans, the Thais became more powerful than their employers. About 1250 a Thai leader established an independent state in the former Khmer province of Sukhothai in the central Menam valley. The Thai trickle became a flood after Kublai Khan's Mongol armies conquered Nan Chao in 1253 and opened it to Chinese settlement. Another Thai state was established in the middle of the fourteenth century with its centre at Ayutthaya, not far north of modern Bangkok. This kingdom conquered and absorbed Sukothai in 1378 and extended its power to embrace most of modern Thailand. In the fifteenth century its pressure obliged the Khmers to abandon Angkor and move their capital south.

Despite, or perhaps because of, their vassalage to China and their historical closeness in Nan Chao, the Thais developed their state on Indian rather than Chinese models. Hinayana Buddhism was taken over from the Mons as the religion of state while the system of government was modeled on the Khmer, who were also the major influence on Thai art. Mon and Khmer also provided the basis for a Thai alphabet. While the Thai language became widespread – at least 80 per cent of the contemporary population of Thailand are Thai speakers – all this suggests that the invaders merged with the existing population to create a society which synthesised Thai and Mon-Khmer elements.

A deliberate attempt at such a synthesis was made by the early Burmese kingdom of Pagan, established towards the end of the ninth century on the middle Irrawaddy. The Burmese, related to the Tibetans, had come south down the river under pressure from the Thais of Nan Chao; the local Mons were prepared to co-operate with the Burmese whom they regarded as a lesser evil than the raiding Thais. Further south the Mon kingdom of Pegu sought Burmese assistance against the eleventh century expansion of the Khmer empire. The defence was successful but it left Pegu subject to the Burmese. The real synthesis of Burmese and Mon, which seems to have followed, was interrupted when the rulers of Pagan unwisely refused homage to Kublai Khan. Mongol armies destroyed the Pagan kingdom and left the Burmese virtually defenceless against the Thai speaking Shans of the highlands. The Mons recovered their independence; their written language now showed a strong Burmese admixture. Only in the sixteenth century did a new centre of Burmese power emerge at Toungoo on the Sittang river to contain the Shan and subdue the Mon.

Maritime Powers in the Indonesian Islands

In the island world to the south and east, the Malayo-Polynesian people remained largely undisturbed by the waves of conquest on the mainland. In central Java a number of conflicting quasi-feudal states emerged; one was sufficiently organised to send embassies to China in the fifth century. The Javanese took what they wanted from Indian contacts but their own culture was essentially resilient. The Philippines, although not entirely without Indian and Chinese contacts, were sufficiently isolated to remain a tribal, animist society until the Spaniards arrived in the sixteenth century.

By the late seventh century, trade through the Straits of Malacca was beginning to rival the portage routes across the Kra Isthmus. Profiting by this, the state of Srivijaya in southern Sumatra developed a maritime empire which controlled both sides of the Straits and extended to the north of the Malay peninsula and into East Java. Srivijaya's hinterland was infertile and lightly populated; its wealth and power were built on tolls and harbour services. A Chinese pilgrim in 671 found it supporting a Buddhist monastery of a thousand monks. In the ninth century a Javanese dynasty came to power in Srivijaya; a century later it defeated an attack by the rising Javanese power of Mataram and burnt its capital.

The geographical scope of the region's trade, and both the extent and the limits of its power politics, were strikingly illustrated in 1025. The Tamil Cholas had just extended their south Indian state by the conquest of Sri Lanka and saw obvious advantages in developing direct trade with China, to which they had already sent a mission. Srivijaya's control of the Straits of Malacca stood in the way of this ambition. The Chola navy was able to project its power across the Indian Ocean, ravage the Srivijayan ports and capture its ruler – an unparalleled exercise of long distance naval power for the eleventh century. But it was not followed up. Srivijaya recovered and, if it never quite resumed its previous imperial status, survived as a maritime power until the thirteenth century.

In the long run the centre of gravity in the island world was bound to shift to Java where the inland states, with their intensive rice cultivation, supported larger populations. By the ninth century one of these states mobilized sufficient manpower to build the gigantic carved stupas of Borobodur, a monument to rival Angkor Wat. As Srivijaya declined, the rising east Java state of Senghasari seized its outposts and contested its control of the Straits. Refusal to acknowledge Chinese suzerainty provoked a Mongol attack in 1293. The attack was abortive but the predominance of Singhasari was replaced by Majapahit. Although it never managed to control the trade routes as thoroughly as Srivijaya in its prime, Majapahit remained the dominant power in the islands for a century. Significantly, its domination was accompanied by an increasing assimilation of the established Hinduism to traditional Javanese beliefs and practices.

The Ming dynasty, which ejected the Mongols from China, at first showed great interest in overseas trade and politics. Early in the fifteenth century, under the leadership of the great eunuch admiral Cheng Ho, massive Chinese fleets – the largest is said to have carried 38,000 men – sailed as far as India and East Africa. The states they visited were duly impressed and sent tribute back to the Emperor, although it may be doubted whether this exceeded the value of the gifts presented to their rulers. Whether these expeditions represented anything more serious than 'showing the flag' is unclear; a change in Ming policy brought them to an abrupt end before China had established itself as a serious player in South East Asia and the Indian ocean.

The Arrival of Islam

Paradoxically, the major impact of these expensive expeditions was to facilitate the expansion of Islam. Muslim traders and missionaries were active in the islands before the end of the thirteenth century and made substantial progress during the fourteenth. Then an exiled Javanese prince established a settlement at the fishing village of Malacca about 1400 and began to take advantage of its key position to dominate the Straits. When Cheng Ho visited Malacca in 1409 he readily offered homage. He and his successors maintained close relations with China, using it as a counterweight to the pressure of the Thai kingdom. Conversion to Islam was another move to mobilize support. By the end of the fifteenth century, Malacca was a great cosmopolitan city controlling both sides of the Straits, a centre of ship-building and the focal point of trade between India and the Red Sea on one side and China, Java and the islands further east on the other.

Supported by Malacca, Islam spread through Malaya and to the coastal cities of Java, where the merchant communities found it a useful focus for their assertion of independence against the waning power of Majapahit. From the coast Islam gradually spread inland but the Javanese, both rulers and ruled, absorbed it in their own manner and resisted the attempts of enthusiastic teachers to convert them to more orthodox ways. By the end of the fifteenth century Islam had also spread to the port cities of the more easterly islands. Soon afterwards it began to penetrate the Philippines where its further spread was to be halted by the Spanish combination of military power and missionary endeavour.

The conversion of the Malays and Indonesians to Islam, and of the Philippines to Christianity, did not result in a major divorce between them and the Hindu-Buddhist peoples of the mainland. Beneath the different systems of beliefs and practices, a common sub-stratum of attitudes and perceptions, and even of values, remained. Surviving through the vicissitudes of centuries, this basic unity provided the foundation for ASEAN, which must be reckoned as one of the more successful of contemporary regional associations.

Japan – Origins

Of all the neighbouring countries which came under the influence of Chinese culture, Japan was most successful in appropriating large elements while preserving its own distinctive and quite different culture. This fact, as well as its key economic role in the contemporary world, makes its history of particular interest.

The origins of the Japanese people are probably to be found in a mixture of Altaic migrants from the neighbouring mainland and others of Austronesian stock from further south. By the time Japanese history begins, about the fourth century AD, there was no consciousness of these origins or of any cultural differences related to them – all the inhabitants of Japan were conceived as one people, except for the aboriginal Ainu. These hunter-gatherers occupied the northern part of the main island, Honshu, and the northern island of Hokkaido. The slow expansion of the Japanese into north Honshu was accompanied by a good deal of fighting with the Ainu and a good deal of absorption of them; presumably the same process had already taken place further south, making the Ainu a third element in the Japanese population.

The early Japanese were organised in clan or lineage groupings, each with their own dependents. The geography of the land, with many small valleys and plains separated from one another by mountains, must have encouraged a degree of separate development. By the sixth century, however, one lineage had established its claim to leadership. This was the Sun family, claiming descent from the sun goddess Ameratsu, and centered in the Yamoto peninsula between modern Nagoya and Osaka; their descendants are still Emperors of Japan. The extension of their power seems to have been based on an adroit mixture of conquest, marriage alliances and the prestige of their mythical descent from the sun goddess; like many archaic rulers, the Sun monarch was as much priest as king. The extent of his effective power outside his own domain is doubtful.

Chinese Influence

The power and culture of neighbouring China was a strong magnet for this embryo state. Confucianism was accepted and Buddhism was encouraged, not without misgivings, in the sixth century. Patronized by the royal house and its officials, Buddhism rapidly became established alongside Japan's native nature-religion, Shinto.

The inflow of Buddhist teachers encouraged an even greater interest in the Chinese model. In the seventh century a deliberate attempt was made to re-organize Japan on the model of Tang China, asserting state control of land, introducing a centralized taxation system and bureaucracy and transforming the local clan chieftains into a court aristocracy. The imitation of the Chinese system, however, was not unthinking. No attempt was made to introduce the Chinese examination system; the power and prestige of the great families made it unthinkable to replace them with mere scholars and they soon acquired hereditary rights to positions in the bureaucracy.

The Japanese Style of Government

A new capital, equipped with splendid palaces and Buddhist monasteries was built at Nara; when the influence of the monks became a problem it was moved to Kyoto in 794 and the monasteries were forbidden to follow. The new system provided the resources on which a sophisticated court culture, marked by a precocious literature and a distinctive, Japanese style of art and architecture could flourish. In the absence of a professional bureaucracy, however, the administration was based on the co-operation of the great families and successive emperors found themselves struggling to maintain their authority against over-mighty subjects. For two centuries, beginning in 857, members of the Fujiwara family dominated the government as Regents and provided wives for Emperors. These, despite occasional struggles to assert themselves, were often reduced to puppets and always occupied with an endless round of religious rituals and empty ceremonies. Ambitious emperors who sought real power adopted the expedient of retiring, usually taking up residence in a monastery, where they could set up their own power apparatus and, as 'retired emperor', try to exercise real influence.

At the same time state control of land was gradually replaced by the growth of hereditary ownership; real power was passing to the strongest leaders of the provincial families who surrounded themselves with armed retainers, the samurai, and paid no more than lip service to the court. The archaic state controlled from the centre was becoming feudalized; indeed, Japanese feudalism sometimes seems more like the European type than any of the other examples of local power to be found around the world at different times.

The Institution of the Shogun

In the twelfth century Japan was disrupted by a series of civil wars between two of the most powerful families, the Taira and the Minamoto, both claiming remote descent from the imperial family. In similar circumstances the Chinese would have concluded that the Emperor had lost the mandate of heaven and he would have been replaced. This option was not attractive to the Japanese. The emperor did not merely have the mandate of heaven; as a descendent of the Sun Goddess he was himself divine. He might be forced to resign but only to be replaced by another member of the

Sun family. Minamoto Yoritomo, who emerged victorious in the civil wars in 1185, therefore devised a typical Japanese solution. He left the Emperor undisturbed in Kyoto and, using the title of shogun (generalissimo) set up an alternative, military administration – the bakafu or camp government – based on his retainers and centred on his own capital at Kamakura. Titles and honours remained with the court nobility at Kyoto but power was exercised from Kamakura. How suited this type of solution was to the Japanese ethos was strikingly demonstrated after Yoritomo's death. A suspicious man, he had done away with his close relatives and left only two young sons. By 1205, the Kamakura regime was controlled by the family of his leading retainers, the Hojo – ironically, turncoat relatives of the Taira. The Hojo used the title of shikken (regent) – not for the Emperor but for the Shogun. Even when the Minamoto line came to an early end in a welter of fratricide and murder, the shikken did not assume the title of shogun. Instead, they used imperial princes to fill this now purely nominal position.

One retired emperor, Go-Toba, was not content to accept this situation but the Kamakura army quickly subdued his troops; even then, the recalcitrant emperor was not killed but simply exiled. By this time the retired emperor was so much a part of the system that the Hojo appointed a brother of the exile as retired emperor, even though he had never reigned as emperor. This, however, was all fiction; Hojo deputies in Kyoto controlled the imperial court and access to it; the shikken confiscated lands from the court nobility and even the imperial family to reward their followers.

The resilience of this complex system was demonstrated when the Japanese saw off two attempts at invasion by the Mongol Emperor of China in 1274 and 1281 – helped by a hurricane which they decided was a divine wind or kamikaze, the word applied to suicide air attacks in the Second World War. The Japanese were, however, under no illusions about Mongol power and the country remained on a war footing for twenty years. This mobilization imposed great costs on the military families – costs obviously not off-set by booty – and the Kamikura regime proved unable to contain their discontent. The weakness of the Japanese adaptation of monarchy became apparent; the locus of power was hereditary and the shikken were no more able to rise above the iron law of dynastic decay than a hereditary monarch.

Profiting by the widespread dissatisfaction, the Emperor Go-Daigo in 1331 attempted to re-assert imperial control. Unfortunately the general on whom he relied, Ashikaga Takauji, seized Kyoto, appointed another member of the royal family as Emperor and proclaimed himself Shogun. Go-Daigo fled with his supporters and for the next half century Japan had two lines of emperors.

The Ashikaga shoguns survived at Kyoto until 1573 but they were never able to establish control of more than a fraction of the country. Central government broke down and the country was controlled by a changing kaleidoscope of daimyo who at this time are best described as warlords. As they fought one another incessantly, they took to supplementing their mounted samurai with levies of peasant foot soldiers. The rigid class stratification of earlier centuries showed signs of breaking down and peasant revolts became common.

The Tokugawa Shogunate

Order was eventually imposed by a succession of three ruthless warlords. Oda Nobunaga, a local lord called in by the Emperor to restore order in Kyoto, extended his authority over half the country. On his assassination in 1582, Hideyoshi, a general of humble origins, seized power and extended his authority over the rest of the country. His humble origins did not incline him to look with favor on the growth of peasant soldiers; in a famous 'sword hunt' he initiated the disarming of the peasantry.

Being careful to observe feudal forms, Hideyoshi managed to keep the support of the warlords and mobilized them for an attack on Korea, intended as a prelude to the conquest of China. The invasions failed and Hideyoshi died in 1598. His leading vassal, Tokugawa Ieyasu – who had managed to stay out of the Korean campaigns – set aside Hideyoshi's infant son and made good his claim to rule in the great battle of Sekigahara. In 1603 he claimed the title of Shogun and established his government in a new castle at Edo, the nucleus of modern Tokyo.

Ieyasu, a cautious and calculating man, was determined to bring an end to endemic civil war and to keep his family in power as Shoguns. The Tokugawa family directly controlled a third of Japan's arable riceland and their supporters at Sekigahara about a quarter. The remainder was in the hands of families which had been their enemies; these 'outside vassals' were always regarded with some suspicion and it was, in fact, their retainers who took the lead in the eventual overthrow of the shogunate and the imperial 'restoration'. That, however, was more than two centuries in the future. Until then the system of control devised by Ieyasu and his early successors worked unfailingly.

The essence of that system was the obligation on the daimyo to spend every second year at court and to leave their families there as hostages in the alternative years; check points were erected on the roads out of Edo to ensure that families were not taken out, nor arms brought in. A secret police system was also set up. Under these constraints, the great lords were allowed to retain their holdings and their samurai; but the independent and warring fiefs of previous centuries were transformed into local government units. Thus the Tokugawa made Japan into an orderly feudal state in which the ambitions of the great lords were concentrated on developing and exploiting the areas under their control. The samurai maintained their military traditions but, in fact, they were transformed into administrators and tax collectors.

Isolation and Development

In their pursuit of stability the Tokugawa rapidly came to regard foreign traders, who had appeared in Japanese ports from 1542, and Christian missionaries as disturbing influences. Christianity, which had won several hundred thousand converts, was eradicated by violent and systematic persecution; two centuries later missionaries discovered a few hundred peasants who had somehow kept their faith alive in secret. At the same time Japan was closed to foreign traders; from 1641 only the Chinese and the Dutch were allowed a very restricted trade at Nagasaki, where the Dutch were kept, like monkeys in a cage, on an artificial island in the harbour. Japanese were forbidden to go abroad and ship construction was restricted to small coasters, bringing to an abrupt end a large and expanding mercantile marine.

The Tokugawa regime was based on an accommodation with the great lords and their retainers and was designed for their benefit. The peasants, deprived of arms by Hideyoshi, were squeezed to support them and the merchants and artisans, in theory, existed to serve them. A revival of Confucianism provided a theoretical basis for this orderly, oppressive state. Later this was balanced by a revival of Shinto and the elaboration of the national myth of the Sun Goddess.

Whatever its defects, the Tokugawa regime gave Japan two great benefits:

First and foremost the Tokugawa brought Japan two centuries of internal and external peace – *the longest period of peace achieved by any country in recorded history.* With peace came prosperity. Rural production increased and rural industries developed. Merchants and artisans flourished, responding to the insatiable demand of the aristocracy who gradually found themselves in debt to ever more prosperous merchants. Financial institutions developed accordingly;

grain markets in Tokyo and Osaka speculated in futures. The great trading houses so prominent in the modern Japanese economy, originated at this time; the Mitsui, who began as brewers in 1620, were bankers to the court and shogun by 1691. By the middle of the eighteenth century, Japan's population had reached thirty million and Tokyo had a million inhabitants, Kyoto and Osaka each half a million. In these great cities a new, more popular type of culture developed, originally to meet the interests of the merchant class but soon attracting the samurai also.

Most important of all, Japan achieved – in its fiendishly difficult combination of Japanese and Chinese scripts – one of the highest rates of literacy in the world; by the time of the 'restoration' 40 per cent of Japanese boys and 10 per cent of Japanese girls were enrolled in more than 11,000 schools. Many attempts have been made to explain the phenomenal success of the contemporary Japanese economy; few give sufficient weight to the long years of Tokugawa peace and development.

The other aspect of Tokugawa Japan which was to prove important for the future was the preservation of local centres of authority, and therefore of initiative. Ieyasu had devised a system of government which ensured peace and made the Shogun's will obeyed throughout. But he had not set out to create a centralized state. Two hundred and fifty great daimyo governed their lands as local potentates, administering justice, collecting taxes and promoting development. Each of them was served by his own samurai administrators, and most of them, whatever they might think of the lowly status of merchants, knew that their mini-states could not survive without the merchants' services and loans.

Thus, when the West burst on Japan in the nineteenth century, the country's response was not dependent solely on the hidebound and traditional central government and its bureaucrats. When they proved incapable of responding effectively, there were alternative and effective sources of power and of action.

Nor were the Japanese taken completely by surprise when Perry's ships showed the American flag in Tokyo bay; their voluntary isolation was by no means absolute. From the beginning they had carefully quizzed the Dutch for information on the outside world. In the eighteenth century they began to study European scientific works with interest and a few daring thinkers called for changes which would facilitate absorption of this new knowledge. By the nineteenth century the Japanese knew far more about Europe and the outside world than the Europeans knew about them.

Ironically, the Tokugawa system, which at first sight looked rigid and inflexible, had produced a society more capable of innovation and measured adjustment than any other in Asia.

CHAPTER EIGHT

BEYOND THE FRONTIERS

History is largely delimited by the availability of records. For this reason the story of humanity in ancient times is largely limited to the three great culture spheres: West Asia/Mediterranean, China and North India. Beyond their boundaries were people without writing or people whose written records have not survived. What little we know of these peoples depends largely on a few enquiring members of the major cultures, whose writings have survived, and on the work of archaeologists. In the Middle Ages a number of these peoples built civilized societies which have left some records; for others, however, we are still largely dependent on outside sources. One way or another, it becomes possible to write at least the outline of the history of the nomads of the Eurasian steppe, of the states which emerged in the Sahel, south of the Sahara, and of the development of advanced cultures in parts of America.

The Nomads of the Eurasian Steppe

Mesopotamia and the Iranian plateau are separated by a chain of by no means impassible mountains from the great steppe which runs for more than three thousand miles from Eastern Europe to Manchuria. When the sparse inhabitants of this vast area learned to ride on horseback, they had the essential mechanism for a pastoral culture which would survive until modern times. By the end of the second millennium BC, they had developed military tactics which made them a continuing menace to the civilized states to the south.

In the long run the impact of the nomads' military superiority was mitigated by their desire to enjoy the fruits of civilisation, not destroy it. The Persian empire was established by Iranians who had migrated forcefully from the north a few centuries before. The preservation of Iranian culture from Hellenization by the successors of Alexander was the work of the Parthians, a kindred people from Central Asia.

Such occasional positive outcomes, however, were no consolation to the villager confronted by a raiding band or the government facing invasion by one of the large federations which the internal dynamics of the steppe generated from time to time. The steppe bordered China, Iran and Europe; only a relatively short passage through the passes of Afghanistan separated it from India. All four had therefore to provide defence against the nomads; their history reflects their success or failure in this key endeavour and the ways in which they approached it. In turn the history of the nomads reflects the impact of the civilized states on them. This impact could operate at long range. Chinese success might persuade a tribe to move off westward, starting a cascade of violent displacement which would eventually result in an attack on Iranian, European or Indian borders. Conflict between tribes might have much the same result.

Throughout the whole of ancient history the steppes of South Russia and Central Asia were occupied by shifting cultures of Indo-European peoples. Further east, the Indo-Europeans gave way to Turkish and Mongol peoples of different origins but the same lifestyle.

The Nomad Impact

The Han Chinese marked the apogee of their power by crushing the H'siung Nu at the end of the first century BC. The defeated H'siung Nu moved off westwards and are often thought to be identical with the Huns who appeared on the fringes of Central Asia soon after. In the fourth century AD, provoked by the eastward expansion of the Ostrogoths, they pushed west and created an empire which extended from the Danube to the Caspian. Attila briefly extended their power to the Rhine and raided into Gaul and Italy. Defeated at Troyes by a mixed force of imperial troops and German allies, he died two years later. His death stimulated the German tribes subject to the Huns to revolt; they put an end to Hunnic dominance at the battle of the Nedao in 454.

Continuous pressure from the east, stimulated by tribal warfare, pushed a succession of nomad tribes across the Russian steppe. By the fifth century, when the Kushans gave way to the White Huns in central Asia, the last of the Indo-Europeans had vanished from the steppe – although the Tocharians remained isolated in Sin-Kiang – replaced by Turks and Mongols. Most of these also eventually disappeared from history, defeated by new and more savage tribes following in their tracks. A few had a major impact on the societies around them. Two, the Bulgars and the Magyars, established themselves in Europe and founded Christian states. The Seljuks led the incursion which eventually transformed Anatolia from the heartland of the Byzantine Empire into the core of a Turkish, Moslem state. Other Turks played a key role in establishing Moslem dominance in north India. Several times Mongol or Turkish tribes established their dominance over north China; two groups, the Mongols and the Manchus conquered all China.

Before the end of the sixth century the Turks had established their dominion from the Aral Sea to the Chinese border. In the next century the Khazars extended Turkish domination over what is now southern Russia. They were succeeded by other Turkish tribes, the Patzinaks and the Cumans. The quarreling Russian principalities never managed to take control of the steppe and consequently found communication with Byzantium difficult and dangerous.

The Turks and Western Asia

The alternative to the Russian steppe for a people pushed towards the west was to turn south into central Asia. With great cities and substantial irrigation areas, central Asia was a prize worth having. Its main disadvantage was that it was not separated from the steppe by any natural, defensible frontier. Before long its latest masters, softened by civilisation, would be subject to attack by a new wave of nomads. At this point the area's second advantage became a tempting option. It was a natural corridor to Iran and beyond that, to Iraq in one direction and to India in the other.

The decline of the Baghdad Caliphate and the weakness of the successor states provided an opportunity for the nomads. A Turkish mercenary general seized control of central Asia in 999 and established the Ghaznavid emirate. From his capital at Ghazni in modern Afghanistan, Mahmud Ghazni devoted himself to raiding India with a combination of nomad ferocity and the fanaticism of recent conversion to Islam. Some of the spoils were used to enrich Ghazni with a Moslem university and libraries and to attract famous scholars.

By 1030 the Ghaznavids had been replaced in central Asia by the Seljuks. Drawing on the manpower behind them on the steppes, the Seljuks extended their power over Iran and Iraq. Their defeat of the Byzantines at Manzikert in 1071 marks the beginning of the decline of the Eastern Empire.

The Mongol Empire

The next great irruption of the steppe peoples was led, not by Turks, but by Mongols. The quarreling tribes, probably numbering less than a million in all, were unified by Genghiz Khan about the end of the twelfth century. Genghiz seems to have believed that he had a mission, given by the Mongol sky-god Tengri, to conquer the world. Like the Chinese Son of Heaven, the Mongol Khan acknowledged no equal; the only possible relationship with him was one of submission and obedience. This ideology was backed by a hardy cavalry, effective strategy and tactics and a policy of punishing resistance with extermination. Baghdad, Kiev, Samarkand and Bokhara were just a few of the great cities destroyed and depopulated. The conquest of China, bitterly resisted over many years, reduced the population by as much as a third.

Those who preferred submission to extermination were subject to tribute payments and military service. As the latter meant an opportunity to share in the spoils of the greatest conqueror the steppe had ever known, submission could be an attractive option for other nomads; Mongol forces soon came to include sizeable contingents of Turks.

On this basis Genghis and his successors spread Mongol power from China to Russia and over Iran and Mesopotamia. Over this vast area the writ of the Great Khan was theoretically supreme and enforced in subordinate Khanates by his brothers and cousins. In fact, the quarrels and conflicts of the Khanates relieved the pressure on neighbouring countries. By 1260 when Kubilai, grandson of Genghis, became Great Khan the position was largely nominal. When Kubilai died in 1294 it was allowed to lapse.

A brief account of the Mongol conquests is apt to give the impression of a series of sudden and unresisted invasions leading to the rapid construction of a great empire. In fact it was not quite as quick as that. The achievement of Ghengis himself was to integrate the steppe peoples, from the Caspian to the Sea of Japan, under Mongol leadership. This was a great achievement and it laid the basis for the triumphs of his successors. But it took nearly thirty years. When Genghis died in 1227 the Mongols had raided many of the civilized lands around them but their power only extended a little beyond the steppe, in Central Asia and the north west of China. It took another thirty years for this power to be extended over Russia, Persia and Mesopotamia. The conquest of Sung China only began in 1258 and took until 1279.

In West Asia, Mongol expansion came to an end when the conquest of Sung China had barely begun. As the Mongols pressed on through Syria, they were confronted by the Mamelukes. These slave soldiers had recently seized power in Egypt and elevated one of their number to be Sultan. In 1260 a Mameluke army under Baibars defeated the Mongols at Ain Jalut in Palestine and put an end to their advance.

The failure to install a successor to Kubilai as Great Khan meant the end of any semblance of a united Mongol empire. For a short time the Mongols had established something like a single state ruling effectively from the Black Sea to the Sea of Japan, a span of well over three thousand miles. Traders, such as the Venetian Polo family, and missionaries such as Carpino, seized the opportunity which this regime provided. The Mongol court entertained Nestorian Christians as well as Catholic missionaries from Christendom, Moslems and Buddhists – all intent on converting the new masters of the world. Their efforts demonstrated the potential apparent in the new nomad state. So did the flourishing of trade between Europe and China, protected by the Mongol regime. If that regime had held together, with its central position and its military superiority, it might have become the link and the hegemon of an Asiatic-European world order.

In fact, however, the nomad society from which the Mongol domination had sprung lacked the structures to make a continued hegemony possible. Determined not to be absorbed by the Chinese, the Mongols used foreign adventurers to supplement their own meagre manpower in controlling and governing the country. Their rule was never accepted and Kubilai's successors were forced out of China by 1368. The Il-Khans in Persia, after dabbling with Nestorian Christianity, accepted Islam and were gradually absorbed. Only on the steppe was the traditional way of life largely preserved. The Golden Horde preserved their domination of Russia until 1480; thereafter superior military technology ensured Russian superiority. Between them, Russia and China put an end to the menace of the steppe nomads.

Sub-Saharan Africa

The Arabian peninsula, largely desert with a few oases and some sparse pastureland on its northern and western fringes, was the source of the series of Semitic peoples who periodically infiltrated the Mesopotamian states. Around the beginning of the first millennium BC the fertile south eastern corner began to be organised in small states which developed irrigation and traded with the more advanced states of Western Asia. The Queen of Sheba was ruler of one of these states; her visit to King Solomon may have been motivated by concern for her trade routes to Phoenicia, on which Israel had a stranglehold.

The origin of the kingdom of Axum – the beginnings of Ethiopia – is traced to the movement of some of these people to the opposite shore of the Red Sea. Its port of Adulis played an important role in the Red Sea trade of the Roman Empire and its connection with India. Converted to Christianity in the fourth century, Axum developed a distinctive culture which has survived into the twentieth century.

Before the arrival of Islam, the Ethiopians had started to spread over the adjacent highlands; these provided a bastion in which they maintained their state and their idiosyncratic version of Christianity. The capital was shifted from Axum to Lasta, where great churches were hollowed out of the rock, and again further south to the province of Shoa. The move to Lasta marked the domination of the Amhara tribes, in which the original Semitic speaking Ethiopians were amalgamated with the Hamitic speaking Agau. The distinction seems to have been relatively unimportant for centuries but in the twentieth century it became an important element in a bloody civil war.

Largely cut off from other Christian states by the surrounding Islamic world, the Ethiopian kings struggled to maintain their independence and to keep control of their country against the fissiparous tendencies of great feudal lords and the obstacles of a difficult terrain. Its original Semitic inheritance, its Christian religion and its developed, feudal state structure marked Ethiopia off from the African people around it. In Ethiopian eyes they were objects of conquest or slave raiding, rather than missionary endeavour or trading relations. Consequently Ethiopia remained an anomaly in Africa, not a source of spreading influence, until the twentieth century.

Kush and the Christian States of East Africa

In 750 BC the border state of Kush, on the southern frontier, had been strong enough to conquer Egypt itself. Driven out of Egypt by the Assyrians in 633 BC Kush maintained its independence and shifted its capital to Meroe, not far from modern Khartoum. Massive slag heaps testify to an iron industry and, according to one scholar, indicate the use of half a million tons of hardwood fuel; perhaps the desert which now surrounds Khartoum is testimony to ecological devastation.

In the fourth century AD, Meroe was weakened by a destructive raid from the neighbouring Kingdom of Axum and then overwhelmed by Nuba tribes from the desert. The Nuba created three successor states which were converted to Christianity in the sixth century. Cut off from mainstream Christianity by the Islamic conquest of Egypt, they maintained a valiant independence for many centuries. Excavation has uncovered two large cathedrals, one of them with many splendid frescoes and a list of twenty seven successive bishops. Christianity does not seem to have spread far south but at Darfur, hundreds of kilometres west of Khartoum, archaeologists have excavated the remains of a building which they think was a Christian monastery. The last of the Nubian kingdoms was only overthrown by the Islamic state of Sennar in 1504.

The Sahelian Cultures

The Sahara was not quite impassable, even before the introduction of the camel in the last few centuries BC, and Saharan oases had been occupied for millennia. The mountains of the Sahara had both iron ore and fuel and evidence of iron working have been found there. It may have been across the Sahara, therefore, that iron working reached the Sahelian zone to the south, although the African smiths had a distinctive technique for producing the high temperatures required. At all events, well before the beginning of the Christian era iron was worked in southern Mauretania and northern Nigeria as well as in parts of East Africa which it may have reached from Kush.

Associated with iron working, and perhaps partly dependent on it, was the emergence first of village clusters and then of cities in the Sahel. Village clusters dating back to the middle of the first millennium BC have been identified in southern Mauretania. Before the beginning of the Christian era, small towns began to appear in the inland delta of the Niger.

The early towns were largely centres used by the cultivators of the surrounding land, with some artisans working in metal and pottery. Endemic warfare created a need for leadership and the ambitions of some of these leaders led to the creation, from time to time, of larger polities, seeking to extract tribute from other towns and impose dues on trade networks. For the most part, existing ruling families were left in control of each town and kept in order by a mixture of intermarriage and hostage taking.

Under these conditions three Sahelian states created successive empires. Ghana, which seems to have originated in the western Sahel around 400 AD, lasted until the eleventh century, when its capital was seized by the same Berber Almoravids who took over Islamic Spain and stemmed the Christian reconquest – a valuable reminder that West Africa was not nearly as isolated as our lack of sources used to make us assume.

The arrival of the camel in North Africa had, in fact, transformed the Sahara into a network of established trade routes along which gold and ivory moved north and textiles, beads, precious stones and luxury goods moved south. A camel could carry nearly a quarter of a ton and caravans of a thousand to two thousand camels were common by the twelfth century, if not earlier. Even larger caravans carried salt from the mines of the desert oases to the towns of the Sahel. The mines and the camel trade were alike controlled by the Sanhaja and Tuareg Berbers of the Sahara.

Along these trade routes Islam came to the Sahel and strengthened the area's links with the wider world to the north and east. Ghana showed it signs of favor. The founders of the next empire, Mali, were Islamic and under their aegis the Sahel became an integral part of the Islamic world. Several Mali emperors made the pilgrimage to Mecca; Mansa Musa (1312–1337) spent his gold so lavishly as he passed through Cairo that he destroyed the price structure there for a year. He brought back scholars and architects; Timbuktu began to acquire brick buildings and to become a centre of Islamic learning. Mali also used its wealth to acquire large horses and suits of armour from North Africa, introducing into West Africa the military style of the European middle ages. It survived, to the amazement of European explorers, into the nineteenth century.

A generation after Mansa Musa's death, a Jewish cartographer in Majorca was delineating his empire on a map intended for use in Christian Europe – another indication of the role of the Sahara and its caravans as a linkage, not a barrier.

By the end of the fourteenth century Mali had begun to disintegrate. It was replaced by a new power based on the Soninke people. Songhai worked in close alliance with the Tuareg of the desert. Drawing on its Islamic linkages, it developed a literate bureaucracy and a system of residents or governors, rather than relying on local potentates. Its power streched from Timbuktu to northern Nigeria and ran far north into the Saharan oases. To the East it bordered on the empire of Kanem around Lake Chad, likewise Islamic and organised by a literate power group.

Around the great empires and threatened by their expansion were numerous smaller states which tended to imitate, as far as possible, their power structures and feed their trade. One of the prime items of trade was the kola nut, an addictive stimulant prized all over West Africa and reputed to be an aphrodisiac; not having been known to the Prophet, it had the additional advantage of not being forbidden by Islam.

Even more important than the kola nut were gold and slaves. From their inception, warring African states, like most states at a similar stage of development, enslaved their captives and used them as cultivators and house slaves. Their dependent, rootless situation made them suitable for the service of ambitious rulers and slave armies developed even before the arrival of Islam.

Slavery therefore became an established institution in West Africa and spread out from the Sahel with other aspects of its culture. Islam re-inforced the established practice; it regarded war with pagans as a religious duty and their enslavement as perfectly proper. When the horses and armour imported from the north gave them a military advantage, the states and empires of the Sahel developed a tradition of regular slave raids on the pagans to the south. Many of the victims found their unfortunate way to the salt mines of the Sahara; a few were transported right across the Sahara and sold in North Africa. Here some of them became the backbone of the military forces in several Moslem states.

Bantu Expansion

South of the Sahel, a slower but more enduring process of development was going on. Starting about the beginning of the

Christian era, Bantu speaking people began a slow expansion from their original homeland in West Africa – probably eastern Nigeria and Cameroon – which eventually led them to settle virtually all of Africa to the south. As they advanced, they drove out or absorbed the Khoisan peoples, hunters and gatherers, some of whom may have begun to keep cattle and sheep. The last distinctive representatives of the Khoisan are the Bushmen of the Kalahari Desert in South Africa and probably the pygmies of the Congo forests. Iron tools to clear the forests were almost certainly one of the keys to the early Bantu expansion and those who settled in the forest areas remained agriculturalists with some fishing and hunting.

Those who spread to East Africa, however, acquired cattle from the people further north. Here some of those who settled eventually came under the dominion of Nilo-Saharan invaders from further north; the recent traumatic explosion of violence in Rwanda is a delayed consequence. Other Bantu cattle herders spread south, probably reaching Zimbabwe and crossing the Limpopo into South Africa sometime during the first millennium. Although cattle were important in their society, they were not pastoral nomads; agriculture provided the basis of subsistence, with cattle merely a source of prestige and, perhaps, a form of investment to be utilized to meet special needs.

The Bantu were organised mainly in warring mini-states; European explorers and settlers in the nineteenth century were inclined to call these tribes but many of them were agglomerations resulting from war and amalgamation, rather than people of common ancestry. Larger groupings began to emerge in some parts as ambitious leaders followed the path of conquest.

State formation in East Africa was stimulated by the development of Arab trading cities on the coast, seeking gold and ivory for export in return for luxury goods. The Arabs merged with the local Swahili speaking population to create the lingua franca of eastern Africa and to bring it tenuously into the trading system of the Indian ocean –

tenuously because behind the coastal cities was the zone of the tsetse fly, in which no beast of burden could survive. Trade was therefore limited to luxury goods which could be carried by human porters.

By the thirteenth century Great Zimbabwe – in the area of the modern state which has adopted its name – had established a flourishing gold trade in the south. Its capital grew into a town of ten to twenty thousand people, adorned with stone buildings whose rude grandeur amazed the first Europeans to see their ruins. In the fifteenth century it lost power to a Shona dynasty further north, the Mwenemutapa, whose wealth and power would impress the invading Portuguese a century later.

Africa on the eve of the European expansion had therefore its own dynamic and a set of distinctive cultures which had some possibilities of positive development. Its sheer mass, and the difficulties of communication between the coasts and the inland, would ensure its independent survival until nineteenth century technology gave the Europeans – and the Arabs – a power which the fragile, warring societies of the interior could not resist.

Archaic Civilisation in America

By 10000 BC or earlier human beings crossed into Alaska from Asia and gradually spread throughout the continent. Cultural differentiation in very different environments, rather than successive waves of immigration, seems to account for the many variations which developed among the American Indian population.

The original hunters and gatherers in southern Mexico and Guatemala domesticated maize before 2700 BC; from here it spread north and south for thousands of kilometres.

Settled farming communities in some areas gradually developed more complex social structures and long distance trading relationships. In Central America, dynastic elites began to unify significant areas and undertake substantial public buildings. Around

Vera Cruz on the Gulf of Mexico, the Olmecs developed a culture with stone sculptures, elaborate calendars and hieroglyphs. The Olmec culture flourished in the early part of the first millennium BC, making it the earliest in Central America known to us; it may well have been the source from which many later developments drew inspiration.

By the end of the first millennium BC Monte Alban in southern Mexico had grown into a densely settled, terraced area with a highly organized population. The Maya people in Guatemala were already building massive pyramids, plazas and causeways and articulating notions of divine kingship on which a complex culture would develop. Somewhat similar developments can be traced in Peru where huge stone ceremonial buildings were erected by the labour of people from dozens of scattered villages as early as 2600 BC.

States in Mexico, Central America and Peru

Amerindian development was therefore following, much later, the same pattern as that of Western Asia and would lead, before long, to the growth of states and empires of a distinctive Amerindian style. It lacked metal smelting, the wheel and the plough but these constraints did not prevent the development of higher cultures. Like the early civilisations in the Old World, these were based on the domination of village agriculturalists by an elite of governing nobles and priests and usually a royal family claiming special relations with the gods.

Great population complexes and political entities that can be called states began to appear in Mexico, Central America and Peru around about the beginning of the Christian era. Ceremonial sites, with temples and pyramids, gradually attracted resident populations and developed into towns and even cities. A major part of the large populations attributed to the greatest of them, however, seems to have been mainly engaged in agriculture to support the elite of nobles and priests and the artisans who produced luxury goods for this elite. Gradually the religious buildings were complemented by the palaces of rulers.

By AD 250 the Maya people in the Yucatan and Guatemala developed great ceremonial centres on sites hacked out of the jungle. Mayan culture was pre-occupied with the cycles of time and developed extraordinarily accurate calendars and an ability to predict eclipses. It also discovered the use of the zero, the only culture apart from India – whence it spread to Europe and Asia – to do so. Mayan rulers decorated the walls of their palaces and temples with elaborate carvings, including hieroglyphs which have recently been deciphered. The picture which emerges shows a society of warring city states, reminiscent in this respect of Sumer, in which one city or another might achieve a limited hegemony for a time – supported by a mixture of conquest and royal marriages – but a unified Maya state never emerged. Much of the art and inscriptions illustrate warfare in which the capture of prisoners and their sacrifice to the victor's gods plays a large part.

This extraordinary culture collapsed about AD 900. The ceremonial sites were deserted, the elites disappeared and the peasantry went on with their basic agriculture. Invasion may have been part of the cause but does not seem the major factor in what, despite many theories, remains the inexplicable death of a high culture. In northern Yucatan, a basically Maya state continued, but possibly under the domination of Toltec invaders from central Mexico, until the fifteenth century. Then it too collapsed; in the next century the Spaniards found only petty chiefs in Yucatan.

In the Valley of Mexico a substantial state emerged by AD 500 centred on the city of Teotihuacan, north east of Mexico City. Teotihuacan at its peak had an estimated population of 200,000 in an area of eight square miles. It was a centre of trade, dominating other city states in central Mexico and probably living in uneasy relations with the rulers of Monte Alban in the distant Oaxaca valley. It was destroyed in AD 650 and no comparable power seems to have replaced it. Toltec invaders from the north established their supremacy until they in turn were overthrown by another wave of invaders, the Chichimecs.

Out of the disorder which followed one of the Chichimec groups, the Aztecs, gradually established their supremacy. From their centre at Tenochtitlan the Aztecs dominated an uneasy empire of city states and tribes stretching from the Atlantic to the Pacific and as far south as Guatemala. Aztec domination, like the Assyrian Empire, was based on military ferocity and the institutionalisation of terror but it had its own peculiar mechanism. No Amerindian civilisation seems to have completely outgrown human sacrifice – as Old World civilisations did – but the Aztecs developed it into the dominant characteristic of their state and society. Their gods demanded literally constant sacrifices of hearts torn from the living bodies of sacrificial victims – without them the sun would die. Aztec warfare was therefore directed primarily to the capture of prisoners and there is even a suspicion that the rebellion of subject states was welcomed – and, one wonders, provoked – to ensure an adequate supply of victims. As many as twenty thousand victims a year may have been sacrificed. Not surprisingly, when Aztec power was challenged by a handful of invading Spaniards, it found little support among the subject peoples.

By the beginning of the Christian era, the first known state in South America developed in the small valleys along the northern coast of Peru. Archaeology suggests that the Moche state, based on extensive irrigation in the valleys was socially stratified and eventually extended over most of the northern coast. Moche craftsmen produced beautiful textiles – preserved in the dry heat of the Peruvian desert – and annealed metalwork. By AD 600 the Moche area and most of the Peruvian coast had fallen under the control of an imperial state based at Wari in the southern highlands. Wari disappeared before the end of the first millennium. Along the northern coast its place was taken by the Chimu who amplified the irrigation schemes to embrace larger areas and carry water over great distances. Inland, a centre of civilisation developed around Lake Titicaca and eventually grew into the empire of Tiwanaku, extending as far as the coast and into northern Chile. This empire dissolved about AD 1200.

The fifteenth century saw the Incas around Cuzco begin their extraordinary career of conquest and integration. Before the end of the century they were masters of all Peru and were extending their empire into the surrounding areas. Their empire was highly organised, with a network of roads and resthouses, messengers, provincial governors and even inspectors. Lacking any form of script, the Incas developed a system of knotted strings, quipu, for keeping records. With a population of perhaps five million the Inca empire was possibly the most closely administered of all the archaic states known to us; at the centre, however, it failed to solve the succession problem. This, together, with its very centralization, helped to make it an easy prey for the small band of Spanish adventurers who descended on it in 1532.

By the time the Old World broke in on the New, Amerindian civilisation had reached a stage of development in government and society, art and culture, roughly parallel to that achieved in West Asia in the third millennium BC. Around the higher cultures other peoples were organized in both tribes and what may best be described as barbarian kingdoms. A large part of the continent, however, was still occupied by hunter gatherers or slash and burn agriculturalists at an early stage of development.

Beyond doubt Amerindian society had potential for further development, although the direction that development might have taken is necessarily unknown. Its technology was insufficiently advanced, and its structures too fragile, to survive the European onset, even without the drastic impact of the Old World diseases against which the Amerindians had no immunity.

Australia and the Pacific

Human settlement in Australia goes back at least 40000 years. The hunting and gathering culture, well adapted to its environment, proved stable but conservative. It was virtually unchanged when European settlement began in the late eighteenth century.

By contrast New Guinea shows traces of forest clearance and root culture as early as 7000 or 6000 BC. Long distance, open water trading began in the New Guinea and adjacent islands as early as the third millennium BC. With the development of the double hulled canoe, settlement and trade spread as far as Fiji.

Navigation skills were at least the equal of boat building. Well before the beginning of the Christian era, a small group of Polynesians ventured further west and settled Tonga; by 300 BC their descendants had settled in Samoa. A distinctive Polynesian culture developed and eventually spread from Hawaii to New Zealand.

The Finns in the Far North

North of the steppe in the forests of northern Russia a vast area was originally occupied by Finnish hunters and trappers. Destined to be largely absorbed, in medieval and early modern times, by the Russians, they play little part in history until two remnants succeeded in forming the nation states of Finland and Estonia in the twentieth century. Other hunters and trappers in northern Siberia survive in small numbers as recognized nationalities in the Russian federation.

Chapter Nine

THE RISE OF THE WEST

In 1500 the impact of the Spanish and Portuguese discoveries on Europe lay in the future. Only the most perceptive of contemporaries would have seen that they might ultimately be more important than events nearer home which were obviously transforming the political landscape of Europe. In 1453 the Ottoman Turks entered Constantinople; their frontier was already on the Danube so the event was mainly of symbolic significance. Europe could clearly see the threat but it was incapable of uniting to meet it. By 1529 the Turks had overthrown Hungary and were besieging Vienna.

The Rise of the Hapsburgs

Meanwhile the continuing marriage diplomacy of the Hapsburgs had brought into being a countervailing empire in the West. Charles V united in his person the crowns, royal or ducal, of Spain, Naples and Sicily, the Netherlands, Austria and Bohemia; in 1519 he was elected Holy Roman Emperor. God, thought his grand-chancellor, the Piedmontese humanist Gattinara, had set the young Emperor on the road to the monarchy of the world. France, almost surrounded by the Hapsburg agglomeration, did not see in it the hand of God; conflict between the two was to be a leading theme of European political history for the next two centuries. The complete dissolution of the concept of Christendom, already eroded by the rise of national states, was marked by the conclusion of an alliance between France and the Turks.

Luther and the Beginnings of the Reformation

Any hope Charles may have had of mobilizing at least the German principalities for a sixteenth century crusade was shattered by Martin Luther.

Luther, a German friar and professor of theology, was outraged by a particularly crass papal fund-raising campaign, in which indulgences (remission of the punishment due to sin) were offered in return for donations. The proceeds were to be divided between the Archbishop of Mainz – who needed the money to pay for papal endorsement of his appointment – and the construction of the new St.Peter's in Rome. In 1517 Luther challenged the notion of indulgences by posting 95 theses on the door of a church in Wittenberg. His theses struck a chord with both the piety and the nationalism of many Germans, resentful alike of the materialism of higher churchmen and the flow of German money to Rome; the protection of the Elector of Saxony prevented his arrest and trial for heresy. By 1519 he had moved to a challenge to papal primacy, by 1520 to much of established religious belief. The printing press ensured the rapid dissemination of his ideas; Luther's command of the German language, his ability to articulate the feelings of Germans resentful of Roman exploitation and, it has to be said, his gift of vituperation ensured their widespread acceptance. Almost certainly without having planned it, he found himself at the centre of a movement for the reform of the Church.

Clearly this movement had to be given form and shape. Luther, compared to Calvin and some of the other reformers, was very much a late medieval man. Having dethroned the pope, he naturally turned to the princes; it was their sacred duty, like a medieval monarch, to reform the Church and to ensure that it stayed reformed – in fact to control it. Most of the German princes found this proposition irresistible, especially when it became clear that reform meant the dissolution of the monasteries, the confiscation of their lands and even the annexation of neighbouring bishoprics. By 1529 a number of significant princes and cities in Germany were united in supporting reforms of the sort called for by Luther ; their protest at the attempt in the Reichstag to restrain the spread of the reform gave rise to the word Protestant. Within a short period most of Germany north of Bavaria was Protestant. So too were Denmark and Sweden.

The Spread of the Reformation

In England, Henry VIII, originally a champion of the papacy, changed his mind when the pope would not grant him a divorce from his wife Catherine. (The pope may have been influenced by the fact that Catherine was the aunt of Charles V and the Emperor's troops were occupying Rome). Henry proclaimed himself Supreme Head of the English Church and appointed as Archbishop of Canterbury Thomas Cranmer who obligingly granted the divorce. Henry also found it convenient to dissolve the monasteries and seize their property but tended to resist changes in ritual and doctrine; only after his death in 1547, and a brief Catholic restoration under his daughter Mary (1553–1558), did England become aligned with the Protestant cause. Even then, Mary's half-sister Elizabeth did her best to keep England at peace with the Catholic powers, notably Spain. Her failure to restrain Drake and other adventurers from plundering forays in Spanish America eventually provoked Phillip II into an attempt to conquer England. The ignominious defeat of the Great Armada signified the rise of England to the position of a first rank maritime power.

Luther's break with Rome was rapidly followed by other, different and more radical teachers. The reformers were united in opposition to the established church and in the conviction that it should be reformed in the light of Scripture. Beyond that, however, they found great difficulty in reaching agreement. Some, like Munzer and the

Anabaptists, became identified with peasant uprisings which were rapidly and bloodily suppressed. Others gradually coalesced around the teachings of John Calvin whose dour regime made Geneva the model and power-house for attempts to convert France and the Netherlands.

In Germany the weakness of imperial power, and the impossibility of controlling either princes or cities, was clear by 1555. The Peace of Augsburg adopted the principle later described as 'cuius regio eius religio' – the prince or the city authorities would determine whether a jurisdiction was Catholic or Lutheran. The compromise satisfied no one – least of all the Calvinists who were left out entirely – but it gave Germany half a century of peace. In 1573 the Polish nobility forced their monarch to accept that they had a similar power on their estates. Even the Hapsburgs found themselves obliged to tolerate the growing Protestantism of the nobility in Austria and Bohemia.

Essentially, therefore, the initial spread of the Reformation was accomplished by enlisting the support of the secular power, royal, princely, civic or aristocratic. Where that power was resolute in supporting the established Church, as in Spain and Italy, the Reformation made no progress and individual reformers fled to more hospitable jurisdictions, or those that seemed such; Servetus escaped the Spanish Inquisition only to be burnt as a heretic in Calvin's Geneva. Where civil power was vacillating or inadequate, the result might be civil war.

In France Protestant, largely Calvinist inspired, churches were organized widely in the south after 1555. Their support came largely from the bourgeoisie and the nobility; they soon came to dominate many towns and even whole provinces where they rarely allowed freedom of worship to Catholics. When their right to organize was threatened by the Crown they resorted to force. Between 1562 and 1593 France was wracked by a succession of civil wars which the last feeble kings of the Valois monarchy were powerless to control. The death of the last Valois king made the Protestant leader Henry of Bourbon the legitimate claimant to the throne. Paris and the Catholic nobility refused to accept him and made an alliance with the King of Spain. At this point Henry decided that 'Paris is worth a Mass' and announced his conversion to Catholicism. Henry's conversion ended the wars and restored peace and unity. His Edict of Nantes in 1598 guaranteed toleration for the Huguenots by making them virtually a state within a state – they garrisoned a hundred small towns at royal expense. The compromise worked for Henry's reign; inevitably it was upset when his successors felt strong enough.

More bitter and prolonged was the strife which broke out in the Netherlands. The government of Charles V burnt some 2000 heretics in thirty years. Most of them were Anabaptists whom everyone else regarded as a social menace. Charles had been born and grown to manhood in the Netherlands; he understood how far he could go. His son and successor, Philip II, was a Spaniard and determined to use Spanish power to make the Netherlands conform. His heavy hand provoked the Protestants to armed resistance under the leadership of William of Orange. They became dominant in the north which in 1581 proclaimed its independence as the United Provinces, the future Kingdom of the Netherlands. The southern provinces, the future Belgium, remained Catholic and, after much hesitation, accepted Spanish domination as the price of preserving their religion.

The war continued until 1609 when a twelve year truce was negotiated. When a final peace was agreed in 1648, Spain had spent more than 200 million ducats as compared with 120 million derived from its American empire. The United Provinces, which had the strongest merchant marine in Europe when the conflict began, profited from the war and Spanish prizes. By 1609 the Dutch were already bidding to replace the Portuguese in the domination of the Indian Ocean.

The Reaction of Church Authority

The initial rapid spread of the Reformation was unprecedented; nothing like it had ever happened in the millennium and a half since the beginnings of the Christian Church. Not unnaturally, Church authority was left floundering as to how to deal with this challenge. Many who did not follow the Reformers were nevertheless sympathetic to demands for the reform of acknowledged abuses within the Church – when Pope Paul III appointed a commission of Cardinals to examine abuses, their criticisms were hardly less stringent than those of the Protestant Reformers.

Pressure from Charles V, searching in vain for ways to preserve the religious unity of the Empire, finally induced the Pope, in 1542, to call a Council at Trent and the reformers were persuaded to attend its second session in 1551–52. But compromise seemed a dirty word to both sides. The Council of Trent formulated a Catholic position and gave impetus to an internal reform of the Church, a Catholic or Counter Reformation. Henceforth Catholic and Protestant defined themselves over against one another; it is only in our own generation that they have begun to think that the things that unite them might be more important than the things that divide them.

The Council's decrees became the programme for the internal reform of the Church. The foundations of the Catholic or Counter Reformation can indeed be traced to origins before Luther but the need felt to resist the spread of Protestantism gave post-Tridentine Catholicism a disciplined and militant orientation quite different from the medieval Church. A new congregation, the Holy Office of the Inquisition, was set up to pursue heresy and heretics; an Index of Forbidden Books listed works which Catholics were forbidden to read without special permission.

More positive in approach was the new religious order of the Jesuits founded by the Spanish soldier, Ignatius of Loyola. The

Jesuits took a special vow of loyalty to the Pope and undertook a long and rigorous spiritual and intellectual training to prepare them to be the champions of resurgent Catholicism. They specialised in education, establishing schools and even universities of such excellence that the nobility and the wealthy unhesitatingly sent their sons there. It was largely thanks to their efforts that Poland, Austria and Bavaria eventually emerged as overwhelmingly Catholic and that Protestantism achieved only minority status in Hungary.

From Reformation to Enlightenment

In retrospect it is obvious that the unity of western Christendom was shattered beyond repair. Such an outcome was unthinkable at the time. Luther and the other reformers did not set out to divide the Church but to reform it all; the champions of the traditional Church were equally determined to suppress what they regarded as heresy. Men so convinced of their own cause did not hesitate to use force either to suppress change or to promote it. The result was persecution of Christian by Christian and a century of intermittent warfare waged in the name of religion – although secular motives were always present and became more predominant as time went on.

Fierce as the religious controversy was, it did not monopolize the attention of the educated. The same centuries which saw religious intolerance at its height also witnessed the first tentative beginnings of science as we understand it. In 1543, the Polish clergyman Copernicus published 'The Revolution of the Heavenly Orbs', suggesting that the earth moved around the sun, rather than the reverse. Copernicus' great leap of imagination only became generally accepted in the next century, after Galileo had used the new invention, the telescope, to see the surface of the moon and much else besides.

Galileo's writings brought him into conflict with the Inquisition and he was forced to recant his assertion that the earth moved round the sun. The Counter Reformation Church had embarked on a fateful course, condemning scientific propositions because they seemed contrary to a simplistic understanding of the Bible, an understanding which it would now condemn as fundamentalism. As it persisted in opposition to new ideas, the Church alienated many of the educated and was forced to rely on power structures to maintain its position; more and more it became a captive of the Catholic monarchs. In many cases the religious commitment of these monarchs was highly doubtful; they simply used the Church as an instrument of royal power.

In the eighteenth century the alienation of the educated produced its inevitable result; Christianity was seen by many as inconsistent with science and philosophy. Newton's Mathematical Principles of Natural Philosophy, published in 1687, seemed to explain the operation of the universe. Newton's conception of the universe lent itself to the idea of God as analogous to a watchmaker – he had made the universe and wound it up, so that there was no need for any further divine intervention. This vague deism became the dominant creed among educated Europeans who liked to consider themselves too 'enlightened' to be Christians. From this it was a short step to active hostility to the Christian churches and their established position in society. Before the end of the eighteenth century the majority of the intelligentsia had become essentially anti-Christian.

Typical of the age was the Encyclopaedia edited by Diderot and d'Alembert. This was not just a compendium of knowledge. It was also an instrument of propaganda which missed no opportunity to criticise Christianity and especially the Catholic Church. Like much of Enlightenment thinking, it was also critical of the existing order in the state although this did not extend to any action to address the gross inequalities of society. Nor did it prevent gross adulation of monarchs who presented themselves as enlightened and were a source of valuable patronage.

The greatest propagandist of all, Voltaire, devoted his life to virulent criticism of the Catholic Church; he died with all the consolations of religion in 1778. Hardly more than ten years later the French Revolution began to carry the ideas of the Enlightenment to their logical conclusion, destroying the established position of monarchs, aristocracy and Church.

Conflict in Europe

The sixteenth, seventeenth and eighteenth centuries were marked by almost continuous warfare between the European powers. In Western Europe the long struggle between Hapsburg Spain and Austria and Valois, later Bourbon, France dominated the sixteenth and a large part of the seventeenth century; it was, at least as much as religion, the basic dynamic of the Thirty Years War (1618–1648). That war devastated much of Germany, destroyed the last Hapsburg attempt to make the Holy Roman Empire a reality and ended with France once more the predominant power in Europe.

Louis XIV set himself to capitalise on this predominance by encroaching on the border territories of the moribund Holy Roman Empire. The prospect of French hegemony soon induced a resistance headed by the Dutch and, after 1688 when William of Orange became King of England, the British. They were successful in containing Louis' ambitions but, when the Spanish Hapsburgs failed to produce a direct heir, they had to accept the installation of a Bourbon on the Spanish throne in 1714. Thereafter, France and Spain were usually allied in the long series of wars throughout the eighteenth century. In Europe these wars had no very decisive result but overseas they established British pre-eminence and stripped the French of most of their Empire.

A second series of wars centred around the Baltic and the ambitions of Sweden to establish and maintain its hegemony there. This brought it into conflict with both Denmark and Russia.

The Rise of Russia

The death of the Tsar Fedor in 1598 brought the house of Rurik to an end and initiated a Time of Troubles in which the throne was briefly occupied by Russian nobles, fraudulent pretenders and a son of the king of Poland, himself a scion of the Swedish royal house. In 1613, however, the nobility agreed on the election of Michael Romanov, son of the Patriarch of Moscow, as Tsar. The Romanov dynasty was successful in consolidating its authority and in winning back territory which had been lost to Poland. For the rest of the seventeenth century, however, Russia continued to be a place apart, its interests at least as much in the east as in the west, its culture and its government more Asiatic than European.

Peter the Great, Tsar from 1689 to 1725, dragged Russia into the European orbit by building a new capital (St.Petersburg) on the Baltic and forcing at least a superficial modernisation on the elite. Once that was done, and exploitation of the country's rich resources increased, Russia's greater numbers ensured its eventual triumph in the Baltic. Throughout the eighteenth century, Russia was gradually established as a leading player in the European power game. The country as a whole, however, changed very little. Poverty and brutal exploitation remained the lot of the great majority of the population, agriculture remained backward and industry, although it grew rapidly, still made only a tiny contribution to the economy. Government remained despotic and arbitrary and the succession to the throne dependent on coup and assassination as well as dynastic legitimacy of a sort. Catherine the Great (Tsarina 1762–96), a minor German princess by birth, assumed the throne when her lover organised a military coup which deposed her husband Peter III and was followed shortly by his murder.

Enlightened Despots

The constant competition and intermittent warfare of the European power game generated a commitment both to military efficiency and to economic development on the part of rulers. In both areas, of course, the commitment was less than complete and not infrequently undermined by a less than perfect understanding of both military power and economics and/or by the opposition of powerful forces within the realm. But, in principle at least, eighteenth century rulers sought to maximise their power by the rational application of knowledge to public affairs. For a time they succeeded in both increasing their control over their subjects and persuading the most articulate of them that the ruler was a personification of enlightenment and even benevolence. They claimed to be, and sometimes were, 'enlightened despots'.

In principle, therefore, European monarchs of the eighteenth century saw no need to consult their subjects; their will was law. The representative institutions of earlier centuries were seen as obstacles to progress and largely fell into disuse. The system was therefore clearly dependant on the will and intelligence of the monarchs and the ability of those they chose to advise and to execute. Less obviously, but no less really, the extent of royal absolutism was often limited by the need to accommodate the interests of the powerful of the realm. The Prussian kings averted any problems by conceding privileges to the nobility at the expense of the peasants. So too did Catherine the Great in Russia; this 'enlightened' despot extended and reinforced serfdom to ensure the support of the nobility. Joseph II of Austria introduced far reaching reforms across many aspects of life. Before very long he had provoked resistance from all levels of society; only his death in 1790 and the accession of his more cautious brother Leopold averted widespread rebellion. In France, Louis XIV had used magnificence and glory to enlist the support of the powerful. As the magnificence and glory faded in his later years and under inadequate successors, and the burden on the lower classes increased, France drifted towards bankruptcy and revolution.

Oligarchic and Aristocratic Alternatives

There were, of course, a few exceptions to the pattern of enlightened despotism. The Netherlands and Switzerland maintained their archaic confederations of republics; Venice and Genoa likewise continued as republics. Poland was an elective monarchy, with royal power so weak that it was not unfairly described as a crowned republic. Between 1772 and 1795 it paid the penalty of its resultant weakness by being partitioned between Russia, Prussia and Austria.

Great Britain's monarchy was hereditary, not elective, but the royal power was circumscribed by a mass of custom and parliamentary privilege as well as by the power of the great aristocrats and merchant families. When this power coalesced with the militant Protestantism of the Puritans the result was a civil war (1642–46) and the execution of Charles I by the parliamentary victors. The Puritan Commonwealth which followed, with Oliver Cromwell as Lord Protector, was not to the liking of most Englishmen and was maintained only by military government. Cromwell's death in 1658 led to the restoration of the monarchy but Charles II understood very well that, if he was to avoid his father's fate, he must rule in co-operation with Parliament and the great families who dominated it.

Charles, adept at manipulation, died in his bed in 1685. His brother James, who succeeded him, was more direct and less adept. He had become a Catholic and was determined to remove the disadvantages to which his co-religionists were subject. Fear of Rome and of James' dependence on Louis XIV of France led to his expulsion in the 'Glorious Revolution' of 1688 and his replacement by his Anglican daughter Mary and her husband William of Orange, Stadholder of the Netherlands.

The Revolution of 1688 brought England firmly into the anti-French camp of which it soon assumed the leadership and set the scene for a series of wars throughout the eighteenth century. At home, it led to the gradual emasculation of the monarchy, a process which was made easier in 1714 when the throne, in accordance with the 1701 Act of Settlement, passed to the nearest Protestant claimant, the Elector George of Hanover. George I was often thought by English opinion to be more interested in his German electorate than his English kingdom. Apart from foreign affairs and military matters, he was prepared to leave the government of England in the hands of the magnates who had brought him to the throne.

The king's ministers learned to function without the king's presence. They 'managed' parliament by a judicious mixture of bribery and blandishment so as to ensure that it supported the measures they found necessary. The eighteenth century saw the firm establishment of parliamentary power in England and the development of a system of government which gave effective expression to the control of the country by the aristocracy and the gentry.

Population and Food Supplies

The eighteenth century saw a significant increase in population all over Europe but it was most marked in the East. Russia, which had 15 million people at the beginning of the century, had reached 50 million at the end; Austria grew from 10 to 30 million, Prussia to 20 million. The three eastern powers now accounted for half the European total of 200 million. Annexation and immigration had contributed but the basic factor was high birth rates and probably some improvement in survival rates. France, which at the beginning of the century had been the most populous country in Europe with 19 million people, had grown to only 30 million, outranked by Russia and matched by Austria.

Increasing population was, fortunately, matched by increasing food supply. Prussian and Polish landlords had long exploited their peasantry to produce surpluses for sale in the West. The Austrian expulsion of the Turks from the Hungarian plain, and the definitive establishment of Russian power in the Ukraine, were followed by the increasing cultivation of those fertile lands.

In the more densely settled West, the opportunities for expanded acreages were limited. Imports from the East met only part of the needs of increasing population; the rest was met by the expansion of new crops, derived from America, and by improvements in agriculture. The potato in the north and corn in the south provided more bulk and nutrients per acre than more traditional crops and made growth in population possible, even in areas such as Ireland, with few resources other than arable land. Holland and England saw the beginnings of an even more significant development; landlords began to practice systematic, improving agriculture, to introduce new crops and new crop rotations and to improve the fertility of the soil. Agriculture was beginning to be seen as a subject for science and technology as well as a way of life.

Europe therefore approached the end of the eighteenth century with a self confidence based on some solid achievements. It had, in fact, despite all the dysfunctions of internecine war and inequitable privilege, established a society capable of generating change and development more rapidly and more continuously than any the world had ever seen before. Europe was gradually coming to realize that there seemed to be no other part of the world which could compare with it either in power or potential.

The Establishment of European Hegemony

Warfare and religious conflict at home did not prevent Europe from exploiting the new opportunities which exploration had opened up. In a few decades after the voyages of Columbus and da Gama the Europeans projected their power around the globe and established the basis on which they would eventually dominate the world.

It did not take long for the Portuguese to realize that, while their tiny kingdom was insignificant in comparison with the powers around the Indian Ocean, their ships were irresistible at sea. The profits of trade could be supplemented by the levies of power; the Portuguese proceeded to seize a few key points from which they could dominate and tax the trade of the Indian Ocean. Before long their ships were pushing on to Indonesia, China and Japan.

The Conquest of America

By comparison with the splendours of the East, the aftermath of Columbus' voyages was at first disappointing. The islands of the West Indies had no wealth to offer and settlement was slow and unrewarding, not least because the local Indians responded to attempts to enslave them by dying – they had no immunity to European diseases. Then in 1519 – the very year in which Luther launched his challenge to the papacy and Charles V became Emperor – Cortez burst in on the Aztec empire in Mexico. With a few hundred Spaniards he attacked and conquered an empire of millions, dominated by a nation of bloodthirsty warriors. The sheer audacity of the venture is breath-taking, its success amazing. The desperate valour of the conquistadors, the superiority of steel over stone weapons, and the leadership of Cortez are all part of the explanation. So too is the nature of the Aztec empire and Aztec warfare, with its emphasis on the capture of victims for sacrifice rather than on killing the enemy to achieve military victory.

But there was also another and more basic factor – the invaders brought with them the Old World disease of smallpox. This, and other European diseases, were unknown in the Americas and the inhabitants consequently had no resistance to them. The first outbreak of smallpox in 1520 prevented the Aztecs from following up the bloody expulsion of the Spaniards from their capital. The rapid spread of the disease decimated the Aztec army and made Cortez's victory possible. So widespread was the devastation that the entire fabric of Indian culture was destroyed; population was reduced to a fraction of the pre-conquest number. The ravages of disease – and the comparative immunity of the Spaniards – perhaps convinced the Indians of the futility of their ancestral culture and religion and the superiority of that offered by the invaders.

Once established in the New World smallpox moved even more rapidly than the Spaniards. By 1525 it had reached Peru, preparing the way for the conquest of the Inca empire by the cut-throat Pizarro and a force even smaller than that which had overthrown the Aztecs.

The government of Charles V moved systematically and carefully to assert its control over the quarrelsome conquistadors and the vast lands they had acquired. Viceroys were appointed to govern Mexico in 1535 and Peru in 1542. The state encouraged and controlled Christian missionaries who became champions of the Indians against the ruthless exploitation of the Spanish settlers. Towns were founded everywhere and universities established at Lima in 1551 and Mexico City in 1553. By the end of the century 250,000 Spanish settlers (or descendants of settlers) administered and exploited an Empire of perhaps nine or ten million Indians and a growing number of African slaves.

Africa and Slavery

In their slow progress down the African coast, the Portuguese established a number of fortified trading posts. Most of the coast was occupied by people at a tribal stage of development although a few small states had begun to emerge. The major African states were far away in the Sahel and the Portuguese had no direct contact with them. The trading posts, however, sucked in gold and slaves which had previously been directed across the Sahara. This weakened the dominant state of Songhai; in 1591 it was overthrown by a Moroccan force which had accomplished the striking feat of marching across the Sahara. Morocco, however, was not able to maintain its supremacy over this distance. Its garrisons were absorbed in the local population and new states were formed in the conquered territory.

Slavery had been endemic in Africa for centuries before the Portuguese discoveries provided a new outlet in the Mediterranean where it had never entirely disappeared. The realization that the Indians were a wasting resource in the Caribbean and perhaps on the mainland made it urgent to find a new source of labour. The trans-Atlantic slave trade began with shipments of perhaps a thousand a year early in the sixteenth century and grew to five thousand by the end. In the seventeenth century, as sugar growing developed, the number grew. By 1700 it had reached 30,000 a year and by 1750 as many as 75,000. The unfortunate victims, or those that survived the horrors of the 'Middle Passage', became the basic population of the West Indies and contributed perhaps fifty percent of the population of Brazil. North America received only a few hundred thousand but the number of their descendants grew exponentially and now exceeds twenty million.

All told, some ten million people were removed from Africa as slaves over a period of almost four centuries. Looking at Africa as a whole, with a total population of fifty million, this was hardly a demographic disaster; but in some areas intensive and persistent raiding produced depopulation. In addition to the human misery involved, a part of the population was brutalized by participation in the victimization of the rest and the normal process of development was corrupted by a vicious and violent traffic. While the European powers – with Britain in the lead by the eighteenth century – were the stimulus, the trade was sustained by Africans who willingly hunted, captured and sold other Africans. In the nineteenth century, it was the Europeans, led and sometimes pushed by Britain, who brought it to an end.

On the east coast a string of small trading towns had developed over many centuries and prospered by a limited trade across the Indian Ocean and with the Middle East. Since they were all Moslem, the Portuguese had no hesitation in attacking and occupying a number of them. The Portuguese remained paramount until 1698 when, weakened by Dutch attacks, they were ejected from the coast north of Mozambique by the Sultan of Oman.

The Portuguese also played a vital role in the survival of Ethiopia which in 1527 had come under attack from an alliance of Islamic states on the coast. The country was ravaged for more than a decade until a Portuguese expedition, led by the son of Vasco da Gama, arrived in the nick of time to destroy the invaders.

European Rivals to Spain and Portugal

The Spanish and Portuguese regarded their discoveries as giving them exclusive rights and actually persuaded a Spanish pope, the notorious Alexander Borgia, to settle the boundary between their claims in 1493. Next year they agreed between themselves on a modification which inadvertently put Brazil in the Portuguese sphere; only in 1500 did Cabral, on his way to India, discover this totally unexpected bonus.

None of the other European countries was impressed by the Iberian claims to exclusive dominion. As early as 1497, the English court had dispatched the Italian John Cabot to find an alternative, northerly route to the East; he failed, but discovered North America, appropriately naming his first landfall Newfoundland. Since it showed no signs of treasure, the English were, for the time being, uninterested; from time to time they made renewed efforts to find either a North West or a North East Passage to the Orient but the Arctic ice defeated them. Jacques Cartier explored the St. Lawrence in 1537, establishing a claim on which France founded a colony in 1603. Fishermen from many European countries began to exploit the resources of the Great Banks, off the coast of Newfoundland.

In the sixteenth century the Europeans in Asia operated in the interstices of local power. The first comers were suitably impressed by the size, wealth, splendour and might of the major Asian states. China alone had a population of one hundred million organized in a single state. India had about the same number; admittedly this was divided into a number of states but the larger of them far outweighed the minuscule power of Portugal in wealth and population. Even Japan had a population approaching twenty million against less than two million in Portugal. Moreover, the advantage the Europeans possessed at sea was notably less apparent on land where superiority in fire power could be offset by the sheer weight of numbers.

No one imagined that the appearance of the Portuguese portended European domination of Asia. Indeed, as the century wore on it seemed doubtful how long Portugal could maintain its position. Perhaps ten thousand Portuguese were scattered around the Indian Ocean, and as far east as Timor, the Chinese coast and Japan, subject to diseases new to them and to the casualties of intermittent warfare. To maintain this number throughout the century required an outflow from Portugal of a hundred thousand –

an enormous effort for a minuscule country. Before the end of the century the waning of Portuguese vigour and power was perceptible.

The decline of Portugal, however, did not mean the end of European domination of the Indian Ocean. Its place was taken by the Dutch and the English, spurred on by their war with Philip of Spain who in 1580 made good his claim to the Portuguese throne. The Dutch conquered Sri Lanka and established a pre-eminent position in Java and the islands of Indonesia. Ousted by the Dutch from Indonesia, the English concentrated on establishing trading settlements along the Indian coast. Before the end of the seventeenth century they found themselves rivalled in this by the French. Neither power was more than a spectator as the last great Mughal, Aurangzeb, extended his empire to include most of southern India and bring the population under his control to 150 million, double that of Western Europe. But his fanaticism and persecution provoked a Hindu reaction. By the eighteenth century the Mughal Empire was in dissolution and India was again divided between warring states.

European Competition in India

The local representatives of the major European countries, France and Britain, realized that the grandeur of the Indian states had become an empty facade and that their rulers could be manipulated to support one intruder against another.

By the middle of the eighteenth century it was clear that no power in the sub-continent was capable of resisting the relatively small armies in the service of the French and British East India Companies. Two thirds or more of the manpower in these armies was Indian, but armed, trained and equipped in the European manner. With 3,000 men of this type, Clive defeated a traditional Indian army of almost 70,000 men mobilized by the Nawab of Bengal at Plassey in 1757. His victory was aided by the last minute treachery of one of the Nawab's generals but the treachery would never have occurred if 3,000 men had not been willing to face 70,000. Clive's victory laid the foundations for the extension of British power over the whole sub-continent. When the British established their superiority over the French, it was only a short step to conquest and empire.

Europe and China

In contrast to India, the China which the Portuguese first encountered in 1516 was a single, unitary state. The decline of the Ming dynasty in the seventeenth century led, not to a new Chinese dynasty, but to the conquest of China by the Manchus. A border people already highly Sinified, the Manchus had little difficulty in organizing an effective administration with Chinese support. Taking over all the prejudice of their Chinese subjects, the Manchu emperors considered their state the most powerful in the world (which it almost certainly was) and the centre around which the rest of the world revolved (which it was not). None of the Europeans who arrived over the seas was inclined to challenge the former proposition; the Russian expansion across Siberia was brought to a halt in 1689 by the Treaty of Nerchinsk.

Manchu China, in fact, could be considered one of the great imperial powers of the eighteenth century, extending its sway over outer Mongolia, Sinkiang and Tibet. The Europeans still treated it with great respect but the balance of power was changing. If China was to maintain its relative position it would have to abandon some of its conservative ways and recover the dynamism it had displayed, half a millennium before, under the Sung.

British Settlement in North America

Whereas European interest in Asia was geared largely to trade, and in Latin America to domination, in north America it turned to settlement. In 1607 the first British settlement was established at Jamestown in Virginia; in 1620 a small group of Puritans – the 'Pilgrim Fathers' – established themselves in New England. By the end of the seventeenth century a hundred thousand Britons had crossed the Atlantic to establish a string of colonies from Maine to South Carolina.

British colonies differed in significant ways from those of Spain and Portugal. First and foremost, the colonists had come, not to conquer or trade, but to settle. Labour was provided by the settlers themselves and by bonded servants from England; only later did the southern colonies turn to African slaves. The colonies developed their own institutions of representative government and were only loosely controlled by the home country. A number of them were established as refuges for dissident sects – and Delaware for Catholics – to exercise their religion without persecution. This did not prevent some colonies from persecuting anyone who did not accept their own form of Christianity but it nevertheless marked a small step on the road to freedom of religion.

Russian Expansion in Siberia

In the seventeenth century the expansion of Western Europe by sea was rivaled by the expansion of Russia by land. In 1581 the Cossack Yermak had crossed Western Siberia. The Khanate of Sibir was overthrown and the Russian frontiersmen pressed on in search of furs and then land to settle. Siberia, like North America, was a colony of settlement. The scattered and sparse hunting and fishing population – probably no more than 200,000 over the whole vast area – could mount little resistance; in two generations the Russians had reached the Pacific. By 1700 the Russian population of Siberia had reached a hundred thousand; by 1800 it was a million. Late in the eighteenth century a few pioneers crossed into Alaska which became Russian territory until it was sold to USA in 1867. Central Asia, with its war-like Turkish tribes and great oasis cities was another matter; Russian penetration did not begin until the nineteenth century.

Resettlement in Eastern Europe

In the eighteenth century, too, German settlement in Eastern Europe was renewed as the Austrians drove the Turks out of Hungary and looked for settlers to fill up the vacant land. The Hapsburgs also encouraged Serbs to migrate from their traditional territory under Turkish control and settle as militia in a military frontier zone in territory historically part of Hungary and Croatia; the ultimate outcome of this settlement was recently played out in the conflicts arising from the dissolution of Yugoslavia.

The Basis of European Domination

By the end of the eighteenth century Europe had come to dominate most of the land-mass which was not already occupied by powerful states and large, prolific populations. Population of European origin had reached 4.5 million in North America and 4 million in the South, almost one million Russians were settled in Siberia, and a beginning had been made on European settlement in Australia and South Africa. Even outside the areas of settlement, the superiority of European power over that of the great traditional empires was becoming apparent. In India, the English had already annexed Bengal and made the Mughal emperor their puppet. Whatever the Chinese might think, their power and wealth were, in fact, already surpassed by Europe and would fall further behind in the century to come. In Africa, Europeans had not penetrated beyond the coast but no inland power had the capacity to resist them when they should decide to do so.

Thus the world had become, for the first time, a single entity rather than a collection of civilisations separated from one another by impenetrable oceans or vast distances occupied by less advanced peoples. And this single entity was dominated by one of those civilisations in a way without any precedent in history.

The rise of Europe is all the more remarkable when one remembers that at the outset of the period, and for the best part of the sixteenth and seventeenth centuries, divided Europe felt itself threatened by the stronger, more aggressive and better organized power of the Ottoman Empire.

At a certain level of analysis, of course, the explanation is clear. Europe, by the end of the fifteenth century, had developed navigation, ship building and gunnery to give its fleets a capacity to sail where ever they wished and to destroy any fleet which challenged them. In the seventeenth century Europe's superiority at sea began to be matched by an enhanced ability to wage war on land; in the next century this also was brought to bear outside Europe.

From the fourteenth century onwards, Europe had been fascinated by the military potential of gunpowder. Despite the dangers – early guns had a nasty tendency to blow up, destroying their gunners rather than the enemy – the gunners and their masters persevered until they had developed effective artillery and hand guns.

Even so, the sixteenth century musket required an elaborate series of operations to load, prime and fire it. Maurice of Nassau, Captain General of Holland from 1585 to 1625, developed a system of drill to ensure these operations were done in unison, culminating in a volley. Maurice then went on to develop a whole system of drills which required armies to march in step to music and enabled them to carry out complex manoeuvres in response to a general's commands.

Once the advantages of Maurice's system had been demonstrated on the battlefield, it was widely copied and improved; by the end of the seventeenth century European armies possessed a cohesion and responsiveness unparalleled anywhere else in the world. The Hapsburgs showed this superiority by chasing the Turks out of Hungary by 1699 but its most startling demonstration was to be by the British and French in India.

Military technology was backed by an array of attitudes, derived from the European experience, which made the European adventurer a different sort of man from most of those he encountered in other continents. From Europe's feudal past he had inherited an aggressive spirit, a willingness to resort to arms and a high regard for courage. Such qualities were not unknown, for example, to the mainly Turkish elite which had established the Mughal empire, to the Mahratta tribes who virtually destroyed it or to the Manchu warriors who conquered China in the seventeenth century. But none of these peoples established the institutions which would perpetuate these qualities from generation to generation.

What difference did it make that the European adventurer was a Christian? Very little, when it came to greed and violence, although no Christian conqueror ever celebrated his triumph with the massive pyramids of skulls used by Tamerlane. But it is probably significant that sixteenth and seventeenth century Christianity was an exclusive religion which claimed a monopoly of religious truth and a unique possession of the right to eternal salvation. These claims inspired a minority of committed Christians – almost entirely Catholic until the nineteenth century – to heroic efforts to convert the pagans. For the average Christian of the time, they often formed the basis for a confidence in divine favor which re-inforced his innate sense of superiority and his expectation of victory.

Thus morale and military technology re-inforced one another to create a culture of superiority which spurred on the European and, before long, depressed his adversary. Almost certainly the positive attitude of the European to problem solving – the product of medieval technology and Renaissance science – added both to his sense of superiority and to his ability to cope with novel situations and new problems. As the centuries progressed, European technology continued to improve and increased its margin over the stagnant technologies of Asia.

Thus when the Mughal Empire dissolved in chaos after the death of Aurangzeb it was the British, not the Marathas, who eventually inherited the imperial role. China still remained the largest single state in the world, but those who knew it realized the weakness behind the facade of magnificence. In Europe itself, the Ottoman Empire was only preserved from destruction by the rivalry of Austria and Russia. By the beginning of the nineteenth century Egypt was virtually independent under an Albanian governor and the rest of North Africa paid little more than nominal courtesies to Istanbul. Persia was in decline and the Muslim states of Central Asia were destined, later in the century, to succumb to Russian expansion. In Africa Britain and the other European powers with interests there were largely content with a few trading stations on the coast. But if they should wish to extend their power, no state or tribe in Africa would be able to resist them successfully.

CHAPTER TEN

THE AGE OF REVOLUTION

In the last quarter of the eighteenth century revolutions in North America and France challenged the assumptions on which European states had built their governmental institutions. Between them, they laid the foundations on which new ideas of government were developed and introduced over the next century and more.

Britain's American Colonies

The triumph of Britain over France in the Seven Years War (1756–1763) left the Thirteen American Colonies of the former free of all external pressures except Indian, which they rightly felt able to deal with. France was obliged to cede Canada and the land east of the Mississippi to Britain and assign her claims to lands beyond the Mississippi to Spain which had neither the power nor the motive to pursue them.

The two million people of European – overwhelmingly British – origin who, along with half a million negro slaves, inhabited the colonies strung along the Atlantic seaboard were organized politically in thirteen colonies each with a Governor appointed by Britain and some form of elected legislature. The occasional tensions inherent in this division of power had been resolved without too much trouble while the overshadowing power of France in Canada concentrated the minds of all concerned. With the French menace removed, the colonists were in a mood to be more assertive and more critical of Imperial controls. It irked them that the British government, concerned to minimize conflict with the Indian tribes, should restrict their expansion across the Alleghany Mountains into the lands ceded by France; the more devout or bigoted Protestants among them were scandalized by the toleration extended – in accordance with the peace treaty – to the Catholic Canadians.

In Britain, the government was in the hands of Ministers appointed by George III with a mandate to enhance the powers of the Crown. They saw no reason why such enhancement should not extend to the colonies. In particular, they asserted the right to make the colonies contribute financially to the liquidation of the war debt and to be less blatant in ignoring regulations which restricted their trade in favor of the mother country. A succession of British governments introduced various revenue raising measures, only to vacillate and repeal them under colonial pressure. The main effect of these efforts was to stimulate political discussion between the educated elites of the various colonies; 'corresponding societies' were established for the purpose and the principle of 'no taxation without representation' became a slogan and before long a battle-cry. The colonists were demanding the rights which they conceived belonged to British citizens – in reality, only to a privileged minority – while the British government was determined to assert a degree of control which categorized a colonist as necessarily a second class citizen.

It did not help understanding that the basic stratum of the American population had been established in the seventeenth century. A white population of less than 300,000 in 1700 had reached 2 million by 1775, mainly by natural increase. The great majority of the colonists were therefore separated from their British origins by several generations. If they still thought of themselves as British they were also aware of differences; it would take only a spark to make the latter loom larger than the former.

The Spark of Revolt

The spark has been traditionally seen as the 1773 'Boston Tea Party.' In reaction to the British insistence on maintaining an import duty on tea, a group of Bostonians threw the cargoes of three tea ships into the harbour. The British government closed the harbour and declared martial law. Next year a Continental Congress representing all 13 colonies met at Philadelphia and proclaimed defiance, although not yet independence. Armed conflict began with a skirmish at Lexington in 1775. Next year a second Continental Congress issued the American Declaration of Independence.

After generations of border warfare with the French and the Indians the colonists were not lacking in military experience. The British found the going harder than they had expected. The colonists were not entirely united in their resistance but the great majority supported it. To subdue 2 million people scattered over such a vast area called for a military effort much greater than the British government was prepared to make. France and Spain seized the opportunity, as it seemed, to reverse their defeat in the Seven Years War; a number of other European powers formed an 'armed neutrality' to contest British efforts to enforce a comprehensive blockade. For a time the British lost control of the sea to the French whose co-operation with the American army forced the capitulation of a small British army at Yorktown in 1781.

War at sea, however, was a type of conflict in which Britain was still fundamentally supreme; early defeats were reversed and it became clear that if Britain could not subdue the revolting colonies, neither could France and Spain defeat Britain. The peace of 1783 recognized these realities. America became independent but the rest of the British colonial empire remained almost undiminished. No one seems to have noticed, at the time, that the war had brought the impecunious French government to the verge of bankruptcy. Certainly no one could have conceived the consequences that were to flow from it before the end of the decade.

Creating a New State

The Americans now faced the complexities of creating a new state and a new nation in the strangest of circumstances. There were 2 million of them, spread along a strip of largely fertile land between the sea and the Alleghany Mountains. Beyond the mountains was a largely unknown continent inhabited by people they regarded as savages. Their origins were European, largely English; their present was full of the confidence of victory; their future was unknown. Nor were they united in their perceptions of what were the positive goals – as distinct from simply ending British rule – their revolution had been designed to accomplish. Many of them saw the revolt in the terms which the American folk memory has now canonized – a struggle for independence and the control of their own affairs proper to free men. Others, whose memory is now preserved only in the more detailed and erudite histories, had envisaged it as also a social revolution directed at landlords and the rich; as usual, they were to be disappointed. Leadership and power in the now independent colonies remained firmly in the hands of the wealthy, educated elites – the Southern landowners and the New England merchants and lawyers.

The Genius of the American Constitution

It is a mark of the maturity and judgment of these men that they rapidly realized that the survival and progress of the new nation required a more substantial political structure than the often squabbling Confederation of 13 independent states which had fought the war and now faced a common and uncertain future. In 1787 a Constitutional Convention met at Philadelphia and after much discussion drafted a constitution which envisaged a new type of state.

Our generation is so accustomed to federal states that it is a shock to learn that the concept was quite unknown before 1787. States were either unitary, with a single supreme authority, or confederations. The latter were established by the agreement of several states which remained sovereign. The Confederation might – usually, not invariably – operate as a single state in its relations with the rest of the world but internally it could only operate on the authorities of the constituent states; it had no authority whatever over their citizens and could neither make laws for them nor impose taxes on them. Its governing body was composed of representatives delegated by the governments of the constituent states and answerable to them; in some cases, its decisions required ratification by each state before they took effect. In effect, a Confederation was as much a permanent alliance as a single state.

The original conception of the American Constitution was to divide the activities of government between the states and the new federal creation and to provide that each of them should operate directly on the citizens in relation to their own sphere of activities. The federal organs were therefore not dependent on the goodwill of the states; the individual citizen had an obligation to the United States as well as to the constituent state. Moreover, the federal organs would be elected by the citizens of the United States, not appointed by the states.

The founding fathers showed less originality in regard to the structure of government: they basically replicated the eighteenth century structure of the British monarchy and the original colonies, with an elected president instead of a hereditary monarch or a governor. Influenced, however, by the writings of the French political philosopher Montesquieu and by the ongoing struggle between George III and Parliament, they enshrined in their constitution the principle of 'separation of powers' between the executive and the legislature. The other distinctive and novel feature of the new American constitution was the role of the Supreme

Court in its interpretation. The Court thus came to decide the actual balance of powers between the federal authorities and the states and between the executive and the legislature. This was largely the work of the first Chief Justice; it may be doubted if the founding fathers envisaged the power which would accrue to the Court or if many of them would have approved of it if they had.

The new constitution was accepted only reluctantly by the states and did not come into operation until 1789. To the surprise of many observers, it provided a durable framework for the new nation as it proceeded to grasp the opportunities now opened to it between the Alleghany Mountains and the Mississippi. By 1800 the white population exceeded five million and the negro had reached a million. Almost all the latter remained slaves; the noble rhetoric which had inspired the Revolution and soon after gave rise to the Constitutional amendments spelling out the rights of the citizen did not extend to them – or, in many respects, to women.

The Looming Problem of Slavery

There was already some anti-slavery sentiment in the North and by 1789 seven states had adopted programmes of emancipation. But the Northern states could afford such magnanimity – they had very few slaves. The South was heavily dependent on slave plantation labour and could not be persuaded to contemplate change, even by the far sighted and prestigious Virginia planter – and slave-owner – Jefferson, author of the Declaration of Independence and second President. For seventy years the shadow of slavery hung over a nation dedicated to freedom. It was finally resolved in a bloody war, leaving behind a legacy of entrenched racial problems, with which the United States is still endeavouring to grapple.

Impact of the Revolution in Europe

Almost from its inception – or perhaps even from the beginning of the struggle for independence – America became for many in Europe a symbol of political emancipation. The educated elites of Europe saw in the American freedom struggle something like a noble echo of their own ideas – not unreasonably so, because the men who had led that revolution, while basing themselves directly on their perception of British constitutional principles, were also, to a greater or lesser extent, children of the Enlightenment and shared many of its ideas and prejudices. Inevitably, therefore, the success of the American Revolution suggested to some people that outmoded and tyrannical regimes might be challenged in Europe as well as in its colonies.

Nowhere was this impact more marked than in France, which had been the first ally of the American colonies and which had provided not only arms but many – by no means always useful – volunteers to serve in their army. The French government, of course, had no particular love for rebellious subjects. It had been motivated by hostility to its traditional enemy, Britain, and had almost bankrupted itself in its attempt to avenge the defeats of the Seven Years War. If it considered itself well rewarded by the destruction of Britain's American empire, it had yet to count the full cost as the state slid further towards bankruptcy and its very support for America gave an additional fillip to those who sought change. A decade after the end of the War of American Independence France was in the grip of a revolution which threatened to reduce the country to chaos and which brought it into conflict with virtually the whole of Europe.

The Significance of the French Revolution

The French Revolution remains as one of the defining events of European and even of world history. From it we derive much of the language and ideology of modern politics. The Revolution is celebrated as the beginning of modern democracy; the massacres and judicial murders, wars and large-scale looting, which horrified Europe and divided France, are largely forgotten.

Two centuries later, it requires an effort of imagination to realize the full novelty of the Revolution. Since 1789, Europe has seen numerous attempts to overthrow the established order and the world even more. Most of these have appealed to some or all of the doctrines of the French Revolution for their justification; a few, notably Fascism and Nazism, have found their rationale in rejecting them while others, like Communism, have claimed to go beyond them.

One thing distinguishes nearly all these revolutions from their archetype; they are made by men (and sometimes a few women) who have planned and contrived them, who have a programme and a vision which they aspire to achieve and at least some notions of how to do so. By contrast the French Revolution appears almost an accident – no one planned it, no one had a full, clear picture of what would emerge from it and certainly no organised group had any notion of guiding it to the outcome which eventuated.

The Origins of the Revolution

The France of the 1780's was faced with some major problems which the government of Louis XVI was ill-equipped to deal with. France was the most populous country in Europe west of Russia and seemed the strongest military power. The French language was the unchallenged medium of diplomatic exchange and the lingua franca of educated Europeans; the prestige of French culture was unchallenged. The despots of central and eastern Europe vied to be seen as patrons of figures such as Voltaire and at least claimed to model their policies on the writings of the French-led enlightenment. France itself, however, did not produce a monarch of the same calibre in the eighteenth century. In consequence, while the will of the king was theoretically supreme, in practice it was trammeled by an immense complex of entrenched privileges, venal administration and conflicting jurisdictions. France might be the most prestigious state in Europe but its government was out-dated and in many ways ineffective.

A chronic problem was raised to the critical level by the cost of the American war. Massive borrowing had pushed the government to the edge of bankruptcy; only drastic increases in taxation could avert it. The weight of taxation fell on the Third Estate, the common people; nobles and clerics were largely exempt. But Louis XVI and his advisers were forced to recognize that the Third Estate was already squeezed so hard that any real increase would have to come from the privileged orders. When half-hearted attempts to enlist their co-operation failed, the king and his advisers resolved to summon a meeting of the Estates General.

This body, representing the three Estates of clergy, nobility and commoners, had not met since 1614. The decision to assemble it generated immense excitement and large and conflicting expectations. The arrangements for its election ensured the predominance of the parish clergy and the country nobility in the first two Estates. For the Third Estate, virtually every male taxpayer had a vote and a voice in the preparation of the *cahiers*, the lists of grievances which were to guide their representatives; no other government in Europe would have contemplated such a widespread franchise or consultation of its people. Louis and his advisers perhaps hoped to enlist the support of the little people in overriding the privileges of the great. But the representatives elected by the Third Estate were not peasants or workmen – they were lawyers and merchants with a sprinkling of professional men and teachers. Many were the sort of people who had imbibed the ideas of the Enlightenment from writers such as Montesquieu, Voltaire, Diderot and Rousseau. Some of them saw the meeting of the Estates as an opportunity to reform the government of France in line with these ideas and in the process to annul the privileges of the nobility. Under their influence the three Estates were transformed into a single Assembly.

From Monarchy to Republic

Faced with increasingly radical demands, Louis vacillated, contemplating the use of military force and then drawing back from it, refusing to accept proposed changes and then yielding to pressure. In October 1789, the King was forced by mob pressure to move from Versailles to Paris; the Assembly followed a few days later. The move delivered real power to the radical politicians, organized in clubs such as the Jacobins and the Cordeliers, who used the support of the Paris mob to bully their more moderate colleagues.

Under this pressure the Assembly and its successors were driven to adopt measures which few members had contemplated at the outset. Feudal obligations were destroyed, nobility abolished, church property confiscated and the clergy turned into elected and paid servants of the state, the historic provinces and other divisions replaced by the 83 departments into which France is still divided. A new constitution limited royal power and made France a constitutional monarchy with real power vested in a Legislative Assembly. Significantly, it was to be elected on a franchise more restricted than that of the Estates General.

As the Assembly and its successors fell increasingly under the control of the radicals, France became a republic, the King and Queen were executed and the country found itself at war with most of Europe. At the same time it was riven by a bitter civil war as cities and rural districts across France resisted the control of the Parisian revolutionaries. The bitterness of the civil war was increased by the radicals' attack on the Catholic religion and those priests who refused to accept the control of the state.

The introduction of conscription, ruthless energy and the genius of Lazare Carnot, the Organizer of Victory, enabled the revolution to survive, to expel the invading armies and to suppress the opposition in blood. Summary justice, or rather vengeance, was exacted on defeated rebels. At Lyons, 2500 were executed by artillery fire under the direction of Fouche, an ex-priest later to be Napoleon's Minister of Police and eventually to play a leading role in his ouster from power after his final defeat at Waterloo.

In Paris, a Committee of Public Safety guided by Robespierre terrorized the legislators with summary trials and rapid executions. To speed up the process the law of 10 June 1794 provided that the accused should only be heard in exceptional circumstances. This simplification at first produced gratifying results; 1376 people were sent to the guillotine in six weeks. But many of the legislators began to wonder if they might be next. Heartened by the success of the armies they saw no need for a continuation of the Terror. On 27 July the legislature voted the arrest of Robespierre and his associates; next day they were sent to the guillotine.

The Rise of Napoleon

Power thus passed from the fanatics and ideologues to the careerists and the profiteers – many of them terrorists – who had somehow succeeded in making a good thing out of the war. A new constitution was drawn up; significantly, while the initial vote remained available to most males, this was only to choose electors, for whom the property qualification was set so high that only 30,000 were eligible in all France. It was now clear that the beneficiaries of the Revolution were the middle class.

Before the new legislature could be elected there was yet another challenge from Paris, organized this time by crypto-royalists. Barras, a former Terrorist made responsible for the defence of the legislature, turned to the Corsican officer whose artillery had recently subdued Toulon. General Napoleon Bonaparte promptly deployed artillery and used its 'whiff of grapeshot', as he described it, on the mob with deadly effect. Although Barras and his colleagues did not at first realize it, the Revolution was over; in future power would depend not on voters but on the army.

The new constitution provided for one-third of the legislature to be elected each year. The five man Directory, which exercised the chief executive power, found the results of such elections inconvenient – they tended to return either royalists or extremist republicans whereas the Directory was intent on holding the middle ground and maintaining its own power. A military coup – excluding unsatisfactory members from the legislature – seemed the easy way out and one was arranged each year until 1799. In that year, the coup was again commanded by General Bonaparte. In the meantime he had won popular acclaim by winning sweeping victories over the Austrians in Italy and had reconstructed the political geography of the peninsula. Next he had led a French army to Egypt, eluding a British fleet under Nelson, and conquered the country in a single battle. Dreams of glory turned to ashes when Nelson destroyed the French fleet, leaving Bonaparte isolated in Egypt while Britain and the Ottoman suzerains of Egypt prepared a counter-attack. Deserting his army, Bonaparte returned to France to find the Directory split, with Sieyes and his supporters, fearful of a return to the Terror, looking for a general to organize a coup.

Bonaparte was happy to oblige but this time he had no intention of playing anything but the star role. When the dust settled, France had a new constitution under which the key powers were vested in a First Consul who was, of course, Bonaparte. The new constitution was approved by 3 million voters with only 1600 against; historians have not found evidence of rigging but over 4 million abstained. Nevertheless there is little doubt that France, exhausted by ten tumultuous years, was happy to commit herself to the new saviour. Just to make sure, Bonaparte retained Fouche, ex-priest and ex-Terrorist, as chief of police.

The Napoleonic Settlement

The First Consul threw himself into the work of governing France with the same daemonic energy and the same cynical realism which had distinguished his military exploits. By 1801 he had negotiated a new concordat with the pope which recognized Catholicism as 'the religion of the majority of Frenchmen' but left the state in firm control of the church, which also accepted the Revolutionary confiscation of church property. Bonaparte had given the peasants, the great majority of the population, the solution they wanted – the restoration of their traditional religion and the guarantee of their acquisitions of Church land. As far as they were concerned, the Revolution was finished, and finished in a very satisfactory manner.

The reconciliation of the Church and of the peasantry was accompanied by an eclectic opening to other, smaller but important elements which the course of the Revolution had alienated. Emigres were encouraged to return and many of them did so, to prosper and make careers under the new regime. Nobles and former Terrorists alike rose high in the administration. The middle class prospered under a government which promoted development and fiscal stability, enforced law and order, kept workers in their place and reformed the chaotic legal system.

The new legal codes, forever associated with the name of Napoleon, were destined to set the standard not only for France but for most of Europe. Unlike the complex of local and conflicting laws and customs which they replaced, they established equality before the law, but not for women. They were unable to manage their own property and subject to discrimination in marriage matters – a single incident of adultery by a wife was sufficient for her to be divorced but she could not divorce her husband for adultery unless he brought a mistress into the house. The standards applied may well have been common before the Revolution; their preservation indicates how far it was from any improvement in the status of women. Nor is it clear that the lowest strata of society – the landless peasants and the urban labourers – were any better off than they had been before the Revolution; the real beneficiaries were the urban middle class and the landholding peasants.

French Hegemony in Europe

Bonaparte's internal settlement was matched by success abroad. First Austria and then Russia were driven to accept peace. Finally in 1802 even Britain, isolated and weary of war, accepted a peace, very favourable to the French. But doubts about Bonaparte's intentions and good faith arose almost immediately; the two protagonists were at war again fourteen months later. It was 1805, however, before Britain found continental allies ready to take the field.

In the meantime Bonaparte had persuaded the French that his status should be changed from First Consul to Emperor. For good measure the puppet republics which had been set up in Italy and Holland were transformed into kingdoms, enabling the Emperor Napoleon, as he now styled himself, to surround himself with suitably titled members of his family. To complete the new structure of Europe, the German states with the exception of Austria and Prussia were formed into a Confederation of the Rhine under French protection. The Holy Roman Empire of the German Nation thus came to an end after 800 years. The Hapsburg Emperor assumed the new and less prestigious style of Emperor of Austria. Already fattened by the absorption of the free cities and prince bishoprics, most of the German rulers were happy to accept their new situation as virtual French vassal states – a status towards which many of them had been moving for the last century or more.

Napoleon expected the members of his family whom he had elevated to royal rank to carry out his commands as if they were French prefects. They strove, with varying degrees of success, to respond to his orders while maintaining the support of their new subjects. His brothers Joseph and Jerome proceeded tactfully as did his step-son Lucien Beauhearnais; they attracted some support and introduced many reforms such as equality before the law. Louis was determined to be a Dutch king and succeeded so well that his imperial brother ultimately drove him from the throne and annexed Holland to France.

For 150 years France had been the premier state in Europe. During all that time, any attempt on her part to transform primacy into hegemony had been resisted by the other major powers. They were not now likely to accept the system which Napoleon had erected but they were deterred by the sheer military power of France and mollified by the sober nature of his rule after the turmoil of the Revolution. If they could be persuaded that he had no further designs on their territories, they might accept the new situation for a time and gradually become accustomed to it. Unfortunately it soon became clear that Napoleon did have further designs on their territories and that his conception of French hegemony was as overbearing as his domination of French government.

What brought this to a head was the British blockade – a traditional war measure for a sea power but one which the British, unable to hit at Napoleon in any other way (after they had rapidly mopped up the French colonies), proceeded to make as tight as possible. Napoleon responded by declaring the Continental Blockade of Britain. The blockade banned British ships and goods from the continent; it aimed to bring Britain to her knees by economic pressure. Its success depended on the co-operation of Napoleon's satellites and the major powers he had defeated. Since Britain was the main source of industrial production and of colonial goods such as coffee and sugar, its enforcement alienated the ruling classes throughout Europe and was a potent source of future conflict; it was also subject to widespread evasion by smuggling.

Resistance in Spain and Russia

In most countries popular support enabled the ruling dynasty to survive defeat without challenge but did not lead to national resistance to the French. Even the areas absorbed into France or made puppet states ruled by Bonapartes seemed to accept their fate with a mixture of some middle class enthusiasm and peasant indifference or passive hostility – manifested mainly in widespread efforts to escape conscription. Consequently, when Napoleon decided in 1808 that the degenerate Bourbons in Spain could well be replaced by his brother Joseph, he saw no reason to expect real trouble. Joseph, who left his kingdom of Naples reluctantly, perhaps had a better intuition of the future. Centuries of decline had done nothing to reduce the fierce pride of the Spaniards or the devotion of the populace to their traditional Catholic religion. A long tradition of hostility to the French was reinforced by the Revolution's persecution of Christianity.

The Bourbons were persuaded to abdicate and the French Marshal, Murat, occupied Madrid. He was met by a bloody uprising which he suppressed with more than a whiff of grapeshot. Joseph, accepted by a gathering of noble and middle class notables at Bayonne (on the Franco-Spanish border) set out for Madrid in high hope. His silent, sullen reception along the way convinced the intelligent Joseph that the country was ready to explode. He was right – resistance was being organized across the country as local leaders came together in committees or *juntas* and priests preached a virtual crusade. They found ready support in the peasants whose miserable lives had not undermined their pride and self-respect. Other peasantries might submit to the violence of marauding French armies living off the countryside; the Spanish would fight back with knife and gun and take frightful revenge on any Frenchman they could ambush. A week after Joseph entered Madrid he learned that Dupont had surrendered a French army of 30,000 men to the Spanish. He promptly retreated north.

In a brief personal intervention Napoleon chased a supporting British army back to its ships and then returned to Paris. The guerilla resistance continued and the British soon returned, led this time by the formidable Arthur Wellesley, eventually to become Duke of Wellington in recognition of his victories. Between them the British and the Spanish tied up 200,000 and more French and satellite troops and slowly drove the French north towards the border; the hardships and deaths of the Spanish theatre began to make war unpopular in France.

Napoleon perhaps should have returned to Spain in person but he was occupied in arranging a marriage with a Hapsburg princess and in trying to preserve an uneasy alliance with Tsar Alexander of Russia. Both efforts were, in different ways, to be failures.

The Hapsburgs, persistently beaten in battle, reluctantly sacrificed the eighteen year old Marie Louise but the marriage did nothing to guarantee their alliance. Nor was Alexander any more reliable. At Tilsit in 1807 Napoleon had made a generous peace with a defeated Russia and dazzled the young Tsar with talk of dividing the Ottoman Empire and sharing the hegemony of Europe. The price, of course, was Russia's adherence to the Continental Blockade, a move far from popular with the Russian nobility; exports from their estates to Britain were a prime source of income. Alexander was well aware of the danger constituted by discontented nobles – he had to reckon the risk of assassination against the danger of defying Napoleon. At the end of 1810 he renounced Russia's adherence to the Blockade. War was now inevitable but it was June 1812 before Napoleon, having assembled an army of 600,000 – about half French and the rest drawn from satellites and unwilling allies – crossed the Russian frontier.

The Russians withdrew before the advancing French, occasionally making a bloody stand and continually wasting the countryside as they went. Napoleon, intent on forcing a decisive engagement, kept up the pursuit which drew him steadily further and further into a virtual wilderness until he reached Moscow, a thousand kilometres from the frontier. The Russians burnt the largely wooden city the same night and their army settled down further east to await his next move. After a month, Napoleon realized that he must withdraw. As he did so the Russian winter, for which his army was totally unprepared, began. The retreat did not stop until the remnant of the army – 40,000 out of 600,000 – reformed on the Elbe.

The Overthrow of Napoleon

The Russian debacle, and the British advance in Spain and into southern France, convinced the powers that France could be beaten. Napoleon was forced back into France. On 4 April 1814, with Paris already occupied by the enemy, his marshals forced his abdication; the senate had already deposed him.

The powers proceeded to restore the Bourbon Louis XVIII and assembled in congress at Vienna to redraw the map of Europe. Napoleon was exiled to the little island of Elba, off the Italian coast, which was assigned to him in full sovereignty. Encouraged by news of the inevitable disagreements at Vienna and rumblings of discontent in France, Napoleon returned to France on 1 March 1815. He made a triumphant progress to Paris and a delirious welcome. The powers not unnaturally refused to believe his protestations that this time the Empire meant peace; they agreed to keep 600,000 men in the field until he was defeated.

Napoleon recognized that he must have a quick victory to maintain his support in France. He struck north with an army of 120,000. At Waterloo, south of Brussels, an Anglo-Dutch army, commanded with Wellington's usual calm skill, held him off in a long day until the arrival of the Prussians turned defeat into rout. Napoleon returned to find Paris in the hands of a committee dominated by Fouche and supported by the legislature. He abdicated and fled to the coast, where he surrendered to the captain of a British warship. This time the powers were determined that he would cause no further trouble – Napoleon was confined on St.Helena, a windswept island in the South Atlantic, where he remained under guard until he died in 1821. Considering that he had shaken their thrones and caused the death of more than a million of their subjects, the monarchs of Europe were, by the standards of the twentieth century, extraordinarily forgiving.

The Impact of the Revolution

The Congress resumed its deliberations. Appropriately, it reassembled in Vienna. For Napoleon and the Revolution had been defeated by the strange, apparently paradoxical 'auld alliance' of Protestant, oligarchic, nationalist England and Catholic, monarchic/aristocratic, cosmopolitan Austria. That alliance dated back to the beginning of the eighteenth century and its reversal in the Seven Years War proved to be only a temporary aberration. The two powers had minimal conflicting interests and much in common. Despite their many obvious differences they shared – apart from the short reign of Joseph II – a respect for traditional rights, actualized in different but equally untidy structures, a reluctance to push confrontations to extremes and the fixed determination of those who knew they would win in the end.

The settlement which the Congress of Vienna endorsed was designed to restore the power structure of Europe to something like its pre-1789 balance, modified to reflect the weight and interests of the major powers in 1815. It has attracted much scorn for its refusal to recognize the aspirations of nationalism and liberalism. But nationalists and liberals were only a tiny minority at the time. After a generation of war and revolution, most people were ready to seek peace and stability in traditional institutions. Despite occasional rumblings of revolt, and a few mercifully short wars, the settlement of Vienna established the basis for a century of relative peace.

Yet in the long run the impact of the Revolution could not be extinguished. With the passage of time its violence and destruction were largely forgotten. If the right of people to a voice in their government has come to seem obvious, the primary credit is often assigned to the Revolution.

Most of the champions of the Revolution were not, by our reckoning, advocates of democracy. Only under pressure and actual fear of the Paris mob would they accept anything like universal manhood suffrage; as soon as possible the franchise would be restricted to ensure the domination of the middle class. The occasional efforts of the Paris mob to ensure that the Rights of Man extended to the right to work and eat were resisted and frustrated as contrary to the prevailing economic philosophy. And, of course, the notion of political or civil rights for women was not even debated; the handful of women who tried to advocate such unprecedented changes received short shrift.

The Revolution was, in fact, made and dominated by the middle class. They were its champions, its managers and its main beneficiaries. In alliance with the more fortunate of the peasantry, who had managed to lay hands on confiscated church or emigre noble lands, they would dominate French political life for most of the nineteenth century. When the Revolution was wound up with Bonaparte's whiff of grapeshot France was dominated by men who had done well out of the turmoil and were determined to preserve their gains. Bonaparte was the answer to their need for stability.

The Revolution had left France a deeply divided country. Napoleon tried hard to remedy the most striking of those divisions. He welcomed the old nobility into his service along with the ex-Jacobins. The return of the Bourbons ensured that the division between monarchist and republican would continue to bedevil French political life for much of the nineteenth century. The legend Napoleon left behind meant that a third force, Bonapartism, would be added to the volatile mixture.

No other division, however, would turn out to be as serious as the division between middle class and working class which the Revolution entrenched and which Napoleon did nothing to undo. As the working class grew in numbers and became more conscious of its grievances, the ground was laid for explosions of violence which reached their culmination in the Paris Commune of 1870 and its suppression – 20,000 men were executed or killed in a few days.

The Revolution's attack on the Church also resulted in a deep division which Napoleon's reconciliation with the Papacy did little to cure. By persecuting the religion of the great majority of the nation the Revolution led the way in creating a quite unnecessary division between liberalism and religion. The defensive reaction of the Catholic Church ensured that mutual hostility became entrenched, to the disadvantage of both sides.

The quarrel with the Church also destroyed the structure of education and charity. Despite some high sounding statements, the Revolution did not succeed in replacing the Church in education. Even after Napoleon had built up a centralized system, adult literacy in 1815 was only 30%, compared with 37% in 1789. In public health, the record was even worse.

But if the limitations of the Revolution seem obvious today, it – or perhaps rather its legend – had set the agenda for the political history of nineteenth century Europe; and from there the tide would continue, in the twentieth century, to flow around the world.

CHAPTER ELEVEN

THE NINETEENTH CENTURY
European Predominance 1815–1914

In 1815 the crowned heads of Europe were not unnaturally resolved to restore the sort of national and international order which they had fought for a generation to defend. Their efforts were rewarded with almost complete success for a generation. Then, in 1848, revolutions exploded across Europe. They were suppressed but industrialisation and widespread, eventually universal, education steadily changed the balance of power within most countries. By 1914 parliamentary institutions and complex bureaucracies alike limited the real power of monarchs and the wielders of power increasingly felt it necessary to pay attention to popular opinion. One result of this, and the progress of industrialisation, was a slow but real improvement in the living standards of large parts of the population. Another was increasing bellicosity as governments found it necessary to bow to popular jingoism fanned by a popular press which had discovered that international crises sold newspapers. The result was the First World War, the death of millions, the destruction of the nineteenth century international order and the beginning of the end of Europe's world hegemony.

The Congress Settlement

A certain realism, and even cynicism, was an integral part of the order which the monarchs and their supporters wished to restore. They saw no need to apologise for that. Not all the wars of the eighteenth century had bled Europe white in the way that Napoleon had done – traditional monarchs had known when to stop fighting in defeat and how to be reasonable in victory.

The Congress of Vienna re-drew the map of Europe, not to restore the states and boundaries of 1789, but to recognize and reconcile the interests of the major powers and to ensure that any new outbreak of revolution could be speedily contained. Russia was rewarded for its key role in Napoleon's defeat by most of Poland. Prussia was compensated for its losses in Poland by the Rhineland, which also opposed a strong power to any revival of French expansion. Austria was dominant in Italy. As for Britain, her sea power was unchallenged and her imperial expansion, in India, Australia and South Africa, made the loss of the American colonies seem little more than an incident.

At the instance of Metternich, the Austrian Chancellor, the powers created the Quadruple Alliance to maintain peace and preserve the status quo. France was admitted to join them in 1818. The first supranational organization in modern European history, the Alliance worked through a series of international congresses called to deal with crises as they arose. Liberal historians have seen the Alliance as repressive but it should not be assumed that a majority of people in most countries sought the overthrow of the restored order. In 1822 the Congress of Verona authorized intervention by France to support the Spanish monarchy against a liberal uprising. The Bourbon army was welcomed in the country where Napoleon's intervention had aroused nation-wide resistance; it quickly restored the traditional power structure and remained there unchallenged for five years.

Britain's Equivocal Position

Britain's oligarchic government was hardly less vigorous than the Continental monarchs in repressing any stirrings of popular discontent – eleven people were killed and four hundred wounded at Peterloo, outside Manchester, when the yeomanry opened fire on a demonstration in favor of parliamentary reform and the repeal of the Corn Laws which kept up the price of bread.

Nevertheless as a Parliamentary government, Britain felt some unease about its association with the absolute monarchs; this increased after 1832 when the first Reform Bill provided for a wider representation of the middle class. British governments, responding to the opinion of the electorate, thus became more inclined to sympathize with the aspirations of the continental bourgeoisie to take control of their governments. Even before this, British sea power had under-pinned the Monroe Declaration by the United States to discourage any European power from assisting Spain to subdue its revolting American colonies.

France from Restored Bourbon to Restored Bonaparte

In France Louis XVIII realized that his continued reign must be based on some concessions to the middle class, the real beneficiaries of the Revolution. His brother and successor, Charles X, attempted a more whole-hearted absolutism and was ejected in 1830 in favor of Louis Philippe, his cousin of the House of Bourbon Orleans. The new king's liberal credentials were beyond doubt; his father had thrown in his lot with the Revolution and even voted for the execution of Louis XVI, before being himself sent to the guillotine.

Louis Philippe, already a wealthy business man, inaugurated a regime appropriately known as the bourgeois monarchy, dominated by the wealthy middle class and dedicated to their enrichment. The Parisian workers, whose ranks had probably accounted for most of the two thousand rioters killed before Charles X abdicated, derived little benefit from the new regime.

The new bourgeois French monarchy and the established one across the Channel found that, against almost all historical precedent, they shared many perceptions and interests; they could work together in international affairs more easily than either of them could work with the autocratic powers to the East. Although much inherited hostility and numerous rival interests remained to be worked out, a major realignment of the European power structure was beginning to take shape.

Louis Philippe, while happy to be known as the bourgeois monarch, was not prepared to surrender real power. This provoked a vocal opposition among the politically active. In 1848 their agitation attracted support from the Parisian working class which rapidly spilled over into violence. Louis Philippe abdicated and a republic was proclaimed. Elections on universal male suffrage produced a conservative legislature which soon came into bloody collision with the Paris workers. Three thousand died in their suppression and ten thousand were sentenced to imprisonment; the Second Republic seemed safe. But the nation had still to elect a president – by universal male suffrage. Only one name on the ballot paper was familiar to the majority of voters – Louis Napoleon Bonaparte, nephew of the former Emperor. They elected him by a massive majority and continued their support in 1852 when, like his distinguished uncle, he exchanged his presidential hat for an imperial crown as Napoleon III, (Bonapartists counted the first emperor's son, who had never reigned in fact, as Napoleon II). So 1848, like 1789, had culminated not in a free republic but in an authoritarian empire.

1848 in Europe – liberalism and nationalism

The events of 1848 in Paris evoked a response across Europe which demonstrated that, despite the resistance of governments, the ideas of the Revolution had now won wide assent among the politically conscious. So too, with ominous implications for the future, had a new sense of nationalism.

For a short time this heady mixture seemed as though it might destroy the Hapsburg empire. There were risings in Prague and

Budapest, Milan and Venice and even in Vienna itself. But the interests and ambitions of the various nationalities incorporated in the Empire were incompatible and could easily provoke conflict. Against these multiple interests, the Hapsburgs were able to re-assert their control without too much difficulty, although Russian assistance was needed to finally subdue Hungary. The Austrian commander, General Haynau, sentenced some hundred Hungarian leaders to death and imprisoned two thousand. This repression earned him the name of butcher among the liberal Britons who lionized the exiled Hungarian leader, Kossuth. They were blissfully unaware that Kossuth and the Hungarians had used summary execution to repress Slovak attempts to assert their independence of the Magyars.

Prussia after 1848

Frederick William IV, King of Prussia, scornfully refused the offer of a German crown from the Assembly sitting at Frankfurt and claiming to represent the German nation – in his mind it was 'a Crown of shame tendered from the gutter.'

Frederick William was a conservative, with no sympathy for liberal claims, but he and his advisers were not therefore committed to the oppression of the poor. Their aim was to make Prussia confident of the loyalty of all its subjects and they recognized instinctively that this meant that they must all have a stake in Prussian society. In this endeavour – in which they were brilliantly successful – the Prussian government became a pioneer of intervention to protect the worker. In 1853 the employment of children under twelve years was forbidden; in Britain the minimum age was eight. Moreover, Prussia, unlike Britain, enforced its rules with an effective inspectorate. Employers were mollified by such measures as financial support for depressed industries – Prussian ministers, inheriting a long tradition of state intervention, were not sympathetic to laissez-faire. This approach, continued and extended by Bismarck, created modern Germany and endowed it with the unique mix of nationalism, economic efficiency and social cohesion which has, after some dreadful aberrations, brought it to a position of predominance in Europe and conceivably in the world.

Italy in 1848

In Italy too 1848 was a year of tumult, uprisings and constitutions. Milan ejected the Austrians and reluctantly accepted help from the King of Sardinia at the price of absorption into his kingdom. A republic was proclaimed in Rome; the Pope, his initial sympathy for the Italian cause destroyed, fled. By early 1849 the Austrians were again in the ascendant. As their troops moved south, President Bonaparte decided that he, rather than the Hapsburgs, should earn the honour – and the support of Catholic voters – of restoring the pope to Rome. French troops overthrew the Roman Republic and a French garrison remained there for twenty years.

By 1856, however, Cavour, the Sardinian prime minister, had enlisted the support of Napoleon III for a war against Austria. France won the battles but Napoleon, appalled at the slaughter and worried that Prussia might intervene, made peace. Sardinia got Milan but not Venice. In the next few years, a mixture of 'popular' uprisings, plebiscites (supported where necessary by bribery and bullying) and military intervention spread Sardinian power and created the kingdom of Italy.

For most of its new citizens, the rejoicing was short-lived. The peasants, the majority of the population, found themselves subject, not only to higher taxation, but also to the conscription of their sons. The new state was clearly dominated by the landowners and the urban bourgeoisie and they rightly expected little from either. In the South, opposition to conscription soon passed over into resistance and brigandage which were brutally suppressed; the Mafia strengthened its vicious hold and the contrast between South and North was re-inforced. Moreover, the new state inherited the anti-clericalism of Sardinia. Monasteries and convents were seized and the clergy, no longer a favoured class, were subject to active discrimination. The Pope, already enraged by the loss of most of the Papal States, was further alienated by these measures and forbad Catholics to participate in civic life. Italy was thus weakened by the hostility or indifference of substantial parts of its population.

The Weakness of the post-1848 Restoration

The uprisings of 1848 ended with the restoration of the old rulers, and apparently of the old order, everywhere except in France. Even there, the Second Empire was not very different from the bourgeois monarchy. In fact, however, the post 1848 situation did differ from the old order. The confidence of the rulers had been shaken and they began to think in terms of maintaining the support of their subjects. Power was beginning to pass from the monarch and his court to ministers and representative assemblies – usually elected on a very limited franchise. Nationalism had been revealed as a new and unpredictable force, which governments would increasingly have to reckon with and which would gradually come to exert a major influence on their policies.

Between 1815 and 1848 the crowned heads of Europe had, on the whole, maintained unity and peace; tension and occasional violence broke out between rulers and a minority of their people, not between states. The next twenty years transformed this situation. The unified Concert of Europe was replaced by a complex of states pursuing conflicting interests and this in turn gave way after 1870 to the creation of two rival and hostile power blocks.

Significance of Nationalism

The Italian ruling elite and its sympathizers abroad regarded the unification of Italy as a great triumph for nationalism and liberalism. The concept of the nation began to take on an almost mystical significance; nations existed as entities with rights which should be acknowledged; if they were not, they might justifiably be pursued by force. A state, or even a boundary, which was not based on nationality was increasingly seen by 'enlightened' opinion as an anomaly and resistance to the demands of nationalists as backward and unjust. Very few realized that whereas in Italy a single nationality occupied a homogeneous territory – with some fuzziness on the borders destined to cause trouble later – further east the map of nationalities was a patchwork quilt. The emerging nationalisms had, as events in Hungary had demonstrated in 1848, conflicting claims and a bloody minded determination to enforce them at the expense of rivals, which would inevitably lead to war and massacre.

The Unification of Germany

The next triumph of nationalism, the unification of Germany, was indeed achieved without massacre but not without war. Indeed, the architect of that unity, the Prussian Chancellor Otto von Bismarck, is famous for his judgment on the Frankfurt Assembly of 1848: 'the great questions of the day will be settled not by resolutions and majorities ... but by blood and iron.' Perhaps few statesman in Europe would have disagreed with him in private but since they did not choose to express such views publicly Bismarck's frankness has made him a byword for cynicism and aggression.

The unification of Germany involved three wars, one with Denmark in 1864, a second with Austria in 1866 and a third with France in 1870. Thanks to the diplomatic skill with which Bismarck ensured that Prussia's opponents were isolated, and the superiority of the Prussian army, all were mercifully short. At the end, Austria was excluded from Germany and the representatives of the German princes, assembled in the Hall of Mirrors in Versailles, hailed the king of Prussia as emperor of a new German Reich.

Prussia, which had annexed a number of north German states foolish enough to support Austria in 1866, dominated the Empire. Moreover, the constitution of the Empire left real power in the hands of the Emperor and the Bundestag, the upper house of the Diet or legislature, in which representatives were appointed by the princes; here Prussia had sufficient votes to command a majority with only limited support from other states. The lower house, the Reichstag, was elected by universal manhood suffrage but its powers were limited.

The new German Empire was thus a mixture which others, especially the British and French, found difficult to understand. It mixed a franchise more generous than most with a legislature dominated by, but not subservient to, the executive. It was a federal state with distinct overtones of a confederation; its constitution assigned to its constituent states powers that the States of the USA or the Cantons of Switzerland had been obliged to surrender to the national government. Yet it undoubtedly possessed a strong central government capable of pursuing its concept of the national interest vigorously. Part, but only part of the explanation, was the dominant position of Prussia. The constitution responded to a genuine sense of regional differences and local loyalties which the Germans found it possible to reconcile with a strong spirit of nationalism. Significantly the current constitution of the Federal Republic of Germany preserves both an upper house with strong powers and the right of the constituent states to nominate the members of that house.

The Emergence of Conflicting Power Blocs

The wars of the period 1854 to 1870, limited as they were by comparison with those to come in the next century, marked the end of the Concert of Europe and the peace it had preserved. It could hardly have been otherwise. The predominance of France in Europe, and the weakness of Germany, had dated back centuries to the disintegration of the Holy Roman Empire as an effective political and governmental entity. The defeat of France and the creation of the new German Empire clearly established the new Germany as the predominant military power in Europe.

Bismarck therefore used all his diplomatic skills to forge alliances and understandings which would support the new status quo. His efforts were doomed to failure because, unlike Metternich and his colleagues in 1815, he had forced the French to surrender territory – Alsace and part of Lorraine – which they regarded as an integral part of France. Germans, in their new-found nationalism, recalled that the former had been German until 1648 and the latter until 1766. Bismarck had fostered this nationalism and the associated anti-French feelings to mobilize support for the new Reich. Now it was impossible to put the genie back in the bottle. The Germans wanted to assert their power and the French dreamed of revenge. Despite all Bismarck's efforts to isolate France, by 1894 Europe was clearly divided into two blocs – France and Russia (to be joined by Britain in 1904) on one side and Germany, Austria and Italy (although it deserted its allies in 1915) on the other.

Remarkably, Prussia and Austria were able to forget the conflicts of the past and forge an understanding which survived until the two states went down in defeat in 1918.

All the European powers except Britain now had very large, conscript armies and these, thanks to the industrial development of the century, were equipped with weapons of far greater destructive power than any ever seen before. Should war come, it would be on a scale never previously seen on earth. Moreover the very size of the rival armies meant that their deployment, even with the aid of the new railway systems, would take time and would be difficult to modify from the plans already prepared. Once governments started to mobilize, they would be reluctant to halt the process for fear that chaos would result and they would be caught at a disadvantage. The control which monarchs and ministers had been accustomed to exercise over generals was thereby weakened. Moreover, most officer corps remained bastions of traditional aristocratic values; even when they gradually came to include an increasing proportion of middle class, these usually absorbed the ethos of their superiors. Aristocratic conceptions of honour and valour, however appropriate they had been when the survival of Christendom depended on desperate hand-to-hand combat with Magyars, Vikings or Moslems, were to prove tragically inappropriate in a warfare of trenches, artillery and machine guns.

The transformation of warfare was only one aspect of massive and interconnected changes in European society which make the nineteenth century a watershed in the history of the world.

The Industrial Revolution

Before the century commenced, technological innovation, already a distinguishing mark of Europe, had begun to accelerate in Britain. Already advantaged by an innovative agriculture, readily available sources of power from coal and metal from iron mines, and an advanced capital market developed to support overseas trade, Britain now experienced an industrial revolution which transformed the basis of production. This transformation occurred first in the textile industry but before long extended to other industries and established Britain's claim to be 'the workshop of the world.' Mining and heavy industry benefited from improvements in transport with the invention of the steam locomotive by Stephenson. The first railway line linked Liverpool and Manchester in 1830; by 1848 Britain's railway network exceeded 5000 miles. By the 1840's industrialization had spread to substantial parts of Europe – Belgium, northern France, the Rhineland and Silesia in Prussia and Bohemia in the Hapsburg empire.

The changes in production methods which were the essence of the industrial revolution meant an immediate increase in productivity and output. Moreover, they reflected and entrenched an even more significant development. Many Europeans were already inclined to take it for granted that problems could be solved; every victory for ingenuity and determination reinforced the conviction that further advances were possible. Technological breakthroughs soon assumed a multiplier function – innovations which had been impossible with the technology and materials of 1800 became possible with those available by 1850 and so on. Change therefore proceeded at an accelerating pace and became the basis for more, and more rapid, change – perhaps the hallmark of the modern world.

For Europe and North America, and hopefully now for much of Asia and Latin America, there is also another hallmark – eventual improvements in living conditions linked with democratisation, a change in political structures which enables some influence on key decisions to be exerted by a majority of the population. These trends, of course, were not apparent at the beginning.

In Britain, the growth of the new factory style production meshed with the reduction in the population supported on the land, a consequence of improved methods of production and the legalisation of the enclosure of common land; this redounded mainly to the benefit of large landowners whereas the commons had helped to support poor rural dwellers. Many of these were now forced off the land and found jobs in the new factories, providing a source of cheap and exploitable labour. Wages were low, hours long and living conditions in the new, industrial towns harsh and unsanitary. Child labour was exploited unconscionably. In short, all the conditions which we now associate with the worst exploitation of labour in developing countries were to be found in Britain as it industrialized and, in due course, in other European countries as they followed its example.

It has been argued that the conditions of the new industrial workers were no worse than those they had left in the countryside. Certainly the life of a poor rural labourer and his family was hard at the best of times, even in Britain, where many observers considered conditions superior to most of Europe. Work was hard, living conditions were poor and sometimes unsanitary and diet often inadequate. Life was very much subject to the pressure and whims of landlords and social superiors. In most parts of the Continent east of the Elbe much of the rural population was still subject to feudal obligations until 1848 or later. But there still remains a strong impression that life in the slums of the new industrial towns, and work in the factories and mines, was even harder. Certainly it was more disruptive of family and traditional group life and had little or no room for the rustic enjoyments of the countryside. And, perhaps most telling of all, the cities could not reproduce themselves – the death rate continued to be higher than the birth rate.

With few exceptions, nineteenth century European capitalists were no more inclined than their current counterparts in developing countries to decrease their profits by raising wages above starvation levels. The relatively new discipline of economics was easily enlisted to support their natural inclination. David Ricardo (1772–1823) formulated the proposition which became known as the Iron Law of Wages. He taught that wages, although they might rise under the impetus of economic expansion, would tend to settle at subsistence level and should be allowed to do so; interference by either state or trade union was wrong. In his later writings Ricardo defined his subsistence wage in terms which make it sound rather closer to the concept of a living wage; these subtleties were, needless to say, cheerfully ignored by employers.

As in many developing countries to-day, the rapid accumulation of profits which new technology and the exploitation of cheap labour facilitated fueled further investment and development, the growth of massive fortunes and the ability of the successful capitalists to influence governments in directions favourable to their interests.

Improvements in Labour and Living Conditions

Although the influence of the entrepreneurs was growing, however, most countries in Europe were not ruled by them. In Britain in the early part of the nineteenth century, for example, it was the great and medium landowners and leading merchants who dominated Parliament. These men also had no great urge to protect the poor. But high among their concerns was to preserve the stability of the society in which they were the major stakeholders; many of them saw that the unmitigated misery of a large and growing class could only be a threat to that stability. In these sentiments they were joined by the more enlightened of the entrepreneurs and by those – probably a minority – who saw the exploitation of the poor as an affront to their Christian belief.

Pressure from the new working class itself no doubt contributed to the growing inclination to ameliorate their condition, although their ability to organize effectively was curtailed by legislative and other restrictions. In Britain, for example, peaceful picketing was not legalized until 1874. By this time, the growth of trade unionism, largely in the guise of mutual benefit or 'friendly' societies, among skilled workers and the extension of the franchise in 1867 had made the votes of the more prosperous members of the working class a matter of concern to the two political parties, Conservative and Liberal, which dominated British politics. Legislation to limit working hours, especially for women and children, and impose minimal occupational health and safety standards gradually produced some improvement in working conditions for most workers. Living conditions were improved by building and sanitary controls, water supplies and sewerage systems and readily available, cheap public transport.

Underlying all these improvements were the advances in science, technology and industrial production which made possible increases in the volume and diversity of output unimaginable in earlier periods. The share of this increased output which went to the workers might well seem inappropriate both to them and to us. It is beyond doubt, however, that by the end of the century, most of them were better off than their ancestors had been at the beginning or, indeed, at any time in the past. They were better fed, better housed and had a little more leisure. Some at least were beginning to feel that they and their fellows were of some account in society and beginning to look for means to make their demands more keenly felt by those who ruled it.

Democratisation, Literacy and the Consequences

The more flexible and intelligent of those rulers were willing to respond and to play the game of politics in ways which would garner them the support of the expanded electorate. Thus Disraeli, a Conservative minister (and later Prime Minister), expanded the franchise in 1867 to 'dish the Whigs.' In the new German empire created in 1871, Bismarck intended to contain the opposition of the middle class liberals by relying on the support of the rural and working class majority.

Many of the working class, however, were already captured by the socialist doctrine of the class struggle. Various formulations of socialism can be traced back at least as far as the French Revolution. Some efforts to give them practical expression in the early stages of the Second Republic in 1848 were suppressed and socialism remained largely a subject for intellectual argument. By 1870 the argument seemed to be largely dominated by Karl Marx and Friedrich Engels. They had published the Communist Manifesto in 1848; after almost twenty years of research in the Reading Room of the British Museum Marx published the first volume of Das Kapital in 1867. Marx's interpretation of history, his argument that capitalist oppression would result in an overwhelming uprising of the workers, above all his assurance that the eventual victory of the proletariat was inevitable, made a powerful appeal to workers who felt themselves oppressed and exploited. The German Social Democratic Workers Party, founded in 1875, was an amalgamation of two established parties, one Marxist in orientation, the other based on the ideas of Lasalle who stressed the use of the vote and the need for universal suffrage.

Three years later Bismarck banned the party and its press; hundreds of party members were imprisoned. He also attempted to steal its thunder. In 1885 he introduced insurance for workers against accident and sickness, in 1889 pensions at 70 years of age. These measures did not prevent the continuing rise of the Social Democrats and Bismarck's proposals to repress them further were the occasion for the new Emperor to dismiss him in 1890. Nevertheless the social legislation of the 1880's did promote a certain basic cohesion in German society which underpinned its strength as a military power, obviously the most formidable in Europe.

The Social Democratic Party maintained a Marxist orientation in principle, as did the French socialist party and most others. In practice, however, these parties came to focus more on immediate benefits for their supporters than on stoking the fires of the class struggle. In Britain the Labour Party, beginning as the Labour Representation Committee in 1900, grew out of the trade unions and was largely dominated by them; its approach to politics was pragmatic rather than ideological. By that date there were socialist or labour parties in at least fifteen European countries as well as strong labour parties in Australia and New Zealand.

Well before the end of the nineteenth century it became clear that the new level of production both required a wider diffusion of education to sustain it and created the relative affluence which made it possible to finance such diffusion without too much strain. The upper classes, who had earlier regarded the extension of education with suspicion as potentially subversive of the social order, were brought to accept it as an economic necessity. Armies based on compulsory military service also saw advantages in literate recruits. Universal education, at least at primary level, was achieved in some countries and in sight in others before 1900.

Of course the suspicions of those who had opposed it turned out to be right. It was not just that a minority of those taught to read turned to Tom Paine and Karl Marx, or the simplified versions for which ardent reformers and good capitalist publishers found a market. Much wider was the influence of a new type of newspaper, geared to the interests, perceptions and prejudices of the newly, and barely, literate. Its success required an ability to gauge and write what they would buy with their hard earned pennies. The new journalism, it was soon realized, could be a potent influence on the attitudes and choices of the majority of voters; but the newspapers, concerned above all with circulation, also saw a need to respond to the attitudes and prejudices of their readers. Politicians found themselves obliged to frame their policies with increasing attention to public opinion mobilized by newspapers.

In foreign relations, as newspapers found that 'patriotic' attacks on other governments appealed to the natural chauvinism of their readers, their influence operated to increase tensions and make compromise settlement of disputes more difficult to accept. Not since Pericles had driven the foreign policy of Athens on the passions he could arouse in the Athenian *demos* had war and peace depended so directly on the skills of the demagogue. The results were to be similar but on a scale more massive than Pericles could have imagined.

The significance of these trends was not lost on the more perceptive observers of society. Helmuth von Moltke, the architect of Prussia's victories over Austria and France, wrote a decade later that the recent wars had been caused by the mood of the people and the activities of party leaders, against the wish of the rulers.

It is hard to reconcile this judgment with the deliberate and planned aggression of Bismarck, Cavour and Napoleon III. But it seems a prophetic anticipation of the jingoistic climate that lay ahead. By the end of the century those who governed, even in states which were less than fully democratic, had to frame their foreign policies with one eye on popular reaction. Many of them were far from guiltless of jingoism themselves; even those who were not felt that they had to take account of the jingoism of the population, fanned by the press.

The Movement of Political Power towards the Majority

The dynasties which had presided over the 1815 reconstitution of Europe still, for the most part, reigned over the same states but the actual government of those states was, with few exceptions, in the hands of elected politicians and bureaucrats who served them. In the two empires of Germany and Austria-Hungary, the powers of the monarch seemed greater than in the liberal, constitutional states of Western Europe but this was largely an illusion or a legal fiction. The Emperors lacked the combination of intellectual power and determination which would have been necessary to dominate their governments in the way which was theoretically still possible. Even in Russia, the absolutism of the Tsar, theoretically untrammelled until 1905, was exercised largely by the bureaucracy.

So real power all over Europe was largely in the hands of the middle class with an occasional sprinkling of the aristocracy. By 1914, however, their supremacy was challenged by the majority lower down the social and economic scale. The gradual extension of the franchise proved irresistible – it embraced all men in France and Germany and was almost as broad in Britain. Middle class politicians still found it possible to mobilize working class votes but this required concessions to working class interests. Moreover the socialist parties were obviously increasing their appeal and their agenda called for the virtual replacement of middle class control of the economy by the power of the state. No one expected that a socialist government would soon come to power but the prospect was that socialist support would increasingly be needed to form governments.

The rise of the socialist parties signified that the control of state power was no longer securely in the hands of either the traditional aristocracy or the newly dominant middle class. In those states which were most successful in terms of international power and national development, power was inevitably passing to the majority. The shape of the future would depend, to a significant extent, on how that majority choose to define itself. As rising national incomes and rising wages increased the living standards and raised the horizons of a growing proportion of workers, the key question was whether the upwardly mobile would maintain their solidarity with the rest of the working class or whether they would take on, along with middle class comforts, middle class attitudes and values. By 1914 it was clear that there was sufficient leakage from class solidarity to boost the votes of the traditional middle class parties but the socialist parties still had reason to hope for the eventual achievement of power through the ballot box.

Europe and the World

One thing on which practically all European voters were agreed was the superiority of Europe over the rest of the world. The century had seen the extension of European power to world domination and no one doubted that this was part of the order of nature – other races were inherently inferior. If the 'white man's burden' included a responsibility not just to govern the rest in their own interest but to prepare them for a time when they could be trusted to govern themselves – and not everyone acknowledged such an obligation – no one thought that such a time was near at hand. For a long time to come, colonies would provide opportunities for settlement and careers for administrators. Both colonies and economic dependencies – which meant the rest of the world – provided cheap raw materials and market outlets which contributed to improved European living standards. Japan, with which Britain concluded an alliance of equals in 1902, was clearly an exception to this general inferiority but one to be reckoned with as a minor player in the European power balance, not a harbinger of the replacement of that balance by a new world order.

Drift into War

The rivalry of the two power blocs was fed by conflicting ambitions beyond their borders. For Austria-Hungary and Russia these ambitions revolved around the slow dissolution of the Turkish Empire and their competing ambitions to dominate the Balkans. Russia, conscious of its origins, viewed itself as the natural ruler of Constantinople, an outcome which would also give it free access to the Mediterranean. The Hapsburgs, in the aftermath of their defeat by Prussia, had reached an accommodation with the Magyars and transformed their Empire into the Dual Monarchy of Austria-Hungary. The deal involved the domination of the other, mainly

Slav, nationalities by the two partners. In 1867, this had seemed possible. A generation later, it seemed much more dubious. The Austro-Hungarian government felt increasingly threatened by Slav nationalism within the Empire and viewed any re-inforcement of it in the Balkans with alarm; the vacuum created by the decline of Turkey must be filled by expansion of Austria-Hungary, not that of Russia or its protégé, Serbia. That state now saw itself as the nucleus of a South Slav state which should include the Croat and Slovene subjects of the Hapsburgs. There were people on its payroll who thought a little murder a small price to pay for such a noble objective. In June 1914 one of them organized the assassination of the heir to the Hapsburg throne in Sarajevo.

The murder of the Archduke Franz Ferdinand, and the Austrian reaction, designed to force Serbia into either subservience or war, was the signal for the rival alliances to be brought into play. No statesman in 1914 possessed the status or the determination which had enabled Bismarck in 1878 to seize the initiative and act as 'honest broker' to resolve differences. Very few, in fact, showed any effective desire to halt the slide to Armageddon.

If Austria attacked Serbia, then Russia would attack Austria and this in turn would bring Germany to the latter's support. Then France would have to support Russia by attacking Germany. Italy was pledged only to neutrality and stayed out for the moment. Britain, bound to France and Russia at least morally, shrewdly waited for Germany to violate Belgian neutrality and so mobilize popular support for entering the war. By 4 August 1914 virtually all Europe was at war. The First Peloponnesian War of European civilization had begun.

Independence in Latin America

By 1815, with the Napoleonic wars ended, Europeans had time to devote some attention to the wider world which had been largely only a backdrop to the titanic struggle with the French. Britain, whose naval power in the recent war had delivered it the colonies of France and its conscripted allies, was prepared to return most of them. France received some footholds on the African coast, on which it would later build a vast if partly barren empire. The Netherlands returned to Java and its posts in the rest of the vast archipelago now called Indonesia and set about bringing the whole area under its control. The Portuguese monarchy, a British ally during the war, remained in control of its coastal stations in East and West Africa and its historic footholds in Asia. Having fled to Brazil to escape Napoleon, the king showed no anxiety to return to Lisbon. When he eventually did so in 1820, he left his son as Viceroy. The Viceroy took the lead in resistance to Portuguese attempts to re-assert control; in 1822 he became emperor of an independent Brazil.

The first and largest of the European empires had been established by Spain in South and Central America. No European power challenged her right to this vast territory but the colonists did. Inspired by the example of the British colonists in North America, they took advantage of Spain's difficulties with Napoleon to proclaim their independence. The restored Spanish monarchy proposed to assert its control by force and the European land powers were sympathetic. They could not give active support after the British made it clear that they would oppose the transport of non-Spanish troops and the United States, in the Monroe Doctrine, declared that such intervention would be regarded as an unfriendly act.

Britain may have been motivated partly by trade considerations but there was also an idealistic sympathy for people struggling for their freedom, especially against one of Britain's traditional enemies. This sympathy was, from our perspective, misplaced. The new states established in Latin America were dominated by a small minority of more or less pure Spanish ancestry who monopolized the wealth and exploited the majority of the population, both Indian and mestizo (mixed blood). Moreover, the new states, lacking any experience of representative government, largely fell under the control of military caudillos or dictators. Latin America may thus claim the melancholy distinction of having introduced the idea of dictatorship to the modern world.

The British Colonies of Settlement

The British experience in North America did not encourage them to contemplate new colonies of settlement. Nevertheless, a settlement was established in Australia in 1788 to provide a place of deportation for convicts previously despatched to America. It took a few venturesome free settlers, some ambitious ex-convicts and a visionary governor to establish that the continent had more potential than a gaol. South Africa, seized from the Netherlands during the Napoleonic War, was retained at the end because of its strategic location on the route to India. British settlement followed, and settlers and authorities alike came into conflict with the existing settlers. These, known as Boers (farmers) or Afrikaaners, were descendents of the original Dutch settlers and French Huguenot refugees. Accustomed to treat the Africans as they liked, the Afrikaaners resented the British abolition of slavery. In 1835 they migrated out of the colony (the Great Trek) and eventually established two independent states, the Orange Free State and the Transvaal Republic.

It was Canada, however, which provided the greatest challenge to British colonialism and evoked the most significant response. Lord Durham's report of 1837 proposed the extension of responsible government with an elected legislature and a cabinet dependent on its support. Canada, and before long the other colonies of settlement, were thus launched on the path to self-government and eventual independence.

French Expansion in Africa

The French embarked on a new colonial era in 1830 when Charles X tried, unsuccessfully, to divert opposition to his rule by invading Algeria. His successor, Louis Philippe, carried on the struggle and France was soon involved in a long and vicious war in the hills behind the coastal plain. By 1880 350,000 European settlers, Italian and Spanish as well as French, in the plains were protected by 100,000 French troops.

The bitter struggle in Algeria did not deter France from embarking on a policy of expansion in West Africa, pushing up the Senegal River and fighting a series of wars with the Moslem states in the interior. Liberty, equality and fraternity obviously did not extend to Africans and in French eyes the Moslem states of the Sahel did not qualify as full members of the international community. This was a sentiment with which the British and other powers interested in Africa could agree, although for the time being they were less inclined than the French to expand the areas under their control.

African and Other Adventurers

In fact, apart from the French, the leading imperialists in Africa in the middle of the century were not European but African and Arab. The historic Christian kingdom of Ethiopia recovered from virtual disintegration under a succession of talented emperors and promptly set about creating its own empire by conquering the Gallas and a large part of the Somalis.

The Egypt of Muhammed Ali and his successors penetrated up the Nile and annexed most of the area which has become the modern state of Sudan; a parallel movement down the Red Sea resulted in the occupation of part of Somalia. The Sudanese adventure came to a sudden halt in 1885 when a religious leader proclaimed himself Mahdi or saviour and mobilized local resistance. The Egyptians were ejected from the Sudan and only returned in 1898 as minor associates of the British, who had in the meantime established a protectorate over their country.

The Sultan of Oman had been overlord of the Moslem towns on the East coast since 1698. This position had become largely nominal but Seyyid Said, realizing its potential, transformed it into real power and in 1840 took up residence in Zanzibar. From here and the other coastal towns, Arab traders penetrated the interior. Well armed and supported by African followers, they dominated the area; they did not seek to rule it but to exploit its potential for slaves and ivory. In the process they made effective rule of any sort impossible; any African group which tried to oppose them was overthrown and destroyed.

An original type of state was created in the Congo by King Leopold of Belgium. Knowing that his country would not support his imperial ambitions, Leopold persuaded France, Germany and even the United States to recognize the Congo Free State, with himself as sovereign. Eventually, however, abuses in the exploitation of the inhabitants aroused a European outcry and the Belgian government was obliged to take over the Free State.

'The Scramble for Africa'

For most of the century, the only European countries with an active interest in Africa had been France, Portugal with its traditional holdings on the East and West coasts, and Britain. The latter preferred to avoid formal sovereignty and confine itself to a few coastal enclaves and informal influence over the surrounding states or tribes. This situation began to change after 1870 when public opinion in the newly unified Germany began to see colonies as a sort of national status symbol. Bismarck resisted these sentiments for a long time but in 1883 gave way. Germany annexed Togo and the

Cameroons in West Africa, Tanganyika in East Africa and South West Africa. A conference of the European powers in Berlin in 1884-85 laid down ground rules which prevented any conflict between the powers as the 'Scramble for Africa' proceeded. Native states and tribes sometimes put up resistance but this was usually overcome without too much trouble; the most bitter struggle was fought between Britain and the white Boer republics. It ended, inevitably, with their defeat and annexation but the concession of self-government within a few years enabled the Afrikaaners to achieve a dominant position in South Africa.

Many aspects of European society were brought together to support late nineteenth century imperialism. Traders looked for new opportunities and feared that if another power expanded its control it would use tariffs and other mechanisms to favor its own nationals. Colonial dominion made new openings for the employment, civil and military, of younger sons of the gentry. Christian missionaries, and the Churches which supported them, welcomed the security given by colonial rule and the suppression of inhuman abuses such as the slave trade. Church and liberal opinion alike sought to defend the interests of the native people against exploitation by colonial powers, traders and the (relatively few) settlers.

European military superiority grew during the century and became definitive with the introduction of the Gatling and Maxim machine guns. At Omdurman in 1898 Kitchener's Anglo-Egyptian force inflicted 20,000 casualties on the fanatical followers of the Mahdi and suffered only 40 itself. British and European opinion appears to have been unmoved by this slaughter, just as on other occasions it had accepted the casualties inflicted on its own troops without question. Human life was still cheap, both the lives of soldiers drawn largely from the poorest sections of the population and the lives of 'savages' who resisted the extension of European rule.

Virtually no one queried the right of the European powers to impose their control on Africans and Asians. The assumption of European superiority was general and justified wars which, if undertaken against another European country, would have been condemned as unprovoked aggression. In a similar fashion, European powers, which already claimed the right to protect their nationals from being subject to the laws of Asian states, were hardly likely to accept the validity of African legal systems.

The Reaction of Africans

What did the African think as he found himself and his fellows subject to European power? That, not unnaturally, seems to have depended largely on what demands the new masters made on him. Taxation, which in many cases could only be paid by finding work for government or settler, was unwelcome but normally bearable. It was a different matter if the new regime took the African's land. This was likely to provoke armed resistance. Short of this, many Africans could see benefits in the education, medical and other services brought by the colonial administrations and in the protection they gave against violence. Education offered a way into new opportunities in the service of the new regime and there was no reluctance to accept them. The African civil servants, even though mostly confined to junior roles such as clerks and postmen, largely constituted the cadre from which the champions and prime beneficiaries of independence would be drawn.

While Africa was the most prominent object of European imperialism in the nineteenth century, it was far from the only one. The islands of the Pacific were taken over by Britain, France, Germany and the United States with little opposition. At the end of the century the last mentioned ejected Spain from her West Indian possessions and from the Philippines and, with some hesitation, become a substantial colonial power.

European Expansion in Asia

Russia gradually conquered the Moslem, largely Turkish, states of Central Asia. The age-old superiority of the nomad horseman over the sedentary peasant and town dweller had come to an end, destroyed by European military technology. This process, from the British point of view, brought the Russians alarmingly close to India. The 'Great Game' of spy and counterspy was played by both sides in the high mountains of Afghanistan until the rise of German power in Europe made them unwilling allies.

Britain's supremacy in India was in fact unchallengeable. France sought compensation in Indo-China, an area with which it had some historic connections going back to the seventeenth century. By 1887 France controlled an Indo-Chinese Union which embraced the three kingdoms of Annam (Vietnam), Cambodia and Laos. Vietnam was not Africa but a historic nation with a unique record of resisting absorption by China despite a thousand year occupation. French rule was destined to provoke resistance until it was finally destroyed.

France would have liked to extend its Indo-Chinese empire to embrace the neighbouring state of Siam (now Thailand). This ambition, however, was frustrated by the opposition of the British who, having conquered Burma, bordered Siam in the west, and the astuteness of the Siamese king. Siam therefore joined Japan and Ethiopia on the very short list of traditional polities which maintained their independence.

Japan's Modernisation and China's Decay

By the middle of the nineteenth century a significant strand of opinion in Japan, well informed on the outside world, was increasingly doubtful of the viability of its established policy of seclusion. They naturally felt vindicated when the Americans forced an opening up in 1854 and the European powers hastened to demand the same facilities. When the Shogun's government showed itself hesitant to adapt to the new reality, they brought about a restoration of power to the Emperor. The new government embarked on a programme of modernization without parallel in history. Mission after mission was dispatched to the West; the structure of Japan's government, economy and defence was transformed in the light of their reports. The cohesion of Japanese society, the manifest urgency of preserving the country from being overwhelmed by Western aggression, the sacred aura of the Emperor and the skilful management of the reformers made it possible to achieve sweeping changes with little opposition.

Japan, having thus demonstrated its ability to modernize, was clearly no object for imperial adventures; by the end of the century it had joined the ranks of imperial powers by seizing Taiwan after a brief war with China. The Japanese victory underlined the weakness of China under the decaying Manchu dynasty.

The size of that country and the rivalry of the European powers deterred any one of them from trying to establish their supremacy. Instead, they joined together in uneasy understanding to impose on China 'unequal treaties' according privileges to their nationals and their trade and giving them footholds on the coast. The Chinese, who still regarded their country as the Middle Kingdom, around which the rest of the world revolved, resented this but were too weak to contest it. In 1911 a revolution led by Sun Yat Sen ousted the Manchu dynasty and proclaimed a republic. Sun and his followers lacked the power to maintain control; China split into virtually independent regions under the control of warlords who were often little better than bandits. Sun led the Chinese National Peoples Party or Kuomintang (KMT) with its centre in Canton; after his death in 1925 the leadership passed to General Chiang Kai-shek.

Japan meanwhile had marked its success by negotiating a treaty of alliance with Britain in 1902 This, the first equal treaty in modern times between a European and an Asian power, acknowledged Japan as a full member of the international community. Japan made its status clear by fighting a successful war with Russia (1904-5) and occupying Korea.

European Hegemony at Risk

Although the European powers did not realize it, Japan's victory over Russia signaled to many Asians the possibility of ending European domination. Unfortunately some in Japan, notably in the officer corps, saw the future in terms of replacing European domination by Japanese.

If the European powers wished to maintain their hegemony of the world then the first requirement was that they should avoid conflict with one another. This, however, they could not or would not do. The World War of 1914-1918 saw the European powers arrayed against one another and using their non-European subjects for support against their European enemies. It marked the beginning of the end of European supremacy.

American Growth and Potential

By the end of the eighteenth century a perceptive observer might well have pointed out that the power structure of Europe and the world was already overshadowed by a new, giant actor; when it realized its full potential, it would dominate the world. He would, of course, have been talking about Russia. The notion that his forecast would be proved true by the United States would probably have struck him as fanciful.

The two million colonists who had set out on the road to independence in 1775 had indeed grown to four million by 1800. That, however. still left them a small country by European standards. In any case, they were pre-occupied with the opportunities for expansion beyond the boundaries formerly imposed by a British government intent on avoiding trouble with the Indian inhabitants. The Americans had no such scruples; many of them were convinced that 'the only good Indian is a dead Indian' and acted accordingly. The scope for expansion was enlarged enormously in 1803 when Napoleon, having forced Spain to restore to France the trans-Mississippi lands ceded by the latter after the Seven Years War, was confronted with the prospect of losing them to the British. To avoid this, he sold the vast territory to the United States for fifteen million dollars.

Settlers who had already pushed across the Appalachians now spread across the Mississippi. Land was made available at a dollar an acre and the American population was growing strongly, largely by natural increase – the flood of migration came later. As the new areas filled up, they were converted from Federal territories to states of the Union.

The expansion of settlement involved constant conflict with the Indian peoples whose rights were ignored by the white settlers. Successive US governments negotiated treaties but largely failed to prevent whites from breaching their conditions. When the Indians were driven to resistance, troops were used to suppress them – sometimes with bitter fighting – and the negotiated treaties abrogated.

Excited by this continuing expansion, many Americans were convinced that it was the 'manifest destiny' of the United States to spread across the continent from the Atlantic to the Pacific. Canada was also included in their ambitions. In 1812, provoked by the high-handed enforcement of the British blockade of Napoleonic Europe, the United States declared war. The conquest of Canada was high on the war aims of many Americans but the attempt met with unexpected resistance. Peace was restored when the defeat of Napoleon removed the original casus belli.

Beyond the purchased territory was land claimed and lightly occupied by Spain; this soon became part of the new nation of Mexico. The United States had contributed to the independence of the Spanish colonies by the 1823 declaration by President Monroe that intervention in the Western hemisphere by European powers would be seen as an unfriendly act. The Monroe Doctrine became the foundation of American foreign policy. Many in the United States, it would often seem to Latin Americans, would come to interpret it as a claim to hegemony.

Some Americans, in their pursuit of new lands, actually pushed beyond the boundaries of the United States into Mexican territory. Here they proclaimed the independent state of Texas which the United States eventually agreed to absorb. This led to war with Mexico which was defeated and obliged to surrender California and the other land north of the Rio Grande. Two years earlier, in 1846, the boundary with Canada had been agreed, bringing the United States to the Pacific in the Oregon Territory.

Population had grown to 24 million by 1850, stimulated now by a steady tide of migration. America became a magnet for poor Europeans – Irish driven out by the potato famine prominent among them and destined to establish their nation as a major constituent of the population. They would be followed by Italians, largely poor peasants from the south, Germans, Poles and many others. Economic hardship accounted for most migrants but there was also a small number of political refugees. Their new home absorbed them all, not always comfortably. The new migrants were at the bottom of the social scale, their labour exploited and their living conditions often crowded and unsanitary. Hope and an expanding economy kept them going, kept the flow coming and the population growing. Opportunity and education made their children Americans, even though their origins were seldom forgotten, and wove diverse strands into one nation.

Slavery and the American Civil War

There was another divide in American society which threatened to tear America apart. The economy of the southern states was based on plantation agriculture, dependent on slave labour. The south was determined to defend its 'peculiar institution'. The northern states, with an economy based on smallholdings and growing industrial development, regarded slavery as morally reprehensible. In 1861 they came to blows, the southern states seeking to secede from the Union and establish the Confederate States of America. Since they accounted for only one third of the population and even less of the industry, the defeat of the Confederate States was inevitable. Nevertheless the war dragged on until 1865 and cost 600,000 lives. It was, although European generals did not realize it, the harbinger of the dreadful trench warfare of 1914–1918.

At this cost, the Union was preserved and slavery abolished. The division between north and south took generations to heal and the freedom of the former slaves was curtailed by discrimination and the terrorism of white supremacist organizations, notably the Ku Klux Klan

Economic Growth

The Civil War did not retard the economic growth of the United States. With a vast and productive territory, a growing population and a rich mineral endowment, growth was rapid and massive. By 1914 the gross national product of the USA was equal to that of Britain, Germany, France, Italy and Austria-Hungary combined. Since its population was only 98 million, as compared with the European powers' total of 238 million, its per capita GNP was much higher. Not only was it a major exporter of primary products, it was increasingly an exporter of manufactures. In total it ran a large favourable balance of trade with Europe which resulted in regular transfers of gold to the United States; by 1914 the U.S. Treasury had accumulated one-third of the world's gold stock.

Moreover, it soon became apparent that America had left behind the imitative phase of industrial development. Stimulated perhaps by the incentive to devise new technological solutions to the problems of a rapidly expanding agriculture, American industry became innovative – a quality strikingly demonstrated by Henry Ford when he used the moving production line to produce cars at a fraction of the previous cost. Ford was more than a technical innovator, he was also an original economic thinker who paid his workers high wages so that they could afford to buy his cars. His approach worked – in 1914 there were more cars in the United States than in all the rest of the world.

Ford's achievement was the more remarkable in as much as the United States was not sympathetic to the social welfare philosophies making headway in European thinking and politics. Perhaps because of the constant inflow of migrant labour, desperate for employment at any remuneration, American labour was poorly organized and highly exploited. A major split was already developing between the political approaches of Europe and America which, almost alone in the industrialized world, had no effective social democratic party.

Russia – Power and Weakness

Russia emerged from the Napoleonic Wars as the predominant military power on the Continent – a position which worried Britain and Austria sufficiently to make them welcome the France of the restored Bourbons as a partner in resisting the far reaching ambitions of Tsar Alexander. Russian military power was real – its population by 1800 had passed that of France, making it the largest country in Europe. It maintained by far the largest armed forces – 800,000 men – whereas none of the other major powers had as many as 300,000. What no one seemed to realize until the Crimean

War made it blindingly obvious was that this power was shallow. Russia was indeed a considerable industrial power at the beginning of the nineteenth century but it was not capable of keeping pace with the development of the Western powers and became steadily more backward by comparison. Even more important, its limited educational facilities retarded the efficiency of its army, including its officer corps, and of its entrenched, conservative bureaucracy.

Russia, in fact, was not fully a European country. While its nobility and its privileged shared in the common European culture, a vast gulf separated them from the peasantry who made up the bulk of the population. The great majority of peasants were serfs, completely at the mercy of aristocratic landlords who regarded them as barely human and treated them accordingly. Peter the Great's effort to modernize and Europeanize Russia had not reached as far as the peasants; indeed, it had increased the gap between them and the privileged who now came to include a substantial number of foreigners. Catherine II bought the support of the nobility by increasing their power over the serfs. In effect, Russia resembled an occupied country in which the privileged class dominated and exploited the bulk of the population like a foreign conqueror.

Not all the privileged class were content with this situation. Alexander's death in 1825 was the trigger for an attempted coup. The Decembrist Conspiracy failed and its leader was executed. Its main impact was to convince Alexander's brother, who became Tsar as Nicholas I, of the need for a more efficient and repressive regime.

Repression and Terrorism

The next Tsar, Alexander II, was convinced of the need for reform if the regime was to maintain itself. In 1861 he issued an edict which began the process of emancipation of the serfs. About half the land was handed over to the mirs or village councils which allocated the right to work defined areas to each individual. The land had to be paid for, usually through a 49 year mortgage. The peasant was no longer tied to the land and could move away if he pleased. This, of course, facilitated movement to the cities and provided labour for industrialization.

Alexander also contemplated issuing a constitution but never brought himself to grasp the nettle. Russia remained a total autocracy, without any restrictions on the power of the Tsar and without any elected legislature. A minority of the privileged class became convinced of the need for change and, in the absence of any recognized means of pursuing their objective, turned to terror. The political history of Russia became a story of conspiracy and repression. In this climate, when even the most moderate criticism of the regime could lead to gaol or exile to Siberia, opposition soon came to be dominated by radical ideas such as anarchism. In 1881 Alexander was assassinated, His successor, Alexander III, reacted by returning to the conservatism and rigorous repression of Nicholas I.

Alexander III also embarked on a policy of Russification. seeking to destroy the national identity of the Ukrainians, Poles, Finns and other peoples by restrictions on the use of their languages. The policy was, of course, largely counter-productive and merely strengthened the resolve of the subject nationalities to escape from the Russian clutches. Even worse treatment was meted out to the Jews. The authorities seem to have used them as a scapegoat to divert the lower classes from their miseries by organizing attacks on their Jewish neighbours. Many thousands of Jews emigrated, mainly to the United States but also to Western Europe and to Palestine – the Russian persecution was a powerful boost to the growth of Zionism and the proposals for a Jewish national home which eventually led to the establishment of the state of Israel.

These nationalistic measures were accompanied by efforts to build up industrial power which achieved a substantial measure of success. Between 1860 and 1913 industrial production grew at an average of 5% per annum. By 1914 Russia was the fourth largest industrial power in the world and the sixth largest trading nation. These rankings, of course, reflected partly the sheer size of the country; most people were still engaged in agriculture and the industrial sector was still a small part of the total economy.

Living and working conditions in the growing industrial towns were appalling, providing a recruiting ground for the more radical political parties. It was in this atmosphere that the Marxist Social Democratic Party split. The majority or Bolshevik faction followed Lenin in advocating violent overthrow of the existing order and the establishment of a dictatorship of the proletariat, led by a small cadre of intellectuals and professional revolutionaries. In 1912 the Bolsheviks were established as a separate party.

Russia's defeat by Japan in 1905 touched off a wave of unrest which shook the Tsarist regime to its foundations. It was suppressed with difficulty and promises of reform. An elected legislature, the Duma, was introduced but Nicholas II, Tsar since 1894, had no intention of yielding real power. Between 1905 and 1914 Russia was a powder keg; another great crisis would inevitably mean an explosion. Russia's involvement in the war of 1914–18 made the crisis and the explosion inevitable.

CHAPTER TWELVE

THE END OF EUROPEAN HEGEMONY
Europe 1914–1945

In August 1914 almost everyone in Europe, including the generals on both sides, expected a short, glorious and, of course, victorious war. The generals were terribly wrong. Engels, the associate of Karl Marx, had known better when he wrote in 1887 that the next war would reproduce the devastation of the Thirty Years War in three or four years and lead to a collapse of the old monarchies. With uncanny accuracy he forecast military casualies at eight to ten million.

The First World War

The original German drive on Paris failed and the two armies in the West settled down into trench warfare, reminiscent of sixteenth century siege warfare but on an incomparably larger scale. The generals on both sides seemed incapable of understanding that to throw infantry against prepared positions backed by artillery and machine guns was to invite massacre. Jingoism disguised as patriotism sent the young manpower of Western Europe into this furnace with terrible results. On the Eastern Front, with its vast distances, the war was somewhat more open but again poor tactics and modern weaponry made for great slaughter. The Russians, poorly armed and led, suffered the highest casualties.

Both sides tried to strengthen their power by enlisting allies. By 1917 Spain, Switzerland, the Netherlands, Albania and the Scandinavian states were the only neutrals in Europe but the war showed no sign of ending in a decisive victory for either side. The deadlock was broken in 1917. In April the United States, provoked by German submarine warfare and the sinking of American civilian shipping, entered the war. The U.S.A. was already a source of loans and resources which kept the Allied war machine going; its entry into the war made a German defeat almost inevitable. In November, however, before American manpower could be trained and transported, Lenin and the Bolsheviks seized power in Russia and sued for peace. Germany insisted on a punitive peace, with vast cessions of territory. Lenin accepted; he knew that the Russians would support whoever gave them peace and he thought that his success in Russia was only the prelude to world revolution which would make this treaty irrelevant.

The peace of Brest–Litovsk gave Germany the opportunity to concentrate its efforts in the West in 1918 but its attack failed. As American re-inforcements began to arrive in Europe and its allies Austria-Hungary, Turkey and Bulgaria asked for armistices, the German High Command urged the government to sue for peace. In a sudden revulsion of feeling the Emperor and the other monarchs were ejected. It fell to the Social Democrats to take the lead in establishing a republic and to ask for an armistice.

The Peace of Versailles

Placing its hopes in the 'Fourteen Points' which U.S. President Wilson had enunciated as the basis for peace, the new German government hoped to negotiate a peace. To its surprise it found that America and its allies insisted on dictating both the armistice and the peace treaty. Many of the terms were not unreasonable but Germany was obliged to acknowledge responsibility for the war ('war guilt') and to accept an unspecified liability for reparations, which were eventually determined at a massive and unrealistic figure. 'If we aim deliberately at the impoverishment of Central Europe, vengeance, I dare predict, will not limp' wrote an economist who had served unhappily in the British delegation at Versailles.

(His name was John Maynard Keynes; twenty five years later, after events had proved him right, he was to be the principal architect of the post 1945 economic framework.) But the leaders of the victors could not afford to listen to such counsel – they had promised their people that the Germans would be made to pay and they lacked the courage to tell them it was impossible.

So the Treaty of Versailles left a heritage of grievance in Germany and did nothing to assuage the fears of France, which rightly expected a German attempt to undo it. France sought security in British and American guarantees but Wilson lost control of the Senate and the Republicans blocked USA ratification of the Treaty. The establishment of a League of Nations – a Wilson idea for the preservation of peace – did little to re-assure France which realized that, without U.S. membership, it would be a toothless tiger.

Both the Turkish and the Hapsburg empires dissolved in defeat. The former was replaced by a number of Arab states, largely under the tutelage of Britain and France as 'Mandates' of the League; this at least gave the Middle East some stability. Austria-Hungary was replaced by a number of weak states based on claims of national identity. In some cases, such claims concealed lack of a common history and consequent friction as between Czechs and Slovaks or deep rooted hatreds as between Croats and Serbs in Yugoslavia. The settlement ignored the advice of the nineteenth century Czech leader, Palacky, that if the Hapsburg empire did not exist it would be necessary to invent it. It left Central Europe and the Balkans divided between quarrelsome minor states and helpless to resist German and Russian expansion.

The Failure of the Liberal State System

The massive death toll of the war traumatized the major protagonists. Perhaps the trauma could have been minimized if the leaders of the victorious powers had delivered on their wartime promises but this they failed to do.

In Britain a brief post-war boom was followed by a slump which pushed unemployment to ten per cent; it did not fall below this figure until the next world war. The problem was exacerbated when the government returned the currency to the gold standard, suspended during the war, at the unrealistically high rate of 4.65 dollars to the pound. This made British exports uncompetitive and entrenched unemployment. An attempt to force down wages led to a short lived general strike and a long miners' strike. Both failed but government and employers lost their appetite for further attacks on wages. Since they had no better ideas of how to deal with the problem, Britain stagnated.

France had financed the war and post-war reconstruction by borrowing, in the expectation that the Germans would pay. This brought on an inflation which reduced the franc to one tenth of its pre-war value before severe economic measures returned it to one fifth. France also returned to the gold standard but at a realistic rate which promoted its exports. Economically, it did rather better than Britain but morale was even lower; the birth rate remained obstinately low, fuelling fears of an entrenched. inability to resist eventual German revenge.

The United States was clearly the major beneficiary of victory. Its casualties were small by comparison with the European powers and the war had transformed it from a debtor to a creditor nation. The mass production assembly line brought products regarded as luxuries in Europe within reach of middle class Americans. Business boomed and the share market was forced up to dizzy heights. American banks lent money to Germany which used it to pay reparations to the victors, who thus met their debt payments to the United States. The international economic system revolved around the United States; any crisis there would have world-wide impact.

The Rise of Fascism

Italy, like the other victors, had suffered massive casualties. Moreover, the promised territorial gains which had lured her to join the Allies were reduced, at the insistence of Wilson, to accommodate the claims of Yugoslavia. At home, workers and peasants alike wondered if the government would keep the promises of improved working conditions and land reform made during the war. Before long they began to occupy factories and farms. With the government reluctant to use force, industrialists and landowners turned for help to a new movement, recruited largely from ex-servicemen and the lower middle class and led by a former socialist editor, turned ardent nationalist during the war. Benito Mussolini never really defined Fascism; at this stage it stood for nationalism and violent opposition to unions and socialists. For the latter purpose he established *squadristi*, groups of toughs who beat up unionists and socialists. By 1922, many cities in central and northern Italy were controlled by them, illegally but effectively; two thousand of their opponents had been killed in the violent struggles which established their power.

Although the Fascist Party had only thirty-five deputies in Parliament, by 1922 Mussolini felt strong enough to threaten to use force unless he was accepted as prime minister. When the government finally made up its mind to introduce martial law, the king refused to sign the necessary decrees. Mussolini became prime minister and proceeded to transform Italy into a fascist state, in which power was concentrated in the Leader, il Duce, and his supporters.

The Fascist state stressed national greatness, militarism, dynamism and violence. It took over from Catholic social theory the idea of corporativism under which workers and employers would come together in corporations to control and agree on conditions in industry; in practice, under Fascism the corporations became an instrument for the employers to enlist the co-operation of the state against the workers.

Mussolini also tried to co-opt the Catholic Church. The Concordat of 1929 recognized the independence of the Vatican City, an enclave measured in acres rather than square miles, and enshrined Catholic ideas on education and marriage in law. The uneasy alliance was soon strained by a quarrel over the Catholic youth movement, which the Fascists saw as a rival to their own. Pius XI became fiercely critical of some aspects of Fascism, virtually the sole source of public criticism within Italy. But fear of Communism and memories of liberal anti-clericalism, from which the Vatican and the Italian church had suffered so much in the past, ensured that the break was never complete.

Fascist propaganda and the insecurity felt by the wealthy in the face of Communism and Socialism ensured a sympathetic reception for the Fascist idea in most of Europe. Military strongmen came to power in Spain, Portugal, Poland and Lithuania in the twenties. In the thirties, partly under the impact of the economic hardship caused by the depression, Eastern European countries gradually abandoned democracy; by 1938 Switzerland, the Netherlands, Denmark and Czechoslovakia were the only countries east of the Rhine and south of the Baltic which remained democracies. Even in Britain, Mussolini attracted admiration from people as prominent as Winston Churchill.

The Threat of Communism

The insecurity of the wealthy in the face of Communism was not without some basis. Lenin had every expectation of extending Communism beyond Russia. In 1918–19 the Communist regime had fought and won a bitter civil war in which the Allied powers had actually landed troops in Russia and given support to the counter-revolutionary or White forces. Only the war-weariness of their people prevented them from becoming more actively involved. The Communist regime lost a war with Poland but extended its power over most of the subject nationalities which had tried to break free. The Tsarist empire was re-constituted as the Union of Socialist Soviet Republics (U.S.S.R.) under the control of the Communist Party, which in turn was controlled by Lenin and the small group of ideologues around him. Moreover, they proclaimed publicly the inevitability of their revolution spreading around the world and in 1919 established the Communist International to pursue this objective. Socialist parties around the world split between those who accepted the leadership of the Russian party and the need for violent revolution and those who adhered to parliamentary methods.

Germany's Problems

In Germany, even before the armistice was negotiated, virtually every major town was in the hands of workers' and soldiers' councils. As it turned out, these supported the socialist led government but this did not prevent two violent attempts by the Communists to take over Berlin as well as armed uprisings in the Ruhr and Hamburg. To defend itself the government was forced to rely on the Free Corps, groups of ex-servicemen armed by the military and less than enthusiastic for a socialist led government. When the Free Corps in Berlin attempted their own coup, the army refused to act and the government was forced to flee. The coup was broken by a general strike. Clearly, in the new democratic republic, the army was more independent of civil authority than it had been under the Empire.

Caught thus between threats from the left and the right, successive German governments grappled with the problems arising from the huge reparations bill imposed on the country. Since they dared not raise taxes to pay reparations, they touched off inflation. This became much worse when the French, dissatisfied with the rate of payment, occupied the Ruhr industrial area. The attempt to exact reparations in kind was frustrated by non-co-operation and strike action. The government supported this financially, again without raising taxes to meet the cost. Germany was soon overwhelmed by hyper-inflation. Savings were destroyed and daily life made almost impossible; wages paid one day were almost worthless the next. The slide was finally halted in October 1923 with the introduction of a new mark, determined to be worth one trillion of the old mark. The episode left a legacy of ruined lives, bitterness and hostility to both the former enemy powers and the Republic which had signed the peace treaty. The military, who had advised surrender, were now blaming the socialists and the Republic for stabbing the army in the back.

A month after the introduction of the new mark, the Bavarian capital, Munich, was the scene of an attempted coup. It was led by an Austrian who had fought in the German army and now led a small group called the National Socialist German Workers Party. The Bavarian police opened fire and the Nazis acquired their first martyrs. Hitler was sent to gaol for a short time and used the opportunity to write *Mein Kampf*, a rambling combination of autobiography and political philosophy in which he set out a programme based on nationalism, racism, anti-Semitism and the glorification of violence and aggression. Had politicians and national leaders, at home and abroad, taken his ravings seriously, Europe might have been spared a second and even more destructive conflict.

Hitler and his Nazis might never have amounted to more than a footnote in history if the state system of the twenties had been capable of grappling with the economic problems which emerged at the end of the decade. Having recovered from the great inflation, Germany gradually worked its way back to a measure of prosperity and international respectability. The constitutional parties dominated the Reichstag and the Nazis, whom Hitler had now decided should seek power through the ballot box, could take only

32 seats in 1924 – and this declined to 12 in 1928 – out of a total of almost 500. The great depression of the thirties changed this situation almost overnight.

The Great Depression

On 24 October 1929 the inherent instability of the New York stock market was suddenly made brutally clear. The bubble of speculation burst with the panic selling of millions of shares. Panic selling continued day after day; the general industrial index fell by more than half in three weeks. Nothing on this scale had ever been seen before and no one knew how to control it. As American lenders began to call in their short term loans to European borrowers and Americans cut back on imports, the crisis rippled around the world. Banks failed and factories began to cut production and dismiss workers; bankruptcies reached unprecedented numbers. As governments grappled with problems for which neither they nor the economists had any solution, they exacerbated the crisis by turning inwards. Tariffs were raised in an effort to protect national industries and preserve employment. This led other countries to retaliate and the mushrooming of tariff barriers reduced international trade and overall employment still further.

The depression struck Germany with particular force because of its dependence on American loans. As unemployment rose to undreamed of heights, many people began to listen to the promises of left and right wing extremists. It was true that there was no unemployment in the Soviet Union, although there was substantial under-employment – there were also millions of prisoners engaged in forced labour under killing hardship but it was easy to minimize or ignore this in the West. Growing support for Communism scared many middle class people and led them to look more favourably on the Nazis and their nationalist propaganda; the party received badly needed money from the big industrialists. Nazi representation in the

Reichstag grew to 107 in 1930 and to 230 in 1932. After much manoeuvring, Hitler became Chancellor in January 1933.

Nazi Power in Germany

The conservatives and the industrialists hoped to use Hitler and discard him but they had underestimated their man. His mesmeric oratory and promises of a great future ensured popular support; his thuggish storm troops and ruthless action supplied an element of force and his unscrupulous political dealings neutralized potential sources of opposition like the army. The exclusion of the Communists from the Reichstag, and the arrest of most of them, gave the Nazis and their nationalist allies an absolute majority in the Reichstag which then voted all power to the Fuhrer. The Nazi party became the only legal party and the states were reduced to subordinate instruments of the national government. Within a year a democratic republic had been transformed into the archetypal totalitarian state.

Many of its members had seen the National Socialist German Workers Party as a blend of nationalism and socialism. Now that the Party had achieved power, they waited in vain for the changes they expected. By early 1934 Hitler saw clearly that he had to choose between the nationalists (and the army) and the socialists. On the Night of the Long Knives his henchmen murdered the leaders of the socialist faction and incidentally underlined for everyone the dangers of differing from the Fuhrer.

Hitler still instinctively knew that he must keep the mass of workers contented and loyal to the Nazi state. The key was to overcome the depression and get people back to work. Public works programmes played a vital role at first; within a few years they were complemented by massive rearmament. Unemployment fell from six million in 1933 to one million in 1936 and to a negligible 34,000 in 1939. The means used did not appeal to orthodox economists; in the short term, at least, they worked. Overseas trade was controlled and operated where possible on a barter system; German science was encouraged to develop substitutes for imports. The threat of inflation was contained by prices and wages controls. Employers and workers were alike absorbed into the Nazi system and if the big industrialists (and the Nazi leaders) did better than the workers at least the latter had jobs, cheap holidays and the gratification of being told that they belonged to the master race which was about to found its thousand year empire.

To preserve the purity of the master race, the Nazi state embarked on a systematic persecution of the Jewish minority, expelling them from the civil service and the professions and forbidding intermarriage. In 1938, in response to the murder of a German diplomat in Paris by a Jewish youth, the Nazis launched Crystal Night, a systematic assault on synagogues and Jewish businesses. Many Jews had already emigrated; those who remained now found that emigration was only possible on conditions which would leave them penniless. Some still left; others remained, unaware that an even grimmer fate awaited them.

Anti-semitism was common in Germany as in other countries. The treatment of the Jews aroused only limited criticism in Germany or abroad. The Germans at least had the excuse that they lived in a police state in which the secret police would soon dispatch critics to imprisonment and mistreatment in a concentration camp. Outside Germany, many people found it convenient to ignore the darker side of the Nazi regime, just as they choose to regard Hitler's talk of German expansion and the thousand year empire as mere rhetoric.

The Destruction of the Versailles Settlement

The establishment of that empire demanded firstly the destruction of the Versailles settlement. In this Hitler had the support of the

German people while the British and French had come to doubt the equity of Versailles and were certainly unwilling to fight for it. Mussolini's attack on Abyssinia in 1935 pre-occupied the democracies; they wanted to use the League of Nations to stop him but were reluctant to employ force or impose effective sanctions. All they succeeded in doing was to induce Mussolini to join with Hitler in the Rome–Berlin Axis and to distract themselves from opposing Hitler's militarization of the Rhineland.

France and Britain were caught in an even more difficult dilemma when the excesses and atrocities following on the election of a new left wing republican government in Spain provoked an army-led rebellion. The rebellion developed into a bloody civil war in which Italy and Germany supported the rebels while the U.S.S.R. and the international Communist movement aided the government. Public opinion in Britain and France tended to favor the government as legitimate and democratic; their governments would not welcome either a Communist or a Fascist Spain. They dithered and General Franco and the rebels won. But Hitler and Mussolini were to be disappointed. Franco was far too shrewd to become their puppet; Spain acquired some of the trappings of Fascism but Franco remained firmly in control. He kept Spain out of the war and afterwards worked his way back into favor with the victors as they came to see anti-communism as a virtue.

Germany had already signed the Anti-Comintern Pact with Japan, now dominated by militarists and nationalists and engaged in an attempt to conquer China. The pact encouraged both parties to continue their programmes of aggression.

In 1938 Hitler took over Austria and began preparations for a move on Czechoslovakia where three million Germans provided a ready excuse for demands for frontier revision. France was bound to Czechoslovakia by long-standing treaties but the government was reluctant to honour its obligations. The British prime minister, Neville Chamberlain, dramatically flew to Munich to negotiate with

Hitler a 'peace with honour'. The Czechoslovak government was persuaded to accept a massive revision of the frontier. (It is said that the German generals were immensely relieved. They had wondered whether the Czechoslovak army, well armed and carefully built up since 1919, might well prove more than a match for the German which had enjoyed only a few years to expand from the small force prescribed at Versailles.) Six months later, in March 1939, Hitler, convinced that Britain and France would not fight, occupied the Czech provinces and established a puppet state in Slovakia.

Britain and France, having failed to fight alongside Czechoslovakia, now gave guarantees to Poland, Rumania and Greece, which would oblige them to fight Germany with far less effective allies. Hitler, mistakenly but understandably, did not take them seriously.

In fact the only way such guarantees could be made effective was by alliance with the U.S.S.R. Since Lenin's death in 1924, that country had been under the control of Josef Stalin who turned the position of General Secretary of the Communist Party into a fearsome personal dictatorship. Eight million people were arrested, the majority to end their lives in the detention camps of the frozen Arctic. Industrial development and the collectivisation of agriculture were pursued successfully at a dreadful cost in human lives and misery. In the late thirties a purge of the leadership saw the execution of the leading 'Old Bolsheviks' and most of the top echelon of the officer corps.

Stalin had enunciated the theory of 'socialism in one country' but, as he maintained the Communist International and used it to control Communist Parties around the world, Britain and France did not trust him and were reluctant to rely on his support to restrain Hitler's advance.

Negotiations for an alliance therefore made little progress. Stalin, distrustful in turn and fearful of finding the U.S.S.R left alone to confront Germany, resolved to make his own agreement with

Hitler. The Non-Aggression Pact announced on 23 August contained secret provisions for the partition of Poland and Russian predominance in Finland and the Baltic States. On 1 September German forces invaded Poland. Hitler was probably surprised when Britain and France honoured their guarantees and declared war.

The Second World War

The German army's blitzkrieg (lightning war) tactics, based on tank attacks supported by the ruthless use of dive bombers, forced the Polish army back to Warsaw in six days. As the Poles withdrew further east, Russian troops entered Poland which was divided between the two new allies.

Germany's sudden and successful occupation of Denmark and Norway in April 1940 shook the complacency of the Allies and brought Churchill to power as Prime Minister in Great Britain. The old warhorse – a minister in the First World War and sponsor of the development of the first tank – was well fitted to epitomize and mobilize the fighting spirit of the British people. Hardly had he come to power when the Germans launched a blitzkrieg attack in the west. Barely more than a month later, they were in Paris and a new French government led by the First World War hero, Marshal Petain, signed an armistice. From the beach at Dunkirk, a flotilla of British yachts and fishing boats evacuated 300,000 men but virtually no equipment.

Churchill's government rejected Hitler's offer of peace and, thanks to the bravery and efficiency of the air force, beat off his attempt to establish air superiority as a prelude to a cross-Channel attack. By mid-September Hitler knew that such an attack was not possible and decided on an attack on Russia.

The Russian armies, demoralized and deprived of many of their best generals by Stalin's purges, were out-maneuvered and surrounded; prisoners were taken by the hundreds of thousands.

Russia was saved by the stubborn bravery of her people and the massive material assistance provided by Britain and America. Stalin cynically appealed to traditional loyalty to 'Holy Russia'. Nazi brutality convinced many who had been prepared to co-operate that German domination would be worse than the Communist regime from which they might have hoped to escape.

Nazi brutality sunk to a new low early in 1942 when it was decided to exterminate the Jews. Transported to concentration camps such as Auschwitz, they were starved, mistreated and eventually gassed by the thousand in specially built installations; the corpses were examined for concealed valuables and gold tooth fillings removed before they were cremated. Six million Jews perished in this way as well as gypsies, captured resistance fighters and even handicapped Germans, considered unworthy members of the master race. Germany, and with it most of Europe, had fallen into the hands of the criminally insane. To their credit, several of Germany's satellites – Italy, Hungary and Bulgaria – resisted demands to hand over their Jews to the Nazis. Among the occupied countries, the Danes managed to transport almost all of them to neutral Sweden and individuals in other occupied countries risked their lives to hide Jews. In France, Fascist elements in the Petain government were willing to co-operate with the Nazis, delivering many Jews to death and leaving scars which can still, from time to time, haunt the French conscience.

While Russians and Germans faced one another from the Baltic to the Black Sea, the war was suddenly given a new dimension by the Japanese. Convinced that America would not accept the establishment of their dominion over East Asia, the militarists who controlled that country launched a pre-emptive strike. Without warning, carrier based aircraft struck the American naval base in Hawaii. Malaya, the Dutch East Indies, Burma and much of Papua New Guinea were over-run in rapid and well conceived campaigns.

Japanese armies seemed poised to invade India and Australia and perhaps even the United States.

Hitler had not been consulted before the Japanese attack but he promptly declared war on the United States. The transformation of America into a full belligerent, coming on top of the attack on Russia, changed the balance of power. The human and material resources arrayed against Germany were now so vast that defeat was virtually certain.

Three years of major, bloody battles forced the German army back from Moscow to Berlin. Over the same period the Americans and the British had forced the Germans and Italians out of North Africa and invaded Italy, which promptly ousted Mussolini and changed sides. A bitter partisan war developed in Northern and Central Italy, as it already had in much of occupied Europe.

Only in June 1944 were Britain and America ready for a massive direct assault across the English Channel. The landing was successful but German defences did not crumble; not until early 1945 were the Allies able to cross the Rhine. Allied bombing was now making life in Germany unbearable, destroying whole cities and killing thousands of civilians. Finally, as the Russians fought their way into Berlin street by street, Hitler committed suicide and the last German armies surrendered.

The final defeat of Germany made that of Japan inevitable. Already driven back from some of her conquests, she now came under massive air attack from island bases as close as 600 kilometres from the home country. Allied air superiority was complete, and used ruthlessly. A fire bomb raid on Tokyo killed 100,000 people and left more than a million homeless.

The Japanese had fought every attack with bitter determination, taking and inflicting enormous casualties. America and Britain were convinced that the traditional warrior ethos inculcated so successfully in the Japanese would lead to continued bloody resistance. This conviction led to a fateful decision. On 6 August

1945, the atom bomb was dropped on Hiroshima, causing unprecedented casualties and introducing the world to a new dimension of terror. Stalin, seeing that the end was imminent, declared war on Japan on 8 August; Russian forces rapidly overran Manchuria. A second atom bomb was dropped on Nagasaki on 9 August. A day later the Japanese government bowed to reality and offered its surrender.

Thus Hitler's attempt at a thousand year empire, and Japan's design of an Asian 'Co-Prosperity Sphere' ended in disaster, with enormous loss of life and destruction for both peoples as well as for most of the countries they had over-run. In 1945 it was not apparent how quickly they would recover from this nadir.

Only gradually, also, did the hidden costs of victory emerge, After 1945, only two significant powers remained on the world scene – America and Russia. Not only Germany and Japan had lost the war. So too had Britain and France. Their colonial empires, and the place which these had guaranteed the colonial powers on the world stage, were doomed. The age of European hegemony was over.

Chapter Thirteen

One World
1945–2004

Introduction

The half century since the end of World War II has seen a transformation of the world which could only be dimly anticipated in 1945. The economic, cultural and political supremacy of Europe was widely felt to be at an end. Europe was divided between American and Russian spheres of influence. What was unexpected was the revival of Europe, the rise of the East Asian economies, and the catastrophic collapse of the Soviet empire.

A new paradigm, building on the outlook of the interwar years but going substantially beyond it, emerged to determine the framework of ideas, attitudes and perceptions within which men and women lived and thought and took decisions. The most striking features of this paradigm were:-

- The pace of change accelerated beyond any thing known previously.
- Wealth accumulated in much of the world at an unprecedented rate. Despite many exceptions, in many countries it was for a time more equally distributed than ever before.
- The position of women in society, especially in Western countries, continued to improve.
- Unequal development produced greater inequalities between countries than ever before.

- Because of transport, communications and political and economic structures, the world functioned as a single entity.
- The erosion of many traditional belief systems left Western society without a commonly and clearly accepted system of beliefs and values.
- Technological precocity increased comfort and welfare – the twentieth century developed a mindset which sought and found technological solutions which previous generations had not looked for.
- Rising expectations became common – men and women expected to live better than their parents. In most democratic countries they expected to use their control of government to achieve this objective.

Above all, the paradigm of the late twentieth century incorporated an openness to change and a less than rational confidence in the benefits of a barely understood science and of technological developments. Not even the manifest threat of atomic destruction could shake the assurance of the majority.

The Post War Economy

Even more than their predecessors in 1918, the men and women of Western Europe and America in 1945 were determined that victory should bring reward. They expected a new economic and social dispensation more favourable to the average citizen. The post-war world order was bound to reflect these aspirations – for a time they were realized to a surprising degree – but it was also bound to reflect the realities of national power and of a social structure dominated by wealth and inherited status.

In their effort to meet the rising expectations of their citizens, governments were aided by the theories of John Maynard Keynes. His General Theory of Employment, Interest and Money, published in 1936, argued eruditely and persuasively that full employment could only be maintained by appropriate government action. Governments should borrow the money which the private sector was reluctant to invest in times of depression and use it for public purposes. By 1945 this view was widely accepted. Its application, coupled with American aid and investment to restore war-ravaged infrastructure enabled the developed countries to embark on an era of prosperity and expansion without parallel in history. Unemployment in most of these countries was kept down to 2% or 3% of the workforce. The exception was the United States where reluctance to adopt full blown Keynsian techniques let unemployment climb to 6%, which still seemed modest after the horrendous rates of the thirties. Full employment and the consequent high spending power meant steadily rising living standards. Advances in technology produced a constant stream of improved and new products on which the newly affluent were happy to spend their money. For a quarter of a century the economies of the developed countries operated in high gear.

Keynes also played a large role in the negotiations at Bretton Woods in the USA which led to the setting up of two international institutions designed to facilitate the better functioning of the international economy. These institutions were the International Monetary Fund (IMF) and the International Bank for Reconstruction and Development (IBRD or World Bank). The IMF was to manage a system of fixed currency exchange rates and make short term loans to countries wIth balance of payments problems. The World Bank was to make long term loans for development. Both these institutions were outside the central framework of the United Nations and controlled by governing boards in which the United States, as the major source of funds, had a predominant vote. Keynes had proposed a third institution, an International Trade Organisation, to facilitate the liberalisation of international trade but this proved too ambitious for governments who could see votes riding on jobs and jobs dependent on protective tariffs. So the post-war economic system was built on tariff protection, with some mutual restraint managed through the General Agreement on Tariffs and Trade (GATT) negotiated some years later. Only after fifty years, in a very different economic climate, was a World Trade Organization created.

In the seventies a number of perverse factors tested the viability of the Keynsian consensus. Full employment re-inforced the bargaining power of trade unions; employers selling in a booming economy had little incentive to resist their demands. Wages and prices both rose, threatening inflation. Some countries, such as Germany, Austria and Japan, managed to control this threat by agreements between employers and employees, backed by governments, to restrain the rise in wages and prices. Others, such as Britain and Italy, succumbed to accelerating inflation.

The problems of the industrial countries were exacerbated when the oil producing developing countries, united in the hitherto rather passive Organization of Petroleum Exporting Countries (OPEC), acted in 1973 to raise the price of oil from $4 per barrel to $15; in 1979–80 it was raised again to $30 per barrel. This added to inflation and destroyed the confidence of the industrial countries.

The failure to prevent inflation in some countries basically reflected the unwillingness of governments to take the steps which Keynes had envisaged for this purpose. Governments regarded measures such as holding down wages and profits as politically impossible – they would ensure defeat at the next election. Some governments turned for a solution to the monetarism of Milton Friedman and the Chicago school which, in effect, represented a return to pre-Keynsian, classical economics. As might have been expected, this provided a cure for inflation at the cost of entrenching high unemployment. At the end of the year 2003 only four industrialized countries had unemployment rates of 5% or less – Austria, Britain, Sweden and Switzerland.

Imports from newly industrialized countries (NIC's) provided manufactures at prices with which the older industrialized countries could only compete behind high tariff barriers. But such barriers were no longer accepted as intellectually respectable by many economists who argued that the comparative advantage of the NICs ought to be given full play, even when it was largely to be found in low wages and bad working conditions. A combination of economic argument, pressure from major producers who might move their production off-shore and consumer demand for lower prices persuaded many governments to lower tariffs and reduce other barriers. By the mid-seventies average tariffs had been reduced from a post-war level of 45% to an average of 5% (although this still included some much higher rates on selected products). Manufacturing in Western countries was ravaged and the growth of unemployment re-inforced.

The Position of Women

In some ways the most striking aspect of the post-war set of values and perceptions was the change in the position of women in society. Almost all societies in the past had taken for granted the subordination of women to men. As late as the nineteenth century even republics such as France deprived women of property rights, made divorce more difficult for wives than for husbands and generally made them subject to their husbands in the same way as minor children to their fathers. The idea of allowing them to vote was widely regarded as a joke. Britain's colonies in Australia and New Zealand were the first jurisdictions in the world to allow women to vote. But the home country was slow to follow suit, eventualy provoking a suffragette movement with a penchant for minor violence. In 1914 they quickly suspended this activity and supported the war effort. Their loyalty was rewarded by the vote for women over 30 in 1918; only in 1969 was the age reduced to 21 in line with that for men. In France women only achieved the vote after the the Second World War.

Before the end of the nineteenth century women, long employed in industry, had begun to penetrate the offices and shops, always in minor and badly paid positions. The massive diversion of manpower to the armed forces in both world wars meant that the employment of women was encouraged by both government and employers. Many women responded to their country's need out of patriotism. At war's end many saw no reason to confine themselves to domestic activities. The boom conditions which followed the Second World War encouraged their continued employment, backed in many countries by improved educational opportunities. Over the next half-century a women's movement gradually emerged to claim equality of opportunity and reward in both economic and social life. Much remains to be done to achieve equality but, compared to previous centuries, the late twentieth century in developed countries might well seem a golden age.

In developing countries, however, the position is different. In a few countries, notably in Asia, a minority of women have managed to use family status, wealth and education to achieve high positions in government and public service; India, Pakistan, Sri Lanka, Bangladesh, Philippines have all had female Prime Ministers; Indonesia a female President. The great majority of women, however, remain caught in the network of traditional customs which enforce their subordination in conditions often degrading and health-threatening. Male domination seems to be entrenched in African society. In the eyes of most Moslems it is sanctioned by their religion; the increasing tendency of Moslem states to revert to Islamic Sharia law will revive old forms of subordination. Ironically, in China, where the Communist state has removed many traditional constraints on women, its 'one child' policy has not only limited their freedom but has sometimes resulted in enforced abortion.

The Bi-Polar Power Structure

The defeat of Germany and Japan was due to the massive superiority of manpower available to Russia and America and the equally massive superiority of the latter in resources and technology. The outcome of the war left these two as the only real world powers; Britain, France and China were such only by courtesy.

Uneasy allies during the war, Russia and America were bound to be suspicious rivals afterwards. Nor was the new institution of the United Nations equipped to control their rivalry. Despite some improvements on the League of Nations, it depended essentially on the decisions of major governments for its effectiveness. If Russia and America found their relations strained, this would be reflected in, rather than controlled by, the meetings of the United Nations.

Such strains were inevitable. The allies had fought with only one common objective – victory – and many different ones. Stalin intended to extend the power of Communism and Soviet Russia as far as possible. Britain and France looked for a restoration of the old order in which their world supremacy was assured. China was locked in a bitter civil war between the Nationalist Government and the Communist party. The American leadership recognized that world order could only be maintained with American participation and naturally equated that with a leading role for the most powerful and wealthy nation in the world. They did not yet, perhaps, realize the full extent of the demands which such a role would generate; certainly the American people did not.

It was Stalin's policy in Eastern Europe, and the contemporary triumph of the Chinese Communists, which clarified American perceptions and mobilized public opinion in support of an active foreign policy. By a mixture of force, threats and chicanery, the Russian occupying forces systematically installed Communist governments in the countries of Eastern Europe.

By 1947 President Truman had had enough. In March he enunciated the 'Truman Doctrine' promising support to 'free peoples' resisting armed minorities or outside pressure. In June, his Secretary of State put forward the 'Marshall Plan' for economic assistance to the war damaged countries of Europe. Visionary but practical, the Plan recognized the need for generosity to promote a speedy recovery. The American assistance in a few years reached thirteen billion dollars, 90% of it a free gift; there would be no repayment obligations to check the recovery. The Plan succeeded beyond all expectations and launched Western Europe on the way to a new level of prosperity. The Organisation for European Economic Co-operation (OEEC), which co-ordinated the work of the Plan, fostered co-operation with significant implications for the future. Stalin refused to allow Eastern European countries to participate and set up Comecon as his own counterpart to the OEEC. But Russia did not have the resources of America and in fact looked to Comecon to exploit the Eastern European countries for its benefit.

Rivalry between USA and USSR was soon expressed in military alliances. The North Atlantic Treaty Organisation (NATO), initiated in 1949, brought together USA, Canada and ten West European countries. It was soon facing the Communist countries organised in the Warsaw Pact. The Cold War had begun and there were no guarantees that it would remain cold, especially as, by 1949, Russia also developed the atomic bomb. The world was thus launched on a nuclear arms race in which vast resources were devoted to ever more destructive weapons. The sardonically named strategy of Mutually Assured Destruction (MAD) assumed that safety from atomic extermination could be found only in the ability to inflict a similar fate on the enemy. Both Russia and America seem to have planned on this basis.

In Asia, America dominated the occupation forces in Japan and set about remaking that country as a democracy. In China, however, Mao Tse Tung led the Communist forces to a complete victory over the corrupt Nationalist government of Chiang Kai Shek; by 1949 the latter was confined to the island of Taiwan. The 'loss' of China was seen in America as a major defeat and led to a vicious witch hunt in which unpalatable advice or even knowledge of China was often equated with guilt. No one seems to have anticipated the problems the Soviet Union would encounter when the Communist bloc included a resurgent China, heir to the claims and the self-esteem of the Middle Kingdom,

One result of Russia's belated entry into the war against Japan was the division of Korea between an American dominated South and a Communist North. In 1950 North Korea launched an invasion of the South which was only repulsed with American help. American success brought China into the war and led eventually to a negotiated settlement which restored the *status quo* of 1950.

By 1950 it was clear to most policy makers in Europe that the shape of the world was changed beyond recognition. European predominance was no longer assured. It was not only outranked by the greater power of America and Russia. It was stripped of much of its own power resources by the independence of its former Asian colonies and against all expectations found them political and increasingly economic rivals, And its concerns were overshadowed by the ingrained hostility of Russia and America and the unavoidable need to take sides in this Cold War which was to dominate the international scene for a generation.

In retrospect, it seems inevitable that Western Europe should have lined up with America which her children had settled and which had adopted and championed many of her values against the strange and dictatorial power to the East. At the outset it was not always so clear. The Communists had a good record in the Resistance, their brief support for Hitler in 1939–40 was conveniently forgotten and the heroic struggle of the Russian people was attributed to Communist rather than national motivation. Moreover, many in Western Europe did not trust the parties of the right and centre to keep their promises of a better life for all. To many such people, only a Communist dominated government seemed to guarantee a state run in the interests of the majority. Postwar elections in Italy and France gave the Communists as much as a third of the votes. To many, especially in America, the threat of a Communist take-over seemed very real. To prevent it, they were willing to support right wing and authoritarian parties and governments. This, in turn, inclined liberals and left wing democrats to align themselves with Communists whose authoritarian and violent aspects they tended to overlook. In no country, however, did the Communist Party obtain a majority at the polls.

Before long the world was divided into two hostile blocs, headed by America and the Soviet Union. Not since the sixteenth century wars of religion had conflict and polarisation revolved so much around ideology. Not all governments, however, were prepared to align themselves with one bloc or the other. In 1955 a meeting of twenty-nine countries at Bandung in Indonesia founded the non-aligned movement, dedicated to pursuing Asian and African, rather than Western or Communist objectives. Prominent in its discussions were Sukarno (Indonesia), Tito (Yugoslavia), Nasser (Egypt) and Nehru (India). Critics were not slow to note that of the four only Nehru could ascribe his power to a truly democratic process and even that exhibited significant flaws.

Western disenchantment with the non-aligned movement grew as its membership expanded and came to include countries such as Cuba which seemed firmly incorporated in the Soviet bloc. Moreover, its demands tended to focus on matters of concern to the Western powers rather than to the Soviet Union. The former increasingly found it necessary to provide aid and make trade concessions to muster non-aligned support while the latter, apart from a few proteges such as Cuba, concentrated on military support for liberation movements. In discussions at the United Nations the

Communist bloc and the non-aligned group often found it possible to support one another against the developed countries.

Towards European Union

With the success of the Marshall Plan the OEEC was developed into the OECD, the Organization for Economic Co-operation and Development. The United States, Canada, Japan, Australia and New Zealand eventually became members of the new Organization which operated as a forum and a respected think tank to harmonize economic policies and promote growth and development.

Some European statesmen, while accepting the need for the global membership of the OECD, were convinced of the need for a distinctively European institution. By integrating the economies of their countries, they hoped to establish a climate of co-operation and make another European war inconceivable. In 1957 they negotiated the Treaty of Rome, setting up the European Economic Community. The new institution was a customs union, pledged to the abolition of all tariffs between member states by 1969. But it was much more than that. The six countries – Belgium, France, Germany, Italy, Luxembourg and the Netherlands – which signed the Treaty of Rome also pledged themselves to the pursuit of 'ever closer union' and accepted a framework of institutions which involved some limitations on their sovereignty. While final decisions on major questions rested with the member governments, the Community was driven by a Commission in Brussels which, although appointed by member governments, developed and pursued its own objectives.

Differences between member governments have slowed the development of the Community and sometimes make the name European Union, which it adopted in 1993, seem a mockery. But its success may be measured by its membership, now fifteen, and by the keenness of ten other countries to join it. With a population approaching 370 million, the European Union is clearly a major player on the international economic stage – by far the largest international trading bloc in the world. Eleven of the fifteen member countries agreed to adopt a single European currency; the problems in the way of this looked formidable and several countries, including Britain, have stood aside but the single currency has now become a reality. So far, however, all efforts to match economic clout with a higher posture in defence and international relations have had only limited success.

Underpinning the Union is a remarkable understanding between France and Germany, established originally by de Gaulle and Adenaur and continued by their successors. It was this established understanding, and the confidence it engenders, which persuaded France to accept the unexpected re-unification of East and West Germany, even though the new Germany is now massively stronger than France in population and economic output.

Decolonisation in Asia

When Japan surrendered in 1945, the colonial powers whose territories it had occupied expected to resume their pre-war possessions. Britain re-occupied Malaya and Singapore without difficulty, although in the former it eventually had to meet a vicious Communist guerilla campaign. Britain also re-occupied Burma but took prompt steps to recognize its independence. The Dutch tried to re-impose their authority on Indonesia by force. They were resisted by nationalists led by Sukarno; these had co-operated with the Japanese and consequently had an armed force at their disposal. The combination of Indonesian resistance and condemnation in the United Nations induced the Dutch to accept Indonesian independence in 1949. In Indo-China, the French stubbornly refused to recognize that the strength of national feeling and the organizing ability and ruthlessness of the Communist resistance made successful re-colonization impossible. The Communist element in the situation ensured American support for the French; Vietnam was thus launched on the long years of war which only concluded with American withdrawal in 1973 and Communist conquest of South Vietnam in 1976.

By contrast, the British were ready to grant India independence. The problem was that Indians were not agreed on the form which that independence should take. The leaders of the major independence movement, Gandhi and Nehru, recognized that the complex of religions in India made it essential for the state to be secular. The Congress Party, which they led, sought to represent all Indians and looked forward to a united India. By 1945, however, a strong element among the Moslems, who constituted a quarter of the total population, had become fearful of domination by the Hindu majority. The Moslem League, led by Jinnah, demanded a separate Moslem state, for which they invented the name Pakistan. The partition which resulted was accompanied by the mass migration of some twelve million people and communal violence which involved a million deaths. Gandhi, the champion of non-violence and racial harmony, was murdered by a Hindu fanatic. One hundred million Moslems remain in India which still retains its secular constitution. Only in recent years has the rise of militant Hindu political parties suggested that the Gandhi-Nehru heritage of a secular state may not be permanent.

Bad relations between the two new states became certain when the Maharajah of Kashmir, a Hindu ruling a Moslem population, decided to accede to India. Nehru, a Kashmiri Brahmin aristocrat himself, could not bear to refuse. The Pakistani leaders saw the whole episode as Hindu aggression. United Nations intervention stopped the border war which followed but Kashmir is still divided and still fuels the hostility between India and Pakistan – a hostility which has inspired both states to maintain large and expensive military forces, to develop atomic weapons and finally to demonstrate their status as atomic powers by test explosions.

The two states developed in very different ways. India has remained a democracy, the largest in the world. It is true that India's democratic achievement is marred by widespread corruption and the manipulation of the voters by self-interested and cynical politicians. Partly as a result of this, India has made less than satisfactory progress in the reduction of poverty and the improvement of living conditions. The poor majority have been promised much but have received little in fifty years. At least they live in a free country in which the not infrequent violence and tyranny of the police are an abuse of the system, not an exercise of it. Slowly, far too slowly, the standard of living is rising. An educated and prosperous middle class now numbers perhaps 200 million out of a total population of a billion. The long monopoly of the Congress Party finally collapsed in the nineties. The government formed by a coalition of minor, largely regional parties collapsed in 1997 and neither it nor Congress gained an absolute majority in the new parliament. The largest party, a Hindu religious party, the BJP, was able to form a coalition government with the support of minor parties. This, in turn, collapsed but another election returned a BJP led coalition to power. In 2004, however, Congress again came to power, with the support of a number of minor parties.

By contrast with India, Pakistan never succeeded in maintaining democratic forms for very long. Politics has been dominated by wealthy landowners and the army. One civilian prime minister, Bhutto, was overthrown and executed by his military commander, General Zia. His daughter, Benazir Bhutto, eventually led her party to victory but has been twice removed from power by Presidential decree. Her successor has been removed by a military coup after apparently trying to organize the assasination of his commander-in-chief. One result of this political chaos was a languishing economy and a failure to develop an effective attack on poverty.

The original Pakistan was composed of two parts on opposite sides of India. Apart from Islam, they had little in common and the eastern province, Bengal, chaffed at the domination maintained by the Punjabis and others in the west. In 1971 it proclaimed its independence as Bangladesh. The revolt was suppressed by the Pakistani army but this in turn was defeated by an Indian invasion. Bangladesh embarked on a precarious independence, one of the most overpopulated and poorest states in the world. Despite this, and despite a series of military coups, it has survived as a viable state.

Economic Development in East Asia

The largely American occupying forces in Japan were commissioned to remake that country as a democratic state. The constitution which they framed accepted the continuation of the imperial house but only as the symbol of the state. Real power was vested in an elected parliament and a cabinet drawn from it. The Liberal Democratic Party, heavily reliant on business interests and their money, dominated the Parliament and mobilized popular support by lavish use of the 'pork barrel'. Cabinets and business both worked in close co-operation with the bureaucracy which was allowed to exercise much of the real, although not the ultimate, power.

Somehow the Japanese, drawing on their tradition of cohesion and national solidarity, found the reserves of courage and skill needed to rise, phoenix-like, from the ashes. By 1950, with China firmly under Communist rule and North Korea launching its attack on the South, informed American opinion was ready to look on Japan as an ally and the potential bulwark of freedom in a Communist dominated north Asia. Japan, for its part, was ready to accept this role within the constraints of the constitution which proscribed military forces. Its government was not unaware of the economic advantage of not having to devote resources to defence and was only slowly persuaded to agree that the constitution might be interpreted to permit some expenditure of this nature. By that time a generation of hard work, co-operation, high savings and careful economic management had brought the defeated and ruined country of 1945 to the top rank of economic power; it is now established as the second biggest economy in the world but in recent years its economy has been stagnant.

Japan perhaps served as a model for the economies of East Asia, four of which – South Korea, Taiwan, Hong Kong and Singapore – achieved such rapid economic growth in the seventies and eighties that they became known as the Asian Tigers. By the mid-nineties they had been joined by Malaysia, Thailand, Indonesia and finally the Philippines and China.

The success of the Asian Tigers posed some uncomfortable questions, both practical and theoretical, for the West. On the practical level, the commitment to promote free trade was brought under severe strain as it became apparent that much of Western industry could not compete with imports from Asia without heavy tariff protection. On the theoretical level, there has been much debate about the reasons for the Asian success. Not unnaturally, many leaders in the Asian countries have laid emphasis on 'Asian values'. This term seems to be a synonym for a selective version of Confucianism, emphasising social discipline and respect for authority. While this is certainly an important factor, critics would also stress the importance of a good education system, high savings rates and heavy foreign investment. Low wages were also a factor in the early stages of industrialisation but in some countries, at least, development has been accompanied by rising wages.

In late 1997 the confidence of the Asian Tigers was rudely shaken by a massive currency crisis. One after another, Thailand, South Korea and Indonesia found it necessary to seek rescue packages from the International Monetary Fund and to accept the stringent conditions attached to them. Other countries in the region were affected by the nervousness this produced and several, including

Malaysia and the Philippines, found their currencies lost fifty percent or more of their value.

Both the devaluation and the attempt to arrest it bear hardest on the poor majority in these countries. Their desperate reaction puts political stability at risk. For several weeks in 1998 Indonesia seemed on the brink of a breakdown in civil order as massive demonstrations pressed for President Suharto's resignation. Suharto finally yielded to this pressure but his vice-president and successor, Habibie, was widely regarded as his friend and protégé. A parliamentary election resulted in a mixture of parties. The parliament elected Abdurrahman Wahid, leader of the largest and best established Islamic movement in the country, as President. His parliamentary party, however, was small. It soon became apparent that his tenure as President was likely to be challenged by the Vice-President and potential successor to the frail Wahid – the daughter of Indonesia's first president, Sukarno. In due course Wahid was forced out and Megawati Sukarnoputri was installed as President. She failed to achieve re-election.

The Asian Tigers are now widely seen to have feet of clay. Scholars and polemicists will argue for a long time about the causes of the sudden and unexpected crash of the Tiger economies. It is already apparent that part, at least, of the explanation is to be found precisely in the 'Asian way' which included not only the Confucian virtues but also corruption, nepotism and cronyism. These factors are deeply engrained in the cultures of these countries and will not be easy to eliminate; until this is done, however, their economic achievements will remain fragile.

Communism and Development in China

Democracy's recruitment of Japan had to be balanced against Communism's success in China. Before long, however, Mao Tse Tung quarrelled with Russia; the two countries' troops clashed on the border and it became apparent that Chinese power might be an offset to Russian rather than a support. Mao proceeded to develop an idiosyncratic version of Communism and to throw China into virtual chaos. The Great Leap Forward attempted to base economic development on backyard industry, especially steel production. Then in 1966 the so-called Cultural Revolution used the youth of the Red Guards to terrorize party leaders and bureaucrats.

Mao's death in 1976 was followed by the rise of one of his old colleagues, Deng Xiao Ping, to supreme power. Deng proceeded to liberalize control of the economy, first in the rural sector and later in the industrial. He was rewarded by a massive increase in output; by the 90's China's growth rates equalled, if they did not surpass, those of the Asian Tigers. This was achieved basically by releasing the acquisitive instincts of a hard working population. But the new policies also resulted in massive unemployment – now thought to be at least one hundred million – and a growing gap between the eastern provinces and the much poorer ones in the west.

Political liberalism was no part of Deng's programme; he intended the Party to stay in control. When, in 1989, students occupied Tiananmen Square in Beijing to press for political reform they were attacked and massacred by tanks. The brutality of the attack drew condemnation world wide. The Chinese leadership might well have replied that there were a hundred thousand revolting students in Beijing alone and similar demonstrations in other major cities; China was threatened with anarchy which would cost far more lives than the Tiananmen massacre.

Worldwide condemnation of the massacre was not followed by any effective measures to force a change of attitude or practice on the Chinese government. Governments realized that this was impractical and their business communities were mesmerized by the apparent prospects for foreign investment. China remains a growing force in the international arena, playing largely by its own rules. It could well be argued that those rules are based only partly on communism; they also incorporate elements of Confucianism and of the ancient concept of China as the Middle Kingdom, around which the rest of the world revolves.

Internally, growth continued at a very high rate. Private enterprise was encouraged and some party apparatchiks used their priveleged positions to make fortunes. Progress was concentrated largely in the eastern, seabord provinces, generating large differentials in income between them and the western provinces. China now shows all the signs of unequal development, the growth of a prosperous middle class and the exploitation of the poor majority which typify many other developing countries. There is no sign that the Communist Party elite is any more committed to improving this situation than elites in other developing countries

China has finally achieved its long-standing ambition to become a member of the World Trade Organisation. It is already a major trading nation. As its GNP and its international trade grow it is bound to exercise an increasing influence on world markets. Its growing resources will support an increasing military budget making its military power even more formidable.

Decolonisation in Africa

One constant theme of the non-aligned countries was the need for rapid decolonisation. After a few unhappy experiences in resisting liberation movements, most of the colonial powers came to agree with them. The nineteenth century Scramble for Africa was now matched by a scramble to get out of Africa.

The decolonisation of Asia had, by and large, returned power to educated and sophisticated elites who blended an understanding of Western culture with a rich tradition of their own. Their values might differ from those of the former colonial power but there was little doubt about their capacity to maintain effective states.

It was otherwise in Africa. In much of the continent the inherited culture was primitive and neither the colonial powers nor the people they educated attached much value to it. Certainly, whatever spiritual or other values it might enshrine, it was much less adapted to assisting its bearers to cope with the world of the twentieth century than the rich cultures of Asia. Of even more immediate moment, in most of Africa the number of people educated in Western learning and experienced in the running of a modern state was minute. Before the war no colonial power had contemplated independence for any of its colonies south of the Sahara in the coming generation; consequently, no preparations had been made for it. The post war groundswell of independence demands – and the support for them by strong currents of opinion at home – took the colonial powers by surprise. The United States, with a traditional hostility to colonialism – as distinct from capitalist investment and economic domination – and a desire to pre-empt Communist gains from liberation struggles, urged rapid movement to independence. Under all these pressures the major colonial powers, Britain and France, began to see independence as inevitable.

In 1957, Britain bestowed independence on the Gold Coast which promptly renamed itself Ghana. The new country was one of the most advanced in Africa, with a long record of education including the first tertiary college in sub-Saharan Africa. The smooth transition to independence encouraged replication; neither African leaders nor colonial decision-makers stopped to think of the differences between Ghana and less developed colonies. In any case Ghana soon began to exhibit less desirable aspects in which the other independent states were quick to follow it.

Prominent among these was the one-party state. African politicians who had led their countries to independence could see no good reason why they should eventually cede power to a rival. The prospect that rival parties would become the focus for tribal hostilities provided a real, but also convenient, reason for the proclamation of single party regimes. In practice, the party usually became a vehicle for the exploitation of the state and its resources by the small elite of party leaders.

Popular dissatisfaction with the results of this exploitation provided the opportunity for the seizure of power by a rival elite – the army. Overwhelmingly, the colonial armies had been officered by Europeans. The armies of the newly independent states were often led by former sergeants, with very limited education or comprehension of the complexities of independence. If things were going wrong – which might mean anything from major economic problems to inadequate pay for the army – their instinct was to push aside the civilians and fix them. Between 1963 and 1967, Africa saw twenty four military coups; in 1975 twenty out of forty one states in sub-Saharan Africa were ruled by military juntas. Inevitably, they found that the problems were not as easy to fix as they had assumed. Many of them yielded to the temptations to use power to enrich themselves and to maintain it by violence and cruelty,

In some cases these problems were compounded by long periods of warfare before independence was achieved. Colonial powers were usually reluctant to grant independence where there was a substantial settler population, The British fought a long war in Kenya before they recognized the inevitability of independence, White settlers in Southern Rhodesia seized power and maintained it through fifteen years of guerilla war before acknowledging defeat. The Portuguese fought bitterly, but ultimately in vain, to repress independence movements in Angola and Mozambique.

The most prolonged struggles were in the north and south of the continent. The French were determined to maintain their presence in Algeria which was home to a million settlers of French origin. Unsuccessful attempts to suppress Algerian guerillas led to the end of the Fourth Republic and the return to power of General de Gaulle. To the horror of the French Algerians, who had seen him as their champion, the General was not prepared to sacrifice the interests of France by continuing an unwinable war; he promptly negotiated Algerian independence.

Even more surprising was the denouement in South Africa where an Afrikaaner-dominated government maintained white supremacy by a regime of restrictive controls and occasional terror. South Africa became the pole-cat of the world, prevented from taking its seat in the United Nations and subject to an increasing variety of sanctions. It remained militarily the strongest power in Africa and stirred up trouble in the neighbouring countries, especially Angola and Mozambique. It was clear that those countries could not overcome it militarily and that the Western powers were unwilling to invest lives and resources in doing so. Finally, however, the white leadership became convinced that their position was untenable and embarked on a peaceful transfer of power. This has so far been surprisingly successful, largely thanks to the constructive approach of the African leader, Nelson Mandela. Released from a long imprisonment in 1990, Mandela became the first President of a multi-racial South Africa. Age has forced his retirement from this office, leaving his successors to cope with the massive problems of development and public order with which South Africa is faced.

Warfare has been endemic in Africa since independence; with rare exceptions it has been within rather than between states. The Ethiopians fought for a generation before accepting the claim of their Eritrean subjects to independence. The Portuguese withdrawal from Mozambique and Angola was followed by long civil wars, tribally based but sponsored by South Africa and the Communist bloc. Belgium's sudden withdrawal from the Congo in 1960 led to a prolonged period of civil strife and the eventual emergence of a predatory military dictator. Mobutu's ouster by another dictator has done little to improve the situation.

In Nigeria, the wealthiest of the African states, with the largest population, tribal tensions are exacerbated by the religious divide between the Moslem north and the Christian and animist south. In

1967 these tensions spilled over into a civil war when the Ibos in the south east made an unsuccessful bid for independence. Nigerian unity was preserved but the country's potential has since been vitiated by ineffective military rule and widespread corruption. Sudan became independent in 1956 as a single entity. Before British conquest in 1898 the area had been dominated by a fanatical, militant Moslem movement, drawing its support from the Arabic-speaking population in the north and intent on converting or enslaving the black tribes in the south. Independence was the signal for the north to resume its oppression of the south. Civil war followed and has continued, with few intervals, until the present. A peace agreement has been negotiated in 2004, but its future is questionable. In the meantime the government is using a predatory militia to attack and drive out the (non-Arab) population of the western province of Darfur.

In much of Africa misgovernment and warfare have been exacerbated by economic problems and natural disasters. Drought has ravaged the Sahel and occasionally other areas. Many years of international research have so far failed to discover the keys to a 'Green Revolution' for Africa to parallel the achievements in Asia. Meanwhile the African population increases rapidly – many African governments have been unsympathetic to population control which can easily be misrepresented as colonialist attempts to keep their countries weak by curtailing their growth. Nor does the male-dominated tradition of African society encourage attention to the health and comfort of women. Weak health services and African attitudes to sex have facilitated the spread of AIDS, which seems to have originated in the continent, until it now constitutes a major threat to health which may soon reach plague proportions.

A generation later, the high hopes of African decolonisation have turned to ashes. Some see faint signs of hope in the abandonment of one-party regimes in a number of states and the contraction, under Western pressure, of state monopolies and controls on enterprise. It is too early, however, to know whether the new generation of politicians and entrepreneurs has the will or the capacity to deliver outcomes more positive than their predecessors. Certainly the way will not be easy and Africa will need all the help it can get from more fortunate parts of the world.

The Islamic Countries and the Middle East

Nowhere was European predominance more resented than in the Islamic countries. Islamic religion and tradition assigned a place to Christians and it was, of course, inferior. All Moslems could agree that their subjection to Christian imperialists was unacceptable; unfortunately they could not agree how to end it. Many in the traditional elite of soldiers, officials and merchants advocated modernisation on Western models; others saw this as inconsistent with the Islamic faith. Probably the mass of the people would have supported the latter view but no one asked them – most Islamic societies were dominated by merchants and landlords in a structure which ante-dated Islam by millennia and with which Islam had made its accommodation in the early years of the conquest. Initially, therefore, there was no question of a mass movement against the West. In the Middle East there was also division between those whose primary focus was Islam and those who were first of all nationalists; moreover there was no agreement among the latter as to whether they sought one Arab state or a collection of smaller states.

The establishment after the first World War by Mustapha Kemal (Ataturk) of a modernizing Turkish state on the ruins of the Ottoman Empire was a triumph of Turkish nationalism rather than of Islam; Ataturk sought Turkey's acceptance in the comity of nations and saw this as requiring substantial Westernization. In Persia, Reza Shah followed the same path rather more cautiously. The Egyptian monarchy and the new states of Iraq and Transjordan were widely seen as British puppets. France ruled Syria and the Maghreb countries and used force to maintain its supremacy.

The British promise in the Balfour Declaration of 1917 to support the establishment of a Jewish national home in Palestine led to a flood of well organized and well financed Jewish migration. Arab Palestinians felt threatened and by 1939 both sides were shooting at one another and at the British. In 1948 the British resigned their Mandate. Ignoring U.N. proposals for a peaceful partition, Jews and Arabs went to war. The Jews won and hundreds of thousands of Arabs became unwelcome refugees in neighbouring Arab countries while others found themselves second class citizens in the new state of Israel.

Arabs saw the West, and particularly the U.S.A., as largely responsible for their humiliation. Arab opinion became even more anti-Western and few Arab governments were able to go against it. Peace with Israel was not possible – only an uneasy truce broken by many incidents and real war from time to time. As Israel, supported by American money and equipment, won these wars it too was disinclined to make the concessions which might have made peace possible. Arab hatred grew with each defeat; Sadat, President of Egypt, paid with his life for daring to make a solitary peace. So, more recently, did Israeli Prime Minister Rabin who had come to accept a framework for peace with Yasser Arafat and the Palestine Liberation Organization. Rabin was killed, not by an Arab, but by a Jewish fanatic. His Labour Party lost the next election by a small margin and it seems virtually certain that Netanyahu and his government sought every excuse not to honour the agreement. An election in 1999 resulted in Netanyahu's defeat but the Labour led government which followed was replaced by a coalition led by Sharon. Under his leadership Israel has expanded settlements in Arab areas and responded to the resulting Arab terrorism with violence. Palestine now teeters on the edge of all out war between Jew and Arab. Neither the United States nor Europe is willing to move beyond ineffectual diplomatic activity to avert the coming storm.

Arab and Islamic frustration with the Palestinian situation provided a catalyst for the mobilization of anti-Western feeling in the Middle East. The West might have treated this with disdain if it had not become dependent on Middle Eastern oil, a dependence strikingly underlined in 1973 by the sudden activation of OPEC and the drastic hike in oil prices. Justified in Arab eyes by American support for Israel in the so-called Yom Kippur war, this action was also welcome to other members of OPEC, who felt they were being exploited by low prices. The OPEC price level could not be maintained indefinitely but even the reduced level at which it eventually settled enhanced the power of the major producers such as Saudi Arabia, Iraq, Iran and Kuwait.

The newly rich countries spent lavishly on welfare and development, on military equipment and, less lavishly, on aid to less fortunate Arab and Islamic countries. Enormous sums remained for investment and these found their way into the Western banks – a constraint on any attempt to wreck Western economies.

Even so, the damage inflicted on those economies was welcome to many in the Islamic world and its new found wealth and prestige raised the morale of many of its people. Programmes of education and development increased the numbers of those who took an active interest in national issues.

The beneficiaries of this development were not the modernizers but the Islamic fundamentalists. The moderate rulers of Egypt found it increasingly necessary to use force against a conspiratorial Moslem Brotherhood. The military rulers of Algeria, threatened with the success of a fundamentalist party, cancelled the pending elections; the resulting guerilla war has claimed thirty thousand lives. The modernizing regime of the Shah in Iran was replaced by an Islamic Republic dominated by Shia ayatollahs, at odds not only with the West and the Soviet Union but also with the nearby states.

Consequently, when Saddam Hussein of Iraq launched an attack on Iran, both the West and his Arab neighbours were prepared to ignore the tyrannical and potentially aggressive nature of his rule and hope for his success. In fact the war dragged on for years and ended in a stalemate. With Iraq's economy in ruins, Saddam tried to recover from the damage by occupying and annexing Kuwait. A coalition, supported by most of the Arab countries and endorsed by the United Nations, was put together by U.S President Bush in 1991. The coalition devastated Iraq and forced her withdrawal from Kuwait. It left Saddam in power and was consequently obliged, working through the United Nations, to spend the subsequent ten years seeking in vain to locate and destroy his alleged arsenal of chemical and biological weapons and wondering about nuclear materials and perhaps weapons in secret preparation.

The defeat of Saddam perhaps gave a fillip to those who sought more effective methods of combating the military superiority of the West, particularly the United States. The key weapon of more fanatical Moslems was the suicide bomber, whom they equated with a martyr. The impact was magnified when the bomber was equipped with a car loaded with explosives. This movement spread throughout the Moslem world. Directed largely against the United States and other Western powers, it was careless of the cost in innocent lives, either Western or Moslem.

On 11 September 2001 the scope of its destructive power was brutally demonstrated when four commercial jets were hijacked and crashed into selected targets in USA, causing massive casualties. The attack transformed the outlook of the United States and its president. George W. Bush (son of the president who had launched the first Iraq war) had been disposed to draw back from international entanglements. He now proclaimed a war on terrorism and launched an attack on the radical Muslim regime in Afghanistan, the Taliban, who were accused of giving shelter to terrorists.

The Bush administration also accused Iraq of sponsoring terrorists and of preserving its arsenal of weapons of mass destruction (WMD). It was able to muster half-hearted support from the United Nations but when this could not be elevated to a clear endorsement launched an attack on Iraq with support from only UK and Australia. The attack was quickly successful and for a short time the Americans seemed to be welcomed as liberators. This initial euphoria soon changed. Spreading resistance resulted in growing American casualties and much greater Iraqi ones. An Iraqi government has been put together with American support but whether the Shia, Sunni and Kurdish elements will hold together remains to be seen.

The war against terror has taken on, for many Americans, the aura of a crusade, justifying curtailment of civil liberties at home and high-handed action abroad. Such action could easily arouse resentment in countries traditionally critical of the United States. More important is the reaction of traditional allies, notably France and perhaps other countries of the European Union.

The revival of Islamic assertion was not confined to the Middle East. Pakistan and Bangladesh, established as Islamic states, are drifting gradually towards a more fundamentalist position. Growing Islamic fundamentalism in Malaysia has been restrained by the determination of the Prime Minister (now retired). Even Indonesia, where masses of believers blend their Islamic beliefs with strands of Hinduism and earlier nature religions, has seen a growth of fundamentalism, so far restrained by the more open approach of the dominant elite. Whether Malaysia and Indonesia will maintain this position is an open question.

These developments have led some in the West to see Islam as the successor to Communism as a threat to Western predominance. For the foreseeable future, this is almost certainly an exaggeration. No combination of Islamic states can muster the power to contest American supremacy and, after the humiliation of Iraq, none is likely to try. Islamic fundamentalism can, however, continue to mobilize attacks on Western interests, property and personnel in particular countries from time to time.

Development Assistance

It was largely in the context of decolonisation that the Western powers devised one of the most remarkable concepts of the twentieth century – the systematic provision of aid or development assistannce from rich countries to poor. There was no precedent for this voluntary transfer of resources, much of it as straight grants and the rest as concessional loans. Of course the donor countries hoped to derive some benefits for themselves – a degree of influence on the recipients, outlets and new demand for their products. These benefits, however were soon curtailed, although never eliminated, by the pressure of recipient countries as a group. In addition, commercial rivalry between the donors led them to devise agreed mechanisms to control or eliminate the more blatant attempts to turn development assistance to their own advantage. Bilateral, country to country, aid was soon supplemented by the creation of multilateral institutions, mostly within the framework of the United Nations. Within the context of the United Nations strategy for a 'Development Decade' a target of 0.7% of the Gross National Product of donor countries was proposed for development assistance. This was accepted by many countries but few reached it.

The original expectations of development assistance were probably over-optimistic. The volume was not sufficient to have a massive impact and donors soon realized that they had much to learn if resources were to be put to optimum use. Criticism came from diverse sources. The growth of voluntary aid agencies provided a small but useful supplement to official resources. Unfortunately many of those involved in such agencies were unshakably convinced of the superiority of their own efforts and missed no opportunity to criticise official aid. In this they were sometimes supported by developing country dissidents, who saw aid as a prop for regimes they hoped to overthrow. With some exceptions when overridden by political or trade interests the official agencies were rigorous in their assessment of their projects – more rigorous, in fact, than most agencies managing investment in the home countries. While good in itself, this provided ammunition for critics. Some of these, in both developing and donor countries, became convinced that aid was a poor substitute for more open trade arrangements. 'Trade not aid' became a powerful slogan but its first impact was to curtail aid rather than liberalize trade.

These pressures, together with the natural reluctance of the public to see its taxes spent on other people, led many governments to draw back from their commitment to development assistance. As more and more Western countries passed under the control of governments with a strong commitment to 'private enterprise', the value of government aid was increasingly subject to question. Few countries now maintain the level of assistance which they achieved earlier. Here again, Africa and more backward countries elsewhere are the ones to suffer; many Asian countries need little aid.

The Disintegration of the Soviet Empire

By the end of the 80's the future of the industrialized, democratic countries seemed bleak. In fact, however, it was the Communist system which was to self-destruct – with breath-taking speed.

In 1985 Mikhail Gorbachov became Secretary of the Communist Party of the Soviet Union, inheriting a poisoned chalice from his gerontocratic predecessors. The Soviet Union was pouring resources into its military, its police and its (duplicated) state and party bureaucracies. So great were the resources required for these purposes that little was left to meet the needs of the civil economy. Life for the ordinary Russian was hard and drab and would remain so until military expenditure could be reduced and productive investment increased. Two decades earlier, Secretary Kruschev had boasted that the progress of the Soviet Union would 'bury' the democracies; Gorbachov knew only too well that it was the ailing Soviet Union which was approaching the graveyard of history.

Gorbachov's strategy seems to have been to combine *glasnost* with *perestroika* and the dismantling of state control over the economy and attracting Western investment. Having neither a strong party base nor wide popular support, he had to manoeuvre within the Soviet power system. As a result, his years of power saw more talk of reform than achievement of it. His policies encouraged ordinary Russians to talk more freely and to hope for improvements in their lives but they delivered very little.

In the Soviet satellites the Gorbachov approach stimulated much more excitement than in the Soviet Union. Gorbachov, intent on maintaining Western good will, was determined that Russian troops would not be used to keep Communist governments in power. When the crunch came, none of those governments had sufficient confidence in their own armed forces to attempt to use them against the mass demonstrations which signaled their downfall. In August 1989, Poland's Communists accepted a Catholic leader as prime minister. In the next few months, Communist regimes across Eastern Europe gave place, with little resistance, to dissidents committed to democracy and free enterprise. By Christmas 1989 the Soviet satellite empire in Eastern Europe had ceased to exist.

The example of Eastern Europe was contagious. Before long the constituent republics of the Soviet Union decided that they also wished to be independent states. Many of the new leaders were Communists or ex-Communists; they represented not so much a craving for democracy as a resurgence of national feeling among the various nationalities dominated by Russia.

By 1991 it was clear that disintegration could not be stopped; broad agreement was reached on the replacement of the Soviet

Union by a much looser association to be known as the Commonwealth of Independent States (CIS). To some of the Moscow *apparatchiks* the prospect was intolerable. They attempted a coup, which failed miserably – its only concrete result was to compromise and ruin Gorbachov and deliver power to Boris Yeltsin, President of Russia.

Yeltsin, no more than Gorbachov, was able to pursue a single minded programme of reform. His own position was derived from popular election but the Duma (legislature) was dominated by Communist deputies who resisted change. His health deteriorated and he finally decided to resign, handing over power to the latest of his many selections as Prime Minister, Vladimir Putin. As expected Putin has now been elected as President. Largely unknown in the West, Putin is a former KGB official. His support in Russia derives, at least in part, from his vigorous prosecution of the bloody war against the secessionist Republic of Chechnya.

In the former Soviet Union, even more than in the states of Eastern Europe, the transition to democracy has therefore been chaotic and uncertain. Unemployment, unknown in the Soviet system, has mushroomed; millions of those employed find their wages unpaid for months. Inefficiency, corruption and budgetary constraints are wreaking havoc in the economy. Crime and violence flourish. The ordinary citizen may sleep better at night because the power of the secret police appears to have been curbed but he knows that the streets are more dangerous and his future problematical.

Any tendency of the Western powers to look with complacency on the dissolution of the Soviet empire has been restrained by the problems it raises for them. Nuclear weapons in massive numbers remained on the soil of Russia, Ukraine and Kazakhstan. With Western, largely American, pressure and financial assistance, these have all been brought under Russian control. But the Russian army and scientific establishments are suffering from lack of resources, drastically reduced living conditions, a breakdown of control systems and low morale. Key scientific staff are tempted to accept well funded appointments in maverick states intent on developing atomic weapons, or to illegally divert nuclear material to them.

Western Europe worried about a less dramatic threat – the prospect of a tide of refugees, stimulated either by economic hardship or by military conflict. So far the tide has not become a flood but the danger remains potent.

It is fairly obvious that the answer to many of these problems is the reconstruction of the ex-Soviet and Eastern European economies to provide growth, increased welfare and full employment. This, after all, was the achievement of the Marshall Plan in Western Europe fifty years earlier. Its benefits could be replicated now, especially as a much larger base – America plus the European Union – is available to finance it. But the vision and generosity which Truman and Marshall had evoked were lacking. The Western Powers were pre-occupied with their own problems and were not prepared even to contemplate the possibility that the economic stimulus involved in a new Marshall Plan might, by kick-starting their sluggish economies, contribute to their solution.

Without such assistance, the transition to a free economy imposed increasing hardship on many people; many of them began to wonder if life was really better than it had been under Communism. This opened the way for 'reformed' Communist parties, usually under a new name, to achieve substantial representation in legislatures and even to form or participate in governments.

Nor was the West ready to grasp the nettle presented to it by the break-up of Yugoslavia into its constituent republics. The result was a bloody civil war which was only brought to an end by economic pressure on Serbia and a NATO-led peace force. Whether the fragile peace thus imposed will survive the eventual withdrawal of the force remains to be seen. In the meantime, Serbia and the ethnic Albanians in the Province of Kosovo came to blows and the

European powers were obliged to recognize, reluctantly, the need to intervene. A massive bombing campaign forced Serbia to accept a NATO peace-keeping force in Kosovo. The Serbian leader, Milosovich, was overthrown and eventually handed over to a UN established War Crimes Tribunal.

The collapse of the Soviet Union and the dissolution of the communist bloc in Eastern Europe meant that the bi-polar power structure was virtually replaced by a uni-polar power structure. No combination of countries is capable of mobilizing military power comparable with that of the United States. In the nineties, the US leadership under Presidents Bush Senior and Clinton seemed to realize that the sheer weight of military power did not mean that the US could resolve all problems to its satisfaction; diplomacy and persuasion were still necessary.

President George W. Bush and his Administration, however, seem much more inclined to rely on military power and to ignore the views of allies and major powers such as Russia and China. Whereas Bush Senior had put together a large combination of countries for the ejection of Iraq from Kuwait, Bush Junior was able to muster only a few allies for a second attack on that country. The US destroyed Iraqi armed power in a few weeks but has since been confronted with a widespread guerilla campaign. The Administration remains reluctant to accept significant UN involvement in the reconstruction of Iraq and this adds to the reluctance of major powers to share the burden of reconstruction

It is clear that neither Russia nor China will easily accept a world order in which the will of the US prevails without challenge. Moreover there are elements within the European Community – notably France – which are disposed to build up European military power to facilitate its acting independently of the US and even acting as a countervailing power on occasion. These elements are by no means in a position to determine EU policy but their existence indicates the potential for an EU-US split. Trade disputes add to the potential for disagreement and misunderstanding.

The Failure of Vision in the West

In the absence of the stimulus that a new Marshall Plan might have provided, Western economies seemed stuck with sluggish growth and high unemployment. Technological developments, particularly in information technology, added to the pressures of competition from low wage countries and the negative effects of Friedmanite economic policies.

Elements in government and among employers, so far from trying to address this problem, began to see lower wages as part of the answer to competing with the newly industrialized countries, ignoring the achievements of the most successful of those countries in eventually increasing wages. By contrast, in the developed countries, a substantial under-class found itself with no prospects except continued poverty which, in some cases, even employment would do little to relieve. For a time, the United States got its unemployment below 5% by accepting low wages; in consequence its poverty rate rose to 13%. Those countries, such as France, which persisted in maintaining social benefits and even tried to increase them, found themselves battered by high unemployment.

The scope which governments found to manoeuvre was reduced by their past success; a quarter century of prosperity and social welfare policies had changed the socio-economic structure. Many of the poor, 'working class' of 1945, and still more their children, had been transformed into middle class before the end of the century. They were prepared to vote for the party which promised them a continuation of the good times and to ignore the growth of unemployment, which they did not at first see as a threat to themselves. Political power in many countries had come to depend on capturing the votes of the middle class which outnumbered not only the rich but also the poor. Politics became increasingly a competition to capture the middle ground; in this endeavour socialist and labour parties became less radical and more centrist. This movement was rewarded with increased public support. For the most part, however, these parties seem to be so mesmerized by post-Keynsian economics that they failed to address the problems of employment and social equity which they are theoretically committed to resolve. The movement of the socialist parties towards the centre leaves part of their traditional constituency unrepresented. A small number of voters have moved further left, supporting more radical parties or joining movements which propose to achieve change by terror. Larger numbers have simply given up voting.

Moreover, a new sophistication in opinion analysis has enabled political parties to discover what policies and programmes could be expected to appeal to the electorate and win their support. This, of course, has serious implications for democracy; it invites political leaders to adopt policies that will get them elected without regard to their merits. If the policies in question are not viable, election confronts the new (or re-elected) government with a choice between bad policy and broken promises. This also promotes increasing cynicism and reduced turn-out on the part of the electorate.

It is a sobering thought that, although Soviet watching was a substantial government and academic occupation, before 1989 neither pundit nor prophet seems to have anticipated the sudden dissolution of the Soviet power structure. Today, no one is predicting a similar crisis in the West. But if the Russian crisis was unpredictable, it is at least possible that an analogous crisis may be brewing in the West, unrecognized until it is too late.

Once this possibility is contemplated, it is easy to identify some of the weaknesses which might make it a reality:

- the growth of an underclass, unemployed or underpaid, and fueled by massive youth unemployment,

- the systematic attack on wages, working conditions and welfare benefits,
- the growth of inequality in incomes and wealth,
- the widespread loss of faith in democratic institutions, leading to the growth of radical and violence-prone groups and to massive abstention from voting.
- the deliberate neglect of public services, welfare, and infrastructure as governments seek every means of containing and reducing taxation.

These and other social problems vary from country to country but hardly any Western country is exempt from most of them. The high hopes of the sixties and seventies have, for millions of people, given way to disillusion and discontent. If the political process will not tackle these problems, the future looks ominous.

The collapse of the Soviet Union and the dissolution of the communist bloc in Eastern Europe meant that the bi-polar power structure was virtually replaced by a uni-polar power structure. No combination of countries is capable of mobilizing military power comparable with that of the United States. In the nineties, the US leadership under Presidents Bush Senior and Clinton seemed to realize that the sheer weight of military power did not mean that the US could resolve all problems to its satisfaction; diplomacy and persuasion were still necessary.

President George W. Bush and his Administration, however, seem much more inclined to rely on military power and to ignore the views of allies and major powers such as Russia and China. Whereas Bush Senior had put together a large combination of countries for the ejection of Iraq from Kuwait, Bush Junior was able to muster only a few allies for a second attack on that country. The US destroyed Iraqi armed power in a few weeks but has since been confronted with a widespread guerilla campaign. The

Administration remains reluctant to accept significant UN involvement in the reconstruction of Iraq and this adds to the reluctance of major powers to share the burden of reconstruction

It is clear that neither Russia nor China will easily accept a world order in which the will of the US prevails without challenge. Moreover there are elements within the European Community – notably France – which are disposed to build up European military power to facilitate its acting independently of the US and even acting as a countervailing power on occasion. These elements are by no means in a position to determine EU policy but their existence indicates the potential for an EU-US split. Trade disputes add to the potential for disagreement and misunderstanding.

CHAPTER FOURTEEN

THE EUROPEANS IN AUSTRALIA

The aboriginal people had occupied Australia for at least forty millennia without being disturbed by overseas invaders. They had developed a way of life well adapted to their environment and maintained it virtually unchanged. Towards the end of the eighteenth century they suffered an invasion by much more advanced people who showed no respect for their rights or their culture. The aboriginal story for the next two centuries is one of tragedy and threatening extermination. The invaders and their descendants spread over the continent and built an egalitarian and innovative society. In the process, however, they subjected the original inhabitants to conquest, disease and exploitation.

Foundation and Establishment

The first Europeans to see the coast of Australia were Dutch, beginning in 1606. They were not impressed. The west coast, which they touched in their journey from Holland to Batavia (now Jakarta) was barren and unattractive. In 1642 Abel Tasman discovered the island which now bears his name – he called it Van Dieman's Land, after the governor who had commissioned his expedition The English buccaneer and navigator, William Dampier, touched on the north-west coast in 1688 and 1699; he shared the Dutch view of it. Cook's exploration of the east coast in 1770 revealed a more promising Australia but did not attract immediate settlement.

The independence of the American colonies in 1783 presented the British government with the problem of the convicts who had previously been sentenced to transportation to those colonies. The choice finally fell on the land revealed by Captain Cook's discoveries in 1770 and named by him New South Wales. Captain Arthur Phillip was dispatched there with fourteen hundred souls, nearly eight hundred of them convicts, in 1787.

The new settlement was fortunate in its first governor. Phillip was not only a competent naval officer, he was a man of character, humanity and vision. He shifted the site of settlement immediately from the barren and unpromising Botany Bay to Port Jackson, a magnificent harbour where, he noted, a thousand ships of the line might lie at anchor. Here Phillip came ashore on 26 January 1788, a date which has become Australia's national day. Thanks to him the infant colony survived the strangeness of its environment and a shortage of food, exacerbated by the loss of a store ship dispatched from England and the lack of farm experience among the convicts, mainly the product of city slums.

The British government had decided, on the strength of reports by Cook and Banks (the botanist on Cook's expedition and a man of considerable influence in London) that Australia was a terra nullius, a no man's land, not effectively occupied by the aborigines whose numbers Cook had drastically underestimated. Phillip treated them with consideration but did not understand them – it does not seem to have occurred to him that the intruders were seizing the aborigines' land. An outbreak of smallpox among them in 1789 reduced the population of aborigines in and around the British settlement by as much as fifty per cent.

A gaol run by naval and military officers inevitably took its ideas of punishment from those services; flogging became a commonplace. Much worse treatment awaited those convicts found guilty of serious crimes within the colony. These were transported again to subsidiary prisons – eventually Norfolk Island, Newcastle, Brisbane and two sites in Tasmania, Port Arthur and Macquarie Harbour – where the regime was notoriously harsher. The commandant was often a sadist; and the prisoners were brutalized by his authority (or sometimes by his failure to exercise it).

When the marine officers objected to undertaking the role of gaolers and other non-military duties, the British government established the NSW Corps for the purpose. Service of this nature was unlikely to attract men of distinction – but it attracted one man, John Macarthur, who was to make a large, if tumultuous, contribution to Australian history. When Phillip returned to England in 1792 the senior officer of the Corps, Major Francis Grose, became administrator. Britain, soon locked in a life and death struggle with Revolutionary France, had little attention to spare for its distant colony; the next governor did not arrive until 1795. The officers of the NSW Corps seized the opportunity; their commander, now administrator of the colony, made them large grants of land and assigned convicts to work it. They formed a cartel to monopolize the purchase of any cargoes which arrived in the colony and resold them at enormous mark-ups. Perhaps the most important cargo was rum; the colony not only consumed it in large quantities but also used it as ready money – money is not in circulation in a gaol and the British government had made no provision for currency in the colony.

Three Governors, all naval officers, struggled in vain to curb the power of the Corps, now aptly known as the Rum Corps. The last of these was Captain Bligh, notorious for the mutiny of his ship, the *Bounty*, and his great open boat voyage from Tahiti to Java. Bligh was a man of violent temper and crude, abusive language. He soon fell foul, not only of the NSW Corps, but of virtually everyone of substance. On 26 January, 1808 he was arrested by a detachment of the NSW Corps. The commander of the Corps assumed the government of the colony and MacArthur, who had initiated the coup, took to styling himself 'Secretary of the Colony.'

Even in the midst of the Napoleonic War, London could hardly ignore this situation. It acted to reassert its rule by sending out a new governor, Lieutenant-Colonel Lachlan Macquarie, accompanied by his own regiment. Macquarie was a man of vision and determination. He saw that the future of the colony could only be built on the work of free settlers but, since immigration was minute, the source of free settlers had to be ex-convicts, or emancipists as they were generally known. He was convinced that once a man or woman had served their sentence – or been released by the governor – their civil rights were fully restored. He appointed the most qualified and gifted of them to responsible positions, even to the court bench, and invited them to share his table. Some of these men, and at least one woman emancipist, made fortunes in trade and died leaving estates worth many millions in today's values. The emancipist architect, Greenaway, adorned Sydney with buildings of real beauty; one is now the Parliament of NSW.

Macquarie, like Phillip, began his rule with a determination to do right by the aboriginal population. Unfortunately, in his case also, knowledge and understanding were not equal to goodwill. When the aborigines, outraged by the overruning of their traditional hunting lands, began to retaliate by attacking isolated Englishmen and killing their animals, the settlers reacted by attacking and massacring aborigines. Macquarie endeavoured to control settler outrages but was rarely successful.

In 1813 three settlers, Blaxland, Lawson and Wentworth, succeeded in crossing the Blue Mountains which for twenty-five years had confined the settlement to a narrow space between the mountains and the sea. There they found vast grassy plains which seemed to offer pasture for the burgeoning herds of the colony. Macquarie built a road over the mountains and established the town of Bathurst. Settlers and their herds poured over the mountains and spread rapidly over the inland plains. In a few years they built a new foundation for the Australian economy. But everywhere they displaced and murdered the aborigines.

Macquarie's policy of advancing the emancipists aroused the opposition of the small number of men and women who were not of convict origin, the so-called exclusives or true merinos – so named with reference to the sheep on which many of them built their wealth. MacArthur, who had pioneered the development of these sheep in Australia, was one of their leaders and used his contacts in London to spread criticism of the governor. The government in London, already perturbed by Macquarie's high expenditure, sent a commissioner to investigate. Mr. Bigge had served as Chief Justice of Trinidad and brought to his task a set of prejudices which made him favourable to the exclusives. His proceedings were offensive to Macquarie who resigned before his report was issued.

Sheep and Self-Government 1820–1850

Bigge's report, however, was satisfactory to the government. Ironically, it called for the promotion of free settlement. Not, however, by ex-convicts but by men of wealth from England. They would receive large land grants in proportion to the wealth they had to invest and convict labour to work them. Emancipists were to be kept in their place and remote settlements established to subdue the more recalcitrant convicts with a harsher regime.

In 1820 Australia had exported 175,000 pounds of wool, in 1830 two million pounds and in 1845 twenty four million pounds. Settlement outran the government's control. Governor Darling tried to confine it within a radius of 150 miles of Sydney. The squatters, as the sheep owners were called, ignored him.

The men who owned the herds of sheep had scant regard for the distant governor or for the aborigines whose land they took over. Resistance was likely to lead to massacre, the whites making full use of their fire-arms to subdue people armed with wooden spears and boomerangs. The use of convict, or sometimes ex-convict, labour as shepherds placed some of the dregs of English society in positions to interact with the aborigines without the restraints which might have applied in towns or more closely settled areas. Aboriginal women were the first victims; when the men retaliated, the whites were quick to react with murder and massacre.

The rapid expansion of flocks increased the pressure for more land. In 1835 settlers from northern Tasmania opened up the area around Melbourne, 'buying' land from the aborigines with trinkets. As news of the fine pasture spread, they were soon joined by others who drove their flocks overland from NSW. Adelaide was settled in 1836, under a complicated scheme which revolved around keeping land prices high and using the money to subsidise the migration of servants and labourers. The planned occupation was soon supplemented by squatters from further east. Brisbane, a convict settlement since 1824, became a free settlement in 1839.

The growth of a free population – even if some were children of convicts – inevitably sparked demands for free institutions, Juries were introduced for civil cases in 1824; it would be many years before they were sanctioned for criminal trials. A nominated legislative council to advise the governor was set up in 1829; it was some years before governors would be convinced that its advice had to be taken seriously. The colonists wanted, in any case, an elected legislative council and an end to transportation. Early in the forties Britain yielded to both demands.

The concession of election to a legislative council led inevitably to demands for further progress. In a confused, three-cornered struggle between conservative and liberal opinion in the colonies and the Colonial Office in London the colonies moved rapidly towards responsible government. By 1856 all the colonies except Western Australia had achieved self-government. No attempt was made by the Imperial Government to reserve to itself powers relating to the native people who were left to the tender mercy of the colonials.

From Gold to Federation

On 12 February 1851 gold was discovered near Bathurst in NSW. A few months later gold was found in Victoria, only just established as a colony, with its own governor, separate from NSW. The news of the gold strikes emptied Sydney and still more Melbourne, as men rushed to make their fortunes. Only a small minority were really successful. Perhaps as many as two-thirds got something, the remaining third nothing at all. This discouraging lottery was not known at the time. By 1853 almost every day brought a ship full of would-be gold miners to Melbourne.

By 1854 Ballarat, in particular, was full of miners who faced the backbreaking work of digging as much as two hundred feet deep in the hope of a 'strike.' Many found the licence fee, the miner's right, more than they could pay. Governor Hotham, supported by his Legislative Council, refused all concessions and sent police and troops to Ballarat. A minority of the miners, probably as low as fifteen per cent, reacted by constructing and manning the Eureka Stockade. Over it they raised the Southern Cross flag and proclaimed the Republic of Victoria. By Saturday night the number in the stockade was reduced to 150 or less. On Sunday morning, 3 December 1854, troops and police attacked and easily overcame the disorganized resistance; twenty two miners were killed and six soldiers.

The Eureka affair, however, was far from over. The thirteen leading rebels were found not guilty of treason by two successive juries. A royal commission, while condemning the miners' action, recommended the reduction of the fee for the miner's licence to one pound per annum. In the end the miners got most of what they contended for, except their Republic. The Eureka Stockade passed into Australian folklore as a symbol for both workers and nationalists.

Gold brought a new source of wealth to Australia and underwrote further development. It also led to a dramatic increase in population. The colonies were already using up to half the revenue from land sales to bring migrants to Australia; the prospect of gold encouraged many more to pay their own passage. Population doubled between 1850 and 1860.

As it became apparent that mining would not support this increased population the thoughts of many turned to the vast areas of land which were locked up in pastoral leases. In the 1860's NSW, under premier John Robertson, pioneered the idea of 'free selection.' The squatter was allowed to pre-empt 25 acres around his homestead; the rest of the land was subject to the right of the would-be settler to select blocks from 40 to 320 acres. The selector was given time to pay for the land and was expected to improve it with fencing and barns. Other states followed the lead of NSW.

Overall the results were largely disappointing. Many of the selectors had neither the skills nor the finance to carve a successful holding out of the bush. Some selectors aimed to cut off a squatter from water or transport and then sell the selection to him at a premium. Many squatters protected themselves by taking up numerous selections in the names of family members and friends. In the end, many people felt that the squatters benefited from 'free selection' more than any one else.

The technological changes of the nineteenth century contributed to the development of the Australian rural economy. Barbed wire enabled the grazier to dispense with the relatively intensive use of manpower in caring for his sheep. An Australian invention, the stump jump plough, made it possible to plough fields without the expensive and back-breaking labour of grubbing out tree-stumps first. But these and similar inventions paled into insignificance with the coming of the railways. These revolutionized the cost of transporting primary produce and therefore the economics of farming and grazing. The export of wheat from Australia became possible so that wheat growing became, in many areas, a supplement or even an alternative to wool. The steamship played a somewhat analogous role in sea transport, reducing drastically the time for a journey between Britain and Australia. Refrigeration made it possible for Australian meat to be shipped to Britain.

British capital financed railway construction and much of the other development. Melbourne and Sydney came to rank among the very largest cities in the southern hemisphere. Dignified with fine buildings, theatres and a university and provided with suburban railways and tramways, they compared with great European cities such as Manchester and Lyons. Melbourne surpassed Sydney in population and became for a time the national financial centre of Australia.

The boom burst early in the 1890's. Drought killed crops and stock; sheep numbers, which had passed a hundred million, were reduced by half. A world-wide depression which reduced demand for Australian exports, notably metals. Reduced demand meant reduced prices so that exporters were caught in a two way squeeze. The depression continued to the end of the decade and beyond.

A large majority of employers saw the solution to their problems in squeezing wages. The squatters were well to the fore in this movement and demanded a reduction in shearing rates. But the shearers were now organized in the Amalgamated Shearers Union, the predecessor of the Australian Workers Union. A bitter fight ensued; the transport industry went the same way. Governments reacted to support the employers, sometimes with force.

The alliance of governments and employers was victorious. The workers responded by seeking to push their interests by political action. The success of the Labor Party exceeded their wildest expectations. Before the decade was over, its parliamentarians were trading support for concessions by another party and looking forward to governing in their own right.

The question of federation came to the fore in the nineties. A series of interstate conventions gradually hammered out a constitution to be put to the people of each colony in a referendum. The Constitution was accepted in each colony, although Western

Australia might well have voted in the negative had it not been for the sudden influx of gold diggers from the eastern colonies after the discoveries at Coolgardie and Kalgoorlie. Finally, it was endorsed, with some amendments, by the British government, and embodied in a British Act of Parliament.

The Australian Constitution enshrined British traditions of parliamentary government which were already familiar from the experience of the colonies. British traditions, however, did not include federal institutions which were essential if the new constitution was to be accepted. For these purposes the Constitution drew mainly on the American model. So the upper house of Parliament was denominated by the Senate and provided equal representation for each state, as the colonies were to be called. Unlike the USA Senate, however, the Australian body had no special powers such as the approval of treaties (seen as an imperial rather than a colonial matter) and key appointments. The Constitution contained an extensive list of Commonwealth powers; all other powers remained with the states. Again on the American model, a High Court was expected to be the usual interpreter of the Constitution as well as the court of appeal; but appeals to the Judicial Committee of the Privy Council were possible.

War and Nationhood

Most of the early governments of the Commonwealth were dominated by liberal protectionists. To remain in power they needed the support of the Labor party. This strengthened the hand of the liberal faction which stood for progressive legislation; shaken by a decade of strikes and industrial troubles these men wished to end the confrontation between employer and labor by concessions. The Labor Party, for its part, had come under the control of pragmatists who had no interest in Marxist ideas of a class struggle; they instinctively saw these as alien to the feelings of the majority of

Australians. They wanted to win elections and introduce legislation which would benefit the workers and the poor; they were prepared to compromise in order to do so. By 1914 they could boast that Labor had held office in the Commonwealth and in every state. Increasingly, Labor's demands defined the main issues of Australian politics. Its success forced the existing parties to sink their differences and amalgamate.

The alliance between Liberal and Labor laid the basis for the new country. By 1914 Australia had given the vote to women, established a Federal Conciliation and Arbitration Court which introduced a basic wage, taken over the administration of Papua and the Northern Territory from Queensland and South Australia respectively, introduced compulsory military training and established an Australian Navy, established the Commonwealth Bank, and resolved the vexed problem of choosing a site for a capital. By any standard this amounts to a considerable achievement for a country of five million people at the end of the world.

Australians, unfortunately, had a full share of the racial prejudice which was almost universal at the time. They regarded Asians as inferior and also a menace to Australian working conditions because of their willingness to work for much lower wages; most Europeans, especially Southern Europeans, were regarded as not much better. The first major legislation passed by the Commonwealth Parliament was the Immigration Restriction Act. Thus was born the White Australia Policy. It was completed by measures to repatriate 'Kanaka' labourers from the cane fields of Queensland to their native Pacific Islands. As for the original inhabitants, they were not a problem. They seemed destined to die out; in the meantime the Constitution itself left aboriginal affairs to the states.

None of the States pursued policies which placed assistance to aborigines at the centre of their concerns. Neither did the Commonwealth when it took over the Northern Territory. Aboriginal outbreaks against their exploitation were met with overwhelming force. The policy developed was to assimilate the children of mixed blood into the main stream population; the aboriginal race and culture were destined to disappear. Half caste children were removed from their mothers and transported hundreds of miles to orphanages where they were given rudimentary education to prepare them for life as stationhands or domestic servants. Contact between parents and children was denied. The hardships and abuses of this policy have recently been documented in the report 'The Stolen Generation.'

Largely ignorant of this shameful situation, many white Australians were proud of their country's growing reputation as a social laboratory. Many shared the brash self-confidence proclaimed by the aggressively Australian weekly, 'The Bulletin,' but few seemed to share its ardent republicanism. Australia welcomed the system of Imperial Conferences begun in 1907 and would have accorded them a wider mandate than other Dominions would accept.

There was little dissent when Britain's declaration of war on Germany in 1914 was seen as involving Australia automatically; the prime minister proclaimed that Australia would support Britain 'to the last man and the last shilling.' The Australian Imperial Force was raised to fight under British control and placed under the command of British generals. Initially recruitment was limited to 20,000 men who were dispatched to Egypt to bolster British and allied power in the Middle East. Camped in the desert outside Cairo, they earned a not unjustified reputation for unruliness. A more solid reputation, for valour and endurance, was built when they landed on Gallipoli together with British and French troops in a vain attempt to force Turkey out of the war. The operation was misconceived and its failure, at the cost of 8,000 Australian (and 12,000 British and French) lives, inevitable. It nevertheless passed into Australia's national legend, regarded by many as the real symbol of Australian nationhood.

After Gallipoli Australian light horse and mounted infantry were employed in the conquest of Palestine and Syria but the main body of recruits were directed to France. As the horror of trench warfare gradually became known in Australia, enthusiasm for the war waned and enlistments slowed down. Hughes, the Labor Prime Minister, made two attempts to secure approval for conscription by referenda. Both failed. They also divided the country badly and split the Labor Party. Hughes and a rump of supporters joined with the Liberals to form the National Party. Hughes remained Prime Minister and prosecuted the war with undiminished enthusiasm.

In all 417,000 men enlisted and 326,000 served overseas. This represented 40% of those eligible to enlist. Sixty thousand died and another 155,000 were wounded. In total, casualties represented two-thirds of those who served overseas. Australian casualties were high because they were almost all front line troops, either infantry or artillery; support services were provided by the British.

Hughes attended the Peace Conference and defended Australian interests, as he saw them, with all the ferocity with which he had promoted conscription. German New Guinea became an Australian Mandate but the islands further north were assigned to Japan.

By 1923 the newly formed Country Party was a recognizable force in politics. Hughes was ejected from the leadership of the Nationals who formed a coalition with the Country Party. Australia, like Britain, had not turned out to be 'a land fit for heroes.' Soldier settlement schemes were inadequately planned and financed and industrial strife was endemic. The Prime Minister, Bruce, decided that the Commonwealth should virtually withdraw from industrial relations in favor of the states. He fought an election on the subject and lost to Labor under Scullin.

Scullin's government began in the same week as the crisis on the New York stock exchange. Divided between ideologues and pragmatists, it failed to deal effectively with the impact of the crisis on Australia. Unemployment rose to 30% and widespread hardship provoked desperation among the unemployed. The Treasurer, Theodore, wanted to deal with the problem by Keynesian type policies of expansion – some years before Keynes published his General Theory! His vision was too advanced for his colleagues. Sir Otto Niemeyer, sent by the Bank of England to advise the government, recommended stringent cost cutting including a reduction in wages and pensions. The Labor premier of NSW, Jack Lang, advocated forcing a reduction in interest payments on overseas bonds. Scullin hesitated but eventually agreed with Niemeyer. It was too late to save his government. Half a dozen Labor members of Federal Parliament defected and formed a separate party loyal to Lang. The Acting Treasurer and former Premier of Tasmania, Joe Lyons, deserted the party and became the leader of a newly named United Australia Party, a combination of the former National Party with Lyons and his supporters. Scullin's majority now depended on the support of the Lang faction; in November 1931 that support was withdrawn and Scullin was badly defeated in the ensuing election.

So, for the second but not the last time, a split in the Labor Party had enabled the conservative forces to control the government.

The Lyons government eschewed radical measures to deal with the problems confronting it. Unemployment was gradually reduced but was still 8% in 1938. The attention of government was increasingly pre-occupied by the looming clouds of war. Fear of Japan had been an element in Australian re-actions since its victory over the Russians in the first years of the century. As the Japanese pressed on with their attack on China in the 1930's Australians realized that they also might be on the Japanese list.

When war broke out in Europe in 1939, Menzies, who had become Prime Minister on Lyons' death some months before, took the view that Australia was bound by Britain's declaration of war. Several divisions were raised to fight overseas as the Second Australian Imperial Force and arrangements were made for volunteers for the RAAF to be trained overseas for service with the RAF. The Australians distinguished themselves in the battle against the Italians and Germans in Libya and in Syria against the Vichy French. The success of Australian troops, however, was not matched by constructive action on the home front. The UAP – UCP government showed increasing signs of disintegration. Having almost lost an election in 1940 it was dependent on two independents to retain office. In October 1941 that support was withdrawn. Labor formed a government with its leader, John Curtin, as Prime Minister. He remained in office until his death in 1945, when he was succeeded by the Treasurer, Ben Chifley.

Three months after Labor came to power, Japan launched its strike on the American Pacific Fleet at Pearl Harbour and begun a rapid drive into South East Asia. British and Dutch resistance collapsed. The newly constructed British base at Singapore surrendered, along with 90,000 troops including an Australian division. The Japanese defeated the American forces in the Philippines; their commander, MacArthur, a former American Chief of Staff, escaped to Australia and was named by the American President as Commander in the South West Pacific. Curtin announced that Australia looked to America, rather than Britain, for support and, in an acrimonious argument by cable, successfully pressed Churchill to return the Australian divisions in the Middle East to take part in the defence of Australia.

The Japanese were defeated by the Americans (with some Australian support) in the naval battle of the Coral Sea in March 1942. Australian troops turned back the Japanese at Milne Bay and on the incredibly rugged Kokoda Trail across the mountain spine of Papua New Guinea. Although Australians did not realize it at the time, the Japanese advance had reached its maximum.

Several years of hard fighting were needed as the Japanese were slowly driven back to their home islands. Even then, only the atom bomb forced their surrender. Australia had three quarters of a million men and women under arms and many hundreds of thousands engaged in munitions and arms manufacture – over three thousand military aircraft were made in Australia, as well as many other instruments of war. So much food and other resources were supplied to American forces that Australia ended the war as a substantial creditor of that country.

The war effort rapidly transformed the employment picture. The war economy was one of full employment and labour scarcity. Curtin and the ministry were determined that if this could be done in war full employment would be maintained in peace. The 1945 White Paper on Full Employment laid out a Keynsian approach and the government even prepared a number of major public works projects to take up the expected slack in employment. In the event they were not necessary although the government proceeded with one major project, the Snowy Mountains HydroElectric Scheme.

One element in the maintenance of a high level of economic activity and employment was an ambitious immigration programme. The war had brought home to government and people alike the need for a higher population as a basis for defence. Begun with an emphasis on British and Irish migration, the programme soon became based on an acceptance of any European. By 1970 two million migrants had come to Australia, more than 80% of them on assisted passages. These migrants supplied much of the workforce on the Snowy Scheme and in the new factories. Their coming gradually modified the narrow chauvinism inherited by the Australian born.

The Labor Party's success in dealing with the problems of war and post-war reconstruction only highlighted the disintegration of the United Australia Party. Menzies put it together again as the Liberal Party and by 1949 mounted a formidable challenge to Labor. The Chifley government had alienated much of public opinion by maintaining wartime controls such as petrol rationing and by attempting to nationalize the banks. Menzies promised, in effect, to continue many of Labor's key policies without the controls and won handsomely, The man who had been ignominiously forced from office by his own colleagues in 1939 was to remain Prime Minister for seventeen years.

Development and Globalization

By 1949 most people in Australia knew they were enormously better off than before the war and expected their good fortune to continue. Their optimism, however, did not extend to the prospects for peace. Reliance on British protection had already proved an illusion. America had a treaty with Australia and New Zealand but carefully preserved for itself the final decision on what action it would take in the event of a threat to those countries. By 1949 all but a small minority of Australians regarded the Soviet Union and Communist China as potential menaces.

The Menzies government saw no answer to these problems but an endeavour to build a closer relationship with Britain and America. Australian troops supported America in defending South Korea against attack by Communist North Korea; they fought with the British against Communist guerillas in Malaysia and against Indonesian infiltration into the Malaysian provinces in West Borneo. When the United States was drawn gradually into Vietnam, Australia followed with a small contribution, first of military trainers and then of fighting men.

A committed anti-Communist, Menzies launched an attack on Communist control of the unions. His Communist Party Dissolution Act was disallowed by the High Court and a referendum to change the constitution was defeated. Effective action against Communism in the unions depended on the so-called industrial groups, informal associations of anti-Communist unionists led by a lay Catholic activist, Bob Santamaria. The groups were not controlled by the Catholic Church and although most members were Catholics, some key leaders were not. The industrial groups, often referred to as the Movement, attained control of a number of unions and became influential in the Labor party. When Labor lost the 1954 election, its leader, Evatt, and Santamaria each blamed the other. The Federal Executive of the Party replaced the Victorian leadership. A number of parliamentarians left the Labor Party and formed the Democratic Labor Party (DLP). They all lost their seats at the next election but a single senator was elected to carry the banner. The importance of the DLP, however, did not rest on a single senator but on the second preferences of its voters. Their preferences were directed, not to the Labor party, but to the Liberal Country Party coalition. For almost two decades, they kept the coalition in power, and Labor in the wilderness.

Preoccupation with anti-Communism did not prevent the Menzies government from presiding over a period of great development. The migration programme was continued, so was the Snowy Mountain Scheme. Commodity prices remained high. Behind the shelter of a high tariff wall and exchange controls. industry and employment expanded. Vast mineral resources in the north of the country were opened up and would soon displace wool as the largest source of export income. Japan was clearly destined to be the main market and a trade agreement was already in place, negotiated in 1957.

Economic policy still gave heavy emphasis to the preservation of full employment – when unemployment rose above two per cent in 1961 the government very nearly lost the next election. Social services were maintained and moderately extended. Overcoming generations of prejudice, the government began to extend assistance to private and Catholic schools.

Menzies retired in 1966, passing power to his hand-picked successor, Harold Holt. The new prime minister is chiefly remembered for his cultivation of the goodwill of American President L. B. Johnson – he proclaimed Australia's loyalty to the alliance with the slogan 'all the way with LBJ.' The Holt government was, however, responsible for introducing an amendment to the constitution to give the Commonwealth power to legislate for aborigines; it received more support than any other referendum has ever done. The Menzies government had already extended social service benefits to all but 'nomadic or primitive' aborigines and awarded them the right to vote. The Arbitration court had accepted their claim for equal pay in the pastoral industry. Underpinning these changes were two important developments. Australians generally were becoming more sympathetic to the problems of aborigines and disposed to recognize an obligation to deal with them. The aboriginal community was finding leaders – frequently of part aboriginal and part European origins – who were not overawed by whites and were mobilizing support, both in their own community and in the more progressive sections of the white community, for radical action to overcome aboriginal disadvantages.

Before the end of the sixties the Ministry began to show signs of weariness. The Vietnam War was already becoming a sign of division. An Australian battalion was sent in 1965 and conscription was introduced to support a larger effort. But the numbers required were not large enough to require the enlistment of the whole of the age cohort available each year; a lottery was used to select the birth dates which would determine liability to service. Many Australians found this 'lottery of death' repugnant. As the cruelty and corruption widespread in the anti-Communist government of South Vietnam became known, opposition to Australian involvement increased and was manifested in massive street demonstrations.

In December 1967 Holt was drowned while swimming off a Victorian holiday beach. The Liberal Party was riven by quarrels and in December 1972 went down to defeat by a revivified Labor led by Gough Whitlam. His government immediately recalled Australian troops from Vietnam and abandoned compulsory military service. Diplomatic recognition was extended to the Communist government of China. The Australian dollar was up-valued. A date was fixed for the achievement of independence by Papua New Guinea, and a Development Assistance Agency created to administer overseas aid. Measures were initiated to improve the situation of aborigines. A Family Court was established and divorce made simpler and easily available. University fees were removed and the Commonwealth began to take more interest in lower levels of education.

The Whitlam government lasted a bare three years, brought down by its lack of experienced and competent ministers, the stagflation caused by the oil shock and its lack of a majority in the Senate. Faced with a hostile Senate which refused to pass his money Bills, Whitlam was dismissed by the Governor General. This unprecedented action divided the country but the Liberal leader, Frazer, won a resounding victory in the election which followed.

The new government talked tough about the need to reform the economy. It slashed government expenditure and presided over the triumph of economic rationalism in the public service. In fact, however, it shied away from any fundamental reform of the economy and relied on the exploitation of new mineral resources. Frazer's tough talk, rising unemployment and growing industrial disputes divided the country. In 1980 a former Liberal established a new party, the Democrats. This party, sometimes along with Greens and independents, came to hold the balance of power in the Senate. In 1983 Labour returned to power under Bob Hawke, the former trade union leader with an outstanding record of negotiating the settlement of disputes.

Hawke's first act was to negotiate an Accord between government, employers and trade unions. Improvements in welfare were used as a trade-off for wage restraint. The Accord did much to overcome the climate of hostility between employers and workers which had developed under the previous government. Unemployment declined from 10 per cent to 6 per cent.

Hawke and the Treasurer, Keating, then took two steps which were quite unexpected from a Labor government. They floated the Australian dollar and abandoned foreign exchange controls. The decision showed the extent to which the government had adopted the free market, economic rationalist ideas of Thatcher and Regan. It made Australia an open economy and reduced the ability of the government to manage it. Australia's high tariff wall was dismantled so rapidly that there was little time for industry to adjust. This caused a rapid growth in unemployment which reached 11% in December 1992.

The result of these decisions was a large increase in foreign debt, mainly due to corporate borrowing overseas, either directly or through the banks. Alarmed by the trend, Keating talked of Australia becoming a banana republic and resolved on a policy of high interest rates; there was little else he could do with the traditional controls dismantled. Interest rates went as high as 20%, causing much misery and a string of business bankruptcies. Keating denominated this 'the recession we had to have.'

When Keating, impatient for the Prime Ministership, overthrew Hawke in December 1991, he faced a revivified Liberal Party. Its leader, John Hewson, presented him with a victory in the next election by developing a policy based on a General Service Tax and other stringent measures such as a time limit on the dole. Keating's formidable attack on these policies brought him victory in 1993 but his policies failed to achieve a significant reduction in unemployment or hold on to the traditional Labor vote. Gough Whitlam had begun the process of adjusting Labor policies to attract the support of the middle class. Hawke and Keating had carried this on successfully but as their economic policies destroyed much of secondary industry and increased unemployment, many of their traditional supporters became disappointed and skeptical. John Howard capitalized on this discontent to appeal to the 'Aussie battlers' and won the 1996 election with a massive majority.

Keating's last achievement was to make provision for the orderly implementation of the Mabo judgment on native title. In this judgment the High Court overthrew the doctrine of terra nullius and found that native title could still exist in large parts of the country. The government's legislation, which has since been amended by the Howard government, represented a compromise consensus between aborigines, pastoralists and mining companies.

Howard had proclaimed his intention to moderate the pace of change and let all Australians be 'relaxed and comfortable' under his government. Many, however, found it impossible to be comfortable with the changes to the social services system, the continuing privatisation, the dismantling of the arbitration system and the introduction of a Goods and Services Tax. Aborigines and their supporters were outraged by the refusal of the Prime Minister to support a Parliamentary apology for the wrongs of the past or to consider compensation to the victims of the forced separation so vividly described in 'The Stolen Generation.'

Nevertheless, in late 1998 the Howard Government survived its first election, although with a much reduced majority. It again succeeded on holding a small majority in 2001. Its record has been marked by the passage of legislation to introduce a General Service Tax and by a departure from Australian policy on East Timor. Australian leadership of the international force sent to East Timor (with Indonesian consent but very much against its wishes), marked a reversal of a policy of friendship with Indonesia dating back fifty years. Its long-term consequences remain to be seen.

Australia followed this by supporting America in Afghanistan and Iraq with small but useful forces. It has also negotiated a free trade agreement with the U.S. although whether this would benefit Australia has been questioned.

Australia therefore entered the third millennium conscious of serious economic problems and of a social division between rich and poor which previous generations had boasted had no place in the

Australian way of life. The sudden growth of Pauline Hanson's One Nation Party was a temporary phenomenon but certainly revealed a mood of disappointment and dissatisfaction among a worrying proportion of voters. While unemployment fell slowly, youth unemployment remained fearsomely high and fostered the growth of a large underclass with little prospect of work and no reason to hope for any improvement in their situation. While many people would like to arrest and reverse this situation there is so far no indication that anyone has the key to doing so. The Labor party has reduced the massive majority with which Howard was elected in 1996 but this has not been able to even sufficiently support a return to government. Despite being led by new leader, Mark Latham, Labour were defeated in the 2004 elections.